The Irish Writers, Authors and Poets Handbook

Lámhleabhar do Scríbhneoirí, d'Údar agus d'Fhilí Gaelacha

Edited by: David Jones
Oscar Duggan

The Irish Writers, Authors and Poets Handbook
Edited by: David Jones and Oscar Duggan

**Dedicated to the authors, writers and poets of Ireland
- past and present.**

Published by **TAF Publishing** 2010

ISBN: 978-1-907522-01-7

Copyright © **TAF Publishing**

The moral right of **TAF Publishing** as author and publisher
has been asserted

A CIP catalogue record for this book is available from
the British Library

Printed in Ireland by Gemini International Ltd

Lámhleabhar do Scríbhneoirí, d'Údar agus d'Fhilí Gaelacha
Curtha in eagair ag: David Jones agus Oscar Ó Dúgáin

**Arna tíolacadh go húdair, scríbhneoirí agus filí Gaelacha
- ón am atá caite agus an lae inniu.**

Foilsithe ag **TAF Publishing**, 2010

ISBN: 978-1-907522-01-7

Curtha i gcló in Éirinn ag Gemini International Ltd

The Irish Writers, Authors and Poets Handbook

Copyright © TAF Publishing 2010

Foreword

Welcome to the first *Irish Writers, Authors and Poets Handbook* for Ireland and Northern Ireland.

Ireland has a long literary history, with great writers of the past like Wilde, Shaw, Joyce and Yeats emanating from our shores. Modern writers like Maeve Binchy, Patricia Scanlon, Cecelia Ahern, Roddy Doyle, Joseph O'Connor and Cathy Kelly are helping to keep Ireland at the top of the best-seller lists.

Thousands of unknown writers and poets, some published - others just hopeful, are producing quality manuscripts; many as participants in creative writing groups in towns and villages across the island of Ireland.

Yet strangely, despite this vibrant literary tradition, no comprehensive writers' handbook specifically for Ireland and Northern Ireland has been available until now.

The Irish Writers, Authors and Poets Handbook for Ireland and Northern Ireland fills this gap. It is a practical guide for writers of all genres. It includes comprehensive listings of publishers, literary agents, local and national newspapers, magazines, literary festivals and events; as well as useful contacts like writers' centres and State sponsoring organisations.

Whether you are an established best-selling author or an aspiring would-be writer, the Handbook is a must for you. It will also be of great reference value to public libraries and writers groups.

David Jones
Oscar Duggan
April 2010

Réamhrá

Fáilte chuig an gcéad *Lámhleabhar do Scríbhneoirí, d'Údar agus d'Fhilí Gaelacha* maidir le hÉireann agus le Tuaisceart na hÉireann.

Tá stair liteartha fhada ag Éire, agus is ón tír seo ar tháinig scríbhneoirí iontacha ón am atá caite ar nós Wilde, Shaw, Joyce agus Yeats. Is de bharr scríbhneoirí nua-aimseartha ar nós Maeve Binchy, Patricia Scanlon, Cecelia Ahern, Roddy Doyle, Joseph O'Connor agus Cathy Kelly, atá Éire fós ar bharr liosta na leabhar sárdhíola.

Tá na mílte scríbhneoirí agus filí nach bhfuil aithne orthu, roinnt díobh atá a gcuid oibre foilsithe agus roinnt atá dóchasach, ag scríobh lámhscríbhinní fiúntacha agus an-chuid díobh mar bhaill de ghrúpaí scríbhneoireachta cruthaitheacha i mbailte agus i sráidbhailte ar fud oileán na hÉireann.

Is ait an rud é nach raibh fáil ar lámhleabhar cuimsitheach do scríbhneoirí, go speisialta d'Éire agus do Thuaisceart Éireann go dtí seo, in ainneoin an traidisiúin liteartha beoga seo.

Líonann an *Lámhleabhar do Scríbhneoirí, d'Údar agus d'Fhilí Gaelacha* maidir le hÉireann agus le Tuaisceart na hÉireann, an folús seo. Is treoir phraiticiúil é do scríbhneoirí a bhaineann le gach seánra. San áireamh ann tá liostaí cuimsitheacha d'fhoilsitheoirí, de ghníomhairí liteartha, de nuachtáin áitiúla agus náisiúnta, d'irisí, d'fhéilte liteartha agus d'imeachtaí liteartha ; mar aon le pointí teagmhála a d'fhéadfadh a bheith úsáideach ar nós ionaid do scríbhneoirí agus eagraíochtaí a bhaineann le hurraíocht Stáit.

Beidh gá agat don lámhleabhar seo, más scríbhneoir sárdhíola tú nó más ábhar scríbhneora tú. Beidh fiúntas ag baint leis, ó thaobh tagartha de, do leabharlanna poiblí agus do ghrúpaí scríbhneoirí chomh maith.

David Jones
Oscar Ó Dúgáin
Aibreán 2010

Acknowledgements/Buíochas

The editors would like to acknowledge the assistance that we received from: Mary McElroy who helped us with the proof-reading; Vivienne Walsh who provided us with Irish language translation assistance; and Proinsias Ó Maolchalain who also gave us direction and advice on this aspect.

www.TAFpublishing.com

Section I

Section II - Directory

By Way of Introduction:

I. The Digital Revolution

It might seem a strange place to start a yearbook, talking about the future. Yet technology changes so fast these days that the future is here almost before it arrives. As authors, writers, poets, editors, publishers, agents, etc., we need to understand the digital age that is already upon us.

Revolutions used to take decades to make any real progress. Stephenson's Rocket was unveiled to the public in 1829, but it took the best part of 50 years before a railway network was in place in Britain.

Time and progress now bear no relation to the tortoise days of the past. Google started commercial life in 1998. In more than a decade, it has taken over the world and changed almost everything.

The first substantial book printed with movable type was *The Gutenberg Bible*. It was completed in 1454 or 1455. The first significant publishing house was set up by the Elzevir family in Holland in 1583. It is conceivable that the last book to be printed and published in the traditional way could be just around the corner.

You think we are exaggerating? Maybe, but consider this: Five years ago Twitter didn't exist, yet today nothing seems to exist without Twitter. It's not just teenagers that use Twitter and other social networking sites like Facebook, MySpace, LinkedIn, and so on. Businesses have latched on to the power of sharing information as a means of building a customer base. Every newspaper, radio and TV show, the music industry, as well as politicians and even churches, now populate social networking sites.

The digital revolution encompasses:
- The Internet or the World Wide Web, which currently means about 2 billion people are connected and contactable in almost every country in the world.

- Instantaneous telecommunications, which means information (images and text) can be delivered to anywhere in the world, for free.
- Electronic reading devices which means anyone with access to the Internet can download an electronic file and start viewing or reading it.
- Print on demand technologies which allows books to be produced locally, economically and in small quantities.
- Google's digitisation of everything, including books; which potentially means every book that has ever been written will be available to download from the World Wide Web.

For authors these developments mean you have a potentially worldwide market for your books over the Internet. You can also profitably print and sell books locally, in your community, without significant investment.

For readers, it means easy access to books without having to leave your living room.

For publishers and bookshops, it means unquantifiable changes to the way you have traditionally done business. Unfortunately it may also mean some having to close down and cease trading.

Of course we've all heard it said that it won't happen. The traditionalists and protectionists behave like ostriches. People won't want to read books on electronic screens, they argue. Google won't be allowed to get away with their plans, they claim. Neither will discerning readers desert the personal service they get from their local bookshop; not for the shopping cart of some anonymous online book catalogue, they hope.

To such people we would like to reunite them with an old friend of theirs. King Canute was convinced he could hold back the tide; he was wrong. So too anybody who thinks the tide of technological progress is preventable; it isn't.

Of course the practice of writing won't really change. People will still want to read good stories. The method of delivery will be different though. Given our busy lifestyles, stories might become snappier, with faster plots and less narrative; the short story might also make a comeback. Issues will also arise over copyright.

The music industry offers an example of what might happen to the literary sector. The days of the super-groups and big record labels are over. More and more groups publish their own material online and establish local and niche followings. Listeners now download infinitely more music to their iPods and MP3 players than they buy in music stores.

A similar technology-led revolution is about to hit the book business. Everyone connected with the industry will be affected. The changes present opportunities and threats to writers, publishers and everyone connected with the book trade. Forecasting how things will pan out is like looking into a crystal ball. One thing's for certain though - everything will be different. The people who succeed in the future will be the ones who utilise modern technology to their advantage. Anybody who gets left behind will go the way of the dinosaur.

We will return to the impact of the digital revolution throughout the book, and we will take a more detailed look at print on demand, blogging, social media and e-books.

II. Becoming a Writer

Writers come in every shape and size, and from every age group and background.

Books and articles can be written about anything and everything, from cookery, DIY, sports, hobbies and culture to business, management, economics, politics, crime, religion, etc. Fiction can be in the form of a short story, a historical romance, a fantasy, a thriller; it can be written for children, teenagers or adults. Poetry, verse, rhyme, even plays and film scripts, all offer opportunities for creative expression. The list of possibilities to write is endless.

It's not only about books either. People write articles for newspapers, journals, magazines, community newsletters, advertising copy and so on. The opportunities to write have never been greater.

There is no qualification or pre-requisite for being a writer, except the ability to express yourself with a reasonable level of literacy. Everyone is entitled to write, many thousands of people earn their living from it, and anyone can become a best-selling author. All it takes is a lot of hard work and a bit of luck.

Not everyone wants to be published though. Many, perhaps most, writers are happy just to write and maybe produce something for consumption by family and friends, their immediate circle or local community.

They say there's a book inside everyone, and everybody has a story to tell. It's not just about telling stories though. Writers are not restricted to novels or short stories. A huge number of non-fiction books and technical manuals are published annually. Opportunities exist to write technical specifications, to report on the news, and express opinions about almost anything. On top of that, the most common form of writing is probably just an exchange of information in the form of e-mails, texts, tweets and blogs. These have largely replaced social letter writing as the modern form of communication.

The Internet has created a plethora of emerging opportunities for people to express themselves and broadcast their opinions. Blogging is a great way to write about things that interest you, to provide specialised information to a broad audience, or just keep family and friends up to date with what is going on in your life.

Computers, laptops and other electronic devices make writing, storage and transfer of text quick and easy. They also give support and confidence to everyone, since we can all now rely on the brilliance of the spellchecker, online dictionary and thesaurus.

If you want to be a writer, the best advice anyone can give you is *write.*

Don't worry if you can't type. A keyboard or laptop are not essential tools. All you really need is a pen and some paper to get you started. The typing bit can follow after you've composed your thoughts. Don't be over concerned with grammatical correctness either. Writing should be for pleasure. The best stories are allowed to flow without interruption, from the hand or fingertip. Editing is for a later stage.

If you are going to write successfully it is important to pick a subject that interests you and that you know something about. There's nothing worse than trying to be creative about a subject that you have absolutely no interest in or knowledge of.

The fun of writing includes researching your subject. There's no substitute for good research. If you want to write about Alsace wines, or Italian motor cars, or whatever it is, then you need some idea of what you are talking about. So too with novels; if your plot is set in the South of France or the slums of Calcutta, it helps if you have some idea of what it's like there.

It helps too to read other people's work. If for example you want to write a crime novel, it would be a good idea to read established crime authors to see how they develop their stories, build profiles of characters and so on. Don't plagiarise though; there's nothing as unbecoming as copying someone else's work.

Creative Writing Courses and Writers Workshops are a good idea to help you get started and create a structure for your work.

First-timers and those new to writing can join their local Creative Writing Group. Most public libraries have an active writing group which usually meets weekly, and they are always delighted to welcome new members. Talking to other writers, picking their brains and sharing ideas are great ways to develop your writing talent and stimulate creativity.

To succeed as a writer requires discipline and hard work. If the objective is to finish your poem or story, or complete your novel or book of non-fiction, then you are going to have to be your own task master. Writing is largely a solo activity. You have to apply yourself and stick to your task. Don't worry if you find the going tough, or your imagination dries up and you don't know what to write. Putting the pen down or closing down the laptop and taking a rest, is good therapy. You can always come back to it later, and you'd be surprised how creative you can be after a break.

People can take years to finish their work and get it to a state that they are happy with. That's the beauty of writing, you can keep playing with it, tinkering with words and phrases until you are happy with them. Writing can be a bit like pottering in the garden, or messing about on the river; it's an enjoyable past-time that doesn't need to have an end result or a deadline.

Remember, writing is very similar to reading; it is best enjoyed rather than endured. So write for yourself, for the fun and fulfilment of doing it, and you are far more likely to produce something that other people will enjoy reading or find useful and helpful.

III. Is There a Book In You?

One of the most striking things about best-selling authors is they are ordinary people. You don't have to be a modern day Casanova, a sporting hero, an explorer, or a member of the SAS to be able to write a good book.

In fact you never need to leave the comfort of your sitting room. Every one of us has a story to tell or something to say. All we need is a bit of imagination or an interest in something, and we have the raw material to write a book, a short story, a newspaper article or a collection of poems.

We met a lady in her sixties recently who'd kept home all her life. She had no experience of writing; yet she'd just written a cookery book. It was full of old-fashioned recipes like liver and bacon, steak and kidney pudding, and so on. It also contained lots of tips on making tasty dishes from the left-overs. It was her first attempt at writing a book. It's perfect for the recessionary times we are living in; and it's selling well right across the country.

That's the beauty of writing; anyone and everyone can do it. You don't have to be educated or professional. For most writers it's a hobby, and like all hobbies they do it in their free time. Some write short stories, others compose poetry, some even tackle a novel. Others write about something that interests them; film reviews, hill walking in Wicklow, World War II tanks, cruise liners, local history. The opportunities to write are endless.

Storytelling is perhaps the most original form of human entertainment. Just listen to the fisherman's tall stories, the after-match descriptions of sports fans, or the 'I said, he said, she said' gossiping of people on the bus or in the pub. Think too of the myths, sagas and folklore of ancient civilisations.

If you fancy your chances at writing, the most important things you need are the three Ds:

- ◆ Diligence
- ◆ Discipline
- ◆ Determination

You need to develop a 'writing habit'. Many successful authors dedicate a certain amount of time each day to writing. They treat it a bit like a part-time job, working to a time table, creating a set of objectives and a daily writing target. Don't be over ambitious though; set targets that are realistic and achievable given your own personal circumstances. If you're working full time during the day, try to set aside an hour in the evening and some time at weekends. If you are commuting, the train or bus journey might give you a chance to do some writing. If you're at home raising a family, maybe the best time is in the morning when the children are at school.

Since writing can be done at any time of the day or night, it really doesn't matter when you sit down to do it. Indeed many a good book has been written in the middle of the night as a past-time for insomniacs.

As well as discipline, diligence and determination, you will need inspiration and creativity.

The two questions most often asked by budding writers include:

- How do I become creative?
- Where can I get my inspiration from?

The answer to these questions is from all around you. Good sources of ideas and inspiration include:

- ◆ Your own experiences
- ◆ Your past
- ◆ Nature
- ◆ Other people
- ◆ Other books
- ◆ TV and radio
- ◆ Travel
- ◆ Research
- ◆ Writing groups
- ◆ The Internet
- ◆ Festivals, etc.

Sit quietly, close your eyes and see what comes into your head. Daydream, let your imagination wander; think what it would be like to win the lottery, to meet a new lover, to find yourself lost in an old castle?

Get a notebook and write down the things that come to mind. Keep writing and turn it into a short story. Give it a title like 'The Day I won The Lottery' or 'Adventures in an Old Castle' - hey presto! You are now a writer.

The question is often asked, "Do I need to work out the entire plot before I start writing?" Some writers do, some don't. Some just write and let the story evolve from day to day. They are more interested in developing the characters than mapping out the plot. Treat your characters like friends; get to know their personalities. Keep their actions and responses to situations consistent; remember people usually act in character. A few surprises though will enhance the story.

Books are not restricted to fictional stories; non-fiction offers far wider opportunities to write. The list of possibilities is endless:

- Cookery
- Sport
- Politics
- Biographies
- History
- Music
- Transport
- Culture
- Fashion
- Memoirs
- Hobbies
- Your Community
- Health
- Religion
- Self-Help
- Brewing or Wine Making

- Travel
- Technical Subjects
- Accidents and Disasters
- Car Maintenance
- Radio and TV
- Celebrities
- Business
- Beauty
- Astrology
- True Crime
- Nature
- Gardening
- Money
- Investments
- DIY, etc.

Writing non-fiction requires experience or knowledge of a subject; or it relies on research and investigation. If you want to write a non-fiction book or technical manual, write about something you are interested in. Check your facts carefully. Present information logically.

Whatever kind of book you are writing, try to keep an end goal in mind. At the end of the day a book with your name on the cover is a huge achievement. Many attempt it, and more and more writers are achieving it.

It has been said there are three basic rules to becoming a successful writer, but no one has yet worked out what they are. As already mentioned, if you really want to be a writer, the best advice anyone can give you is to get writing. That is the only way you are ever going to succeed.

Is there a book in you? Of course there is; you just have to let it out.

IV. Becoming Creative

Everyone is capable of being creative; but they need to allow themselves to be. That's not meant to be a smart statement to placate people who feel they have no chance of being a writer. It is meant to encourage them. It's a simple truth; you can be creative if you allow yourself to be. That's because creativity is closely related to confidence.

If you want to be creative, the first thing you have to do is believe in yourself. You have to trust your hunches and inspirations, and let them develop.

Try the little exercise we outlined in **Chapter III**. Sit quietly, close your eyes and see what comes into your head. Allow your imagination to wander; give it free reign to go wherever it wants to. Don't hold it back, let it come up with an idea, any idea and then see where that idea takes you. Jot down the ideas that come into your mind and make up an imaginary story that links them all together.

Try another approach - list the numbers 1 to 20 down the left hand side of a page, and build a story in steps as it comes to you. When you think of a beginning, describe it beside number 1. When you get the end, describe it beside number 20. Fill in the rest of the story in sequence from 2 to 19. Take your time. There's no hurry. Let your imagination fill in the gaps.

You can use this approach for fiction and non-fiction. If you're writing non-fiction though fill in facts beside each number rather than ideas.

A variant of this approach to encourage creativity is called clustering.

Clustering is a mapping technique that allows the imagination to wander in all directions. See diagram opposite.

Example of a Cluster built around the Subject of War

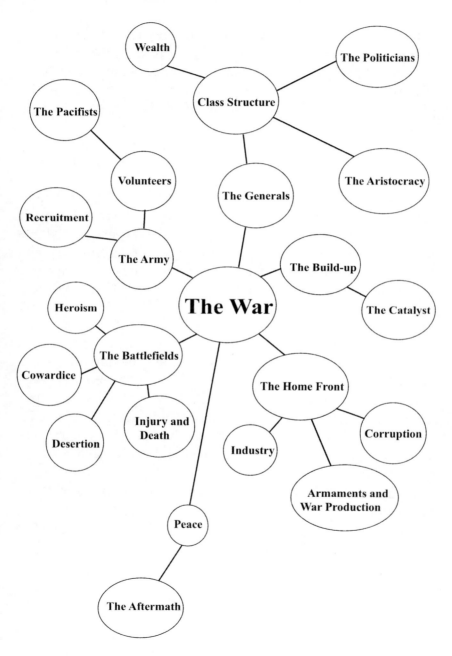

A variant you might adopt is **The Time Cluster** - starting with the original nucleus of the idea, create three time zones around it - Past, Present and Future. Allow these time zones to develop by writing down connections as they spring to mind.

You can also create clusters that help build characters. For example:

Relationship Cluster - starting with a central character build up relationship connections, for example: Father, Mother, Childhood, Siblings, Lovers (past and present), Teachers, Friends, Enemies, Boss, Workmates, Neighbours and so on - you can use this list of relationships to stimulate your imagination.

Activity Cluster - start with the central character and build connections about the things he or she does or has done in his or her life. Use the following list to start you off: Career, Hobbies, Travel, Holidays, Skeletons in the Cupboard, etc.

Personality Cluster - build connections around your character based on his or her personality.

Appearance Cluster - build connections around your character based his or her appearance.

Use the clustering approach if you get stuck when you are writing. You can use a combination of all these techniques or you might even develop an approach of your own.

Inspiration is different to creation. Creativity is original thinking. Inspiration is thinking that has been influenced or encouraged by something else.

You can get inspiration from anywhere. It's all around you, but you have to open your eyes and ears and let it in. Watch out for things of interest, particularly unusual things. Encourage your mind to watch everything that is happening around you. Focus on the detail as well as the broader picture. Listen in to other people's conversations; you'd be amazed how interesting and inspiring they can be. Study people's faces and clothes. Watch their body language, facial expressions and mannerisms. Read newspapers and magazines, tune into the news, find out what's going on in your community or locality. Be alert; keep your eyes wide open, and your ears pinned back. That's the best way to be inspired.

Keep a notebook of ideas and inspirations. Write down things that happen, take notes of overheard conversations. Jot down strange coincidences, funny events and anecdotes. Many famous writers have based their entire stories on things they overheard in coffee shops, airport terminals, doctor's waiting rooms, etc.

V. Getting Published

Many writers have no ambition to be published. They write purely for personal pleasure or out of interest for a particular subject; or perhaps for the entertainment or interest of family and friends. Others write for consumption by a society or club that they belong to, or for the local community in which they live. They may sell their work, but to a closed circle rather than the wider world.

Other writers have a greater ambition for their work. They seek to be published, to be sold on a national or even international level.

There's more than one way to skin a cat; and like all things in life there are several different routes a writer can take to getting published.

The traditional route is to submit your work to an agent or publisher in the hope that they will like it and promote it for you. This puts the onus in the hands of the agent or publisher by giving them the power to select or reject your work.

For some writers the only true test of worth is to be accepted by a publishing house. Others see this selective process as an insult to their work. They point out that agents and publishers very often reject work that subsequently goes on to become an international best-seller. Indeed many of the world's leading authors suffered rejection after rejection before they were eventually published.

The great advantage of the traditional agent/publisher route is that it sets and maintains standards. When a book has been released by a recognised publishing house, you know it will be produced to a high level of quality.

One consequence of becoming published in the traditional way is that ownership of the rights to the work usually transfers to the publisher or agent. In such cases they benefit more from the long-term success of the work than the author does. Of course, in fairness to the publisher, it must be pointed out that they are taking the commercial risk by putting up the cost of editing, printing, marketing and distribution. Should the book fail they, not the author, stand to bear the loss.

For this reason the traditional model is often known as risk publishing or trade publishing.

If this is the route you want to take then you are going to have to submit your work for consideration by a literary agent or publisher.

It's up to you which route you take, agent or publisher. Most successful authors have an agent, but some prefer to deal directly with the publisher. Agents take a commission from the revenue generated by your work, so going directly to the publisher could save you some costs. It needs to be understood though that many publishers, particularly of fiction, will only accept submissions via an agent. In the first instance therefore it is probably best to try to seek an agent. If that fails you can try approaching a publisher directly.

Literary agents represent an author they choose to work with. If they like your work they will undertake to try to find a publisher for you. They will negotiate your contract, secure an advance if possible, and agree your royalty levels. Having an agent working on your behalf gives you a greater chance of getting published. The fact that the agent has selected your work is a recommendation. Agents have established relationships with publishers. They know which publisher is more likely to accept your genre, and the fact that they are recommending you will more likely get you onto a publisher's shortlist for consideration.

Some writers prefer to approach publishers directly. This may be because they haven't been able to secure the services of an agent, or because they prefer to retain their independence.

Whichever course you chose, agent or direct to the publisher, you need to prepare your work for submission. This is a critical process. How well you do it will have a serious impact on your chances of success. **Chapter IX - Submitting Your Manuscript** explains how to go about submitting your work.

VI. The Publishing Process

If you are thinking about getting a book published it would be as well to have an understanding of how the publishing process works.

Obviously each publisher will work slightly differently depending on their size, management structure and so on, but the general process will be as follows:

- Manuscripts will be submitted by agents, other publishers (possibly overseas publishers) and authors. Manuscripts sent in by authors are known as direct commissions; they are often rather unkindly referred to as the 'slush pile'.

- New manuscripts are vetted within the Editorial Department. The first review is carried out by a Commissioning Editor (sometimes known as the Acquisitions or Acquiring Editor). His or her job is to decide whether the manuscript is worth further consideration.

- The Commissioning Editor presents suitable manuscripts to an Acquisitions Meeting attended by other editors, as well as production, marketing and sales representatives. The meeting decides whether to bid for the manuscript and agrees possible author advance, royalties and publishing rights that are to be sought (domestic, international, etc.).

- Assuming the manuscript gets the go ahead, it then goes to the Rights Department where selling rights (including domestic rights, serialisation rights, television and film rights, and translation rights) are agreed. An Advanced Information Sheet is completed. This includes preliminary details about the book: title, ISBN, format, extent (page count, word count), agreed rights, etc.

- The next stage is Structural Editing where the book is edited 'as a whole'. This includes reviewing narrative, chapters, pacing, characterisation, writing style, any illustrations, appendices, bibliography and so on.

- After this comes Copy Editing which focuses on the text. Spelling, syntax, grammar, punctuation, paragraphing, facts, figures and consistency are checked and corrected.

- Once this is done a First Proof is produced. This is checked by the author and a proof-reader.
- Any revisions are incorporated into a Second Proof. Prelim pages (dedication, copyright, acknowledgements, etc.) are added. So too are contents and index pages.
- Further proofs may follow until the Final Proof, which is the end of the 'Editing' process.
- Next the book goes into the Design Stage. The size and layout, cover, jacket, binding and any embellishments are designed, reviewed and finalised. This is often referred to as the 'Blads' (book layout and design stage).
- The book now goes into Production. A technical specification is prepared, the book is type set, and page-proofs are generated and checked. The book is then printed, bound and packed.
- Cover price is agreed. Marketing and Sales plans are prepared. Press packs, reviews and advertising are sorted out.
- Advance selling may take place.
- Warehousing and Distribution of the book then follows.
- Everything is under the watchful eye of the Accounts Department; one area of which, The Royalties Section, looks after author advances and royalties.

Things don't happen in haste. Caution and attention to detail are the cornerstones of successful publishing. Publishing a book is a time-consuming and expensive process; that's why publishers are very selective about the manuscripts they accept.

Impatient authors should be aware that the whole process from submission to publishing can take a year or more to complete. That's assuming that your manuscript gets taken on, which is a lengthy process in itself.

L191, 765

VII. Literary Agents

The literary agent's role is to represent the author, to help promote their career, find them a publisher, and negotiate rights, advances and royalties. They may also help arrange media interviews, book signings, TV appearances, book reviews and so on.

In simple terms: publishers publish books, agents represent authors; the agent is there to get the best deal for the authors they represent.

It might seem a surprise to realise that the agent is actually working for the author, given that the agent initially selects the author(s) they want to work with. The legal arrangement though is that the agent represents the author. The fine detail of the working arrangement will be subject to a written and agreed agency contract.

Agents get paid on the sale of their client author's books and rights. Their usual commission is 15% of domestic sales and 20% of overseas sales. What this does mean, for the author, is that the agent has a vested interest in working with you and for you. They don't get paid until you get paid.

Agents may work alone, or work for a literary agency - some of which might employ 50+ agents.

Many publishing houses, particularly publishers of fiction, deal only with agents and don't take unsolicited manuscripts directly from authors. So if you are a first-time author hoping to get your novel published, you should first try to obtain an agent.

Getting an agent is a bit like getting a job; you've got to work hard at it. The steps involved are as follows:

- Prepare your submission well - see **Chapter IX - Submitting Your Manuscript**.
- Approach agents who specialise in your genre.
- Try to get a name, rather than just sending a 'Dear Sir or Madam' letter.
- Check first to see if the agency has any preferred guidelines for submitting manuscripts. Follow the guidelines carefully.

- Have a good title for your book.
- Write a blurb for the back cover.
- If possible get testimonials from writers groups, other writers or experts in the field you are writing about.

Remember, for fiction there's no point approaching an agent until your book is more or less complete.

For non-fiction, getting an agent is less important as publishers are more willing to consider proposals and submissions directly from writers.

Looking for a publisher for your book?
See **www.WritingandPublishing.info**
Free advice and information about self-publishing

VIII. Protecting Your Work

Your original work is protected by copyright.

Copyright law is complex and is affected by international legislation. In simple terms you have copyright to everything you write. All you have to do is claim it.

Titles and ideas are not protected by copyright. If you want to protect them you would probably have to do so via trademark and patent legislation.

The easiest way to claim copyright is to include at the bottom of each page the word 'Copyright' and the internationally recognised symbol © followed by the year of origination and your name (e.g. Copyright © 2010 John Smith). It is a good idea to use both the word and the symbol as some countries or jurisdictions only recognise one or the other.

If you are publishing your own work you can include the following statement somewhere on the first few pages:

The right of <<Insert your name here>> to be identified as author of this work has been asserted by him/her in accordance with the copyright, design and patents acts pertaining.

All rights reserved. No reproduction, copy or transmission of this work may be made without written permission from the author.

No paragraph of this work may be reproduced, copied or transmitted save with written permission of the author or in accordance with the provisions of the copyright acts pertaining.

This work is made available subject to the condition that it shall not, by way of trade or otherwise, be lent, sold, hired out or otherwise circulated without the author's prior consent.

Any person who does any unauthorised act in relation to this work may be liable to criminal prosecution and civil claim for damages.

Theft of copyright is unusual, but it does occasionally happen. Should there be a dispute over your work, it would be essential for you to be able to prove the date of your original copyright claim.

The best way to do this is to send your manuscript to yourself by registered post. Place your work in a sealed envelope and sign your usual signature across the seal. Address the envelope to yourself. Take it to a post office and send it by registered post. Make sure the Post Office date stamps the receipt. Also ask them to date stamp across the seal. Keep the receipt somewhere safe.

Do not open the envelope when you receive it. Keep it safe with the receipt.

In the event of a dispute, hand the unopened envelope and Registered Post receipt to a Notary Public, Commissioner of Oaths or Court Official to open. They will be able to verify the date of origination from the Post Office date stamp and registered letter receipt.

Authors, poets and other writers are advised not to sell their copyright even to a publisher. It is far better to licence the publisher to publish your work. Licensing should be for a defined period (10, 15, 20 or 25 years); try to avoid indefinite licenses.

Should the book go out of print, then subject to certain terms and conditions, you should be able to claim back your copyright from the publisher.

Remember, your copyright is valuable; don't give it away cheaply.

IX. Submitting Your Manuscript

Some points to keep in mind when submitting a manuscript for consideration by an agent or publisher include:

1. Research the market to identify publishers or agents who are appropriate for the type of work you want to submit. For example there's no point submitting a romantic novel to a technical publisher, or vice versa.
2. Prepare your presentation carefully, check for spelling mistakes, make sure your work is tidy and well laid out.
3. Use white paper (80gsm bond is a good choice).
4. Start with a title page (no need to be illustrated). Include book's title and sub-title, your name, address, phone details and e-mail address.
5. Print on a single side only, and double space your text.
6. Use a standard 12 point font that is clearly legible; Times New Roman is ideal.
7. Set the margin at 3cm all around the page (header, gutter, footer and fore-edge).
8. Start each chapter on a new page.
9. Indent paragraphs, but only insert a blank line for a change of subject or theme, or for a new location.
10. Be consistent with headings, sub-headings, use of capital letters and variant spellings.
11. For plays use capitals for character names, leave a line between different character speeches, and italicise stage directions.
12. Set out poetry exactly as you would expect to see it in print.
13. Number pages (at the top right hand or bottom right hand corner). Start from the first page of the text and number consecutively. If you need to add a subsequent page (for example after page 21 , number it 21A, 21B and so on.
14. If illustrations are to be used include them, preferably inserted in the appropriate places.
15. Number 'prelim' pages (copyright, dedications,

acknowledgements, contents, etc.) with small Roman numerals (i, ii, iii, etc.).

16. Include your name, address and contact details on the last page.

17. Send copies not original pages.

18. Send a stamped addressed envelope only if you want your submission returned.

19. Don't fasten, staple or pin pages together. Punch with a single hole and use a toggle.

20. Don't use binders. Place the pages in a manila folder. Write the book's title, your contact details and number of pages submitted on the outside.

The listings for **Book Publishers** in **Section II** include publisher's requirements for submissions. You can usually find the guidelines for submission on the agent's or publisher's website. If not you can write to them, e-mail them or phone to ask for their guidelines.

Follow the publisher's or agent's guidelines for submission. There's no point submitting an e-mail if they state that e-mail submissions are not accepted. Most publishers won't accept a full unsolicited manuscript. They will probably want a synopsis (a summary of the plot) and a copy of the first few chapters to show how you write. To the agent or publisher these are a sample, a taster to see if the full manuscript is worth requesting.

X. Writing a Synopsis

Most authors find writing a synopsis extremely difficult. How do you condense a 100,000 word manuscript into three or four pages? The answer is - with difficulty.

Writing a synopsis forces you to look at your work as a whole. It makes you think about it. What kind of story is it? What is it really about? What is its main theme? Why would anyone want to read it?

Take time writing the synopsis. Keep it brief; it needs to quickly generate interest in your work. Bear in mind, agents and publishers get hundreds of unsolicited manuscripts. You have to sell your work and stand out from the crowd. If you are submitting fiction, identify the genre (romance, historical, crime, thriller, sci-fi, etc.), outline the plot, describe the characters, explain the nuance or twist in the tale, and say what it is about your work that will make it appeal to the targeted reader.

If you are submitting sample chapters, prepare them carefully. Read them over at least three times, check for spelling mistakes and unnecessary wordage.

For fiction include the following in your synopsis:
1. Type of Novel (genre) - Choose from:
   - Crime
   - Thriller
   - Science fiction
   - Horror
   - Fantasy
   - Humour
   - Satire
   - Chic-Lit
   - Lad's-Lit
   - Romantic
   - Historical
   - Erotic

2. Brief Summary (maximum 150 words) outlining the plot and major characters.

3. Detailed Summary (maximum 500 words) to include:
- Setting - when and where the story is based
- Main characters - brief description, their role in the story and relationship to each other, any distinguishing characteristics
- Sequential outline of the plot and how it unfolds, chart the highs and lows of the story and how they impact on the main characters
- Brief statement of what is interesting or unusual about your novel, any dramatic turning points, any twist in the tale, punch line, etc.

4. Write your synopsis in the third person and in the present tense.

Non-fiction

The approach for non-fiction is different than for fiction. You can submit a non-fiction proposal before the book is written, to see if any publishers are interested in your project. You can send your proposal (at this stage it's called an Initial Pitch) directly to a publisher. Select the publisher carefully though to ensure they publish books in your chosen genre (for example military history, cooking, self-help, etc.).

The Initial Pitch should be no more than two pages. It should include an overview of the book you are proposing to write. Describe the subject or topic. Discuss its findings or conclusions and explain the research that you are undertaking. Define the target market and describe how your book differs from other books about your subject. Outline too any new ground that it covers, or gap in the market that it fills. Include a chapter breakdown and probable word count.

If the Initial Pitch succeeds a publisher may express an interest in your proposal.

If not you can try sending a Second Pitch when the book is nearing completion.

The Second Pitch needs to be a more detailed synopsis (same format as the Initial Pitch). It should be accompanied by a concise description of each chapter (100 words for each chapter), as well as a sample chapter in full.

The golden rule, before you send in your submission, is check it carefully. Make sure there are no spelling mistakes and don't be too verbose.

It often helps to get your submission reviewed before you send it to publishers or agents. Remember, you only get one shot at the target.

XI. The Covering Letter

A covering letter should accompany your manuscript submission.

Try to avoid 'Dear Sir', or 'Dear Sir/Madam' letters. If at all possible your submission should be addressed to a named individual in the publishing house or literary agency you are approaching.

You can probably find the name of the appropriate person by researching the publisher's or agent's website. Check the Publisher and Agent listings in **Section II** of this Handbook, as they contain many contact names. Alternatively you can call the publisher or agent, explain that you want to submit a manuscript and ask who you should send it to.

If you can't find a name, then address your letter, as appropriate, to: The Fiction Editor, Non Fiction Editor, Children's Editor or Poetry Editor at XYZ Publishers, or to The Literary Agent at XYZ Literary Agency.

The purpose of a covering letter is to introduce your manuscript and convince the publisher or agent to read it.

As previously stated, for non-fiction you can submit a proposal before your work is completed. For fiction your work needs to be more or less finished.

Your covering letter should be set out as follows:

- Your name, address and contact details should be at the top
- The letter should be dated
- It should start with a short sentence explaining why you are writing to the addressee:
  I am pleased to submit my manuscript for your consideration.
- It needs a brief biography of yourself; keep it relevant to the work.
- It needs a short (75 word) description of your work to include:
  - Its genre
  - Major theme
  - Plot description

- Page and word count
- Status: Finished, started, half-written, etc.
- You need a concluding sentence explaining that you have included a synopsis and sample chapters according to the publisher's or agent's guidelines.
- If you want your submission returned, explain that you have enclosed a stamped addressed envelope. Make sure it is big enough to contain your manuscript and contains the correct value stamp for the size and weight.
- Finally your letter should be signed by you.

Custom dictates that you should approach only one agent or publisher at a time. If you do decide to submit to more than one publisher or agent it is considered best to advise them of this. Be aware though, this may put them off spending much time on your manuscript unless they feel it is exceptionally good - no one likes the concept of a 'Dutch auction'.

Keep a list of agents and publishers to whom you have sent your submissions; keep dates and record of any replies, follow up calls or correspondence.

XII. Dealing With Rejection

After you've submitted your manuscript you have to exercise unlimited patience.

It usually takes months before you hear anything back from an agent or publisher. This can be a testing time as you wait to hear what they think of your book. It is also frustrating because, until you hear back, you can't really approach another publisher or agent.

Unfortunately the most likely response from an agent or publisher to a new author is going to be 'thanks but no thanks'. This doesn't mean your story is poor or your writing style is weak; it simply means it is not what the agent or publisher is looking for at that particular time.

Literary agents and publishing houses are not infallible. It's amazing how often they fail to spot a potential best-seller. It might surprise you to know how many times John Grisham was rejected by publishing houses, before he was finally accepted.

The rejection letter will probably be short and sweet, something like:

> *Thank you for your manuscript which we read with interest. We are sorry to have to tell you that we have decided not to take it any further.*

Publishers and agents receive thousands of unsolicited manuscripts every year, so it stands to reason they will have to reject most of them. They are very busy and are unlikely to explain why they haven't chosen your submission. Neither are they likely to give any feedback, hints or tips about your writing style.

Rejection letters are as much a part of being a writer as is the click-click sound of a keyboard. Indeed lots of best-selling authors received scores of rejection letters before they finally got accepted by a publisher.

Don't take rejections personally. They are not a reflection of your ability or capability. They do not signify that you are useless or un-publishable.

Try to look upon rejection letters as milestones towards your goal of getting published. The more rejections you notch up, the closer you are to success.

Keep trying, keep writing and keep submitting manuscripts. 'If at first you don't succeed, try, try and try again' should be adopted as the motto of all writers. It really is amazing how many famous authors saw their manuscripts turned down over and over again before they finally got accepted.

Remember, there's more than one way to skin a cat.

See **Chapter XIV** on **Assisted Publishing**. More and more writers are choosing this route; not just because they unable to find a publisher, but also because they retain control over their books, and keep much more of the sales revenue than they would with conventional publishing.

Looking for inspiration or help with your writing?
Go to **www.WritingandPublishing.info**
For advice and and tips on successful writing

XIII. Alternative Ways to be Published

The traditional route to getting published via a literary agent and/or a publishing house doesn't work for everyone.

There are several reasons why you might want to consider an alternative. You may have been unsuccessful in finding a publisher to take on your work, you might wish to keep more of the sales revenue from your book for yourself, or you might want to keep permanent control of your copyright.

You might also intend to be published on a small scale, and plan to sell your books locally, or within a club, community or family group. People write family memoirs, local histories, collections of poems, short stories etc., that aren't of interest to large publishing houses, but still have the potential to sell to a niche market.

Whatever the reason, the alternatives you can consider are presented below:

Vanity Publishing is where you pay a publishing house to print and publish your book. In reality this means going to one of several companies that specialise in vanity publishing. This approach is not recommended unless you are rich and have money to burn.

Firstly it is invariably expensive. You may be asked to pay a considerable sum of money for a large quantity of books, most of which will probably never sell. Some Vanity Publishers ask that you print several thousand copies, justified on the basis that printing such a large quantity keeps unit costs down. Others offer a 'Package' approach, which includes lots of 'added value services and a listing in their catalogue', but very few actual books. It is not unheard of to pay out €1,500 plus and get less than 20 books. Others just keep your manuscript on file and only produce a book if they actually get a sale. In this case you've paid out a considerable sum of money to produce a fancy electronic image and very little else.

Secondly you often have to give up the rights to your work.

Check the Copyright clause carefully. If it says rights are reserved and copies cannot be made without the permission of the publisher then run a mile - unless of course the publisher is taking the risk with their own money to publish the book.

Vanity Publishing is treated with disdain by the publishing industry. Book distributors, wholesalers and bookshops don't support vanity-produced books. It is almost impossible to get a review in the media. To put it bluntly, you are very unlikely to be taken seriously, and your money will almost certainly end up being wasted.

Self-publishing is where you go it alone, publish your book yourself and retain all the rights.

To do that you need to:

- Arrange your own cover design, typesetting, ISBN, bar code and print-ready PDF
- Organise your own printing and binding
- Arrange legal deposits
- Organise your own marketing, sales and distribution.

It can be done, and many people have done it successfully; but it requires a degree of technical competence, across a variety of disciplines, that most authors do not possess. Indeed no single individual can be expected to excel at all the required disciplines to write a book, get it into print, and market and sell it successfully. It also implies risk, because if anything goes wrong it is all on your head.

You'd be amazed how many household names had to get books published by doing it themselves. Writers like Rudyard Kipling, Virginia Woolf, Mark Twain, D.H. Lawrence and Beatrix Potter all started out self-publishing. In Ireland James Joyce and Roddy Doyle did it on their own. More recently *Shadowmancer* by G.P. Taylor was originally self-published before being spotted by Faber & Faber. It went on to become an international best-seller.

The poet and artist William Blake published his own work. He went so far as to make his own paper, mix his own inks and even got his wife to sew on the covers. Luckily you don't have to go to that extreme, but self-publishing, by doing it all on your own, can still be an onerous undertaking.

Assisted Publishing is a rapidly growing alternative to the traditional publishing house route. It is also seen as an easier option to publishing on your own. With Assisted Publishing, authors retain all rights to their work, and all books produced belong to them until they are sold. A specialist publishing partner takes on the work of cover design, typesetting, ISBN, etc., organises printing and binding, and helps with marketing, sales and distribution.

More and more writers are turning to Assisted Publishing to get their books produced. It is the fastest-growing sector of the book publishing market and is now accounting for a rapidly increasing percentage of new titles being produced in Ireland, the UK and America.

For these reasons Assisted Publishing is described in more detail in the following chapter.

Thinking about self-publishing?
See **www.WritingandPublishing.info**
Free advice and information about going it alone

XIV. Assisted Publishing Explained

Not surprisingly, recent advances in electronic media and digital printing technology have impacted on the traditional publishing model. One area where these advances are reflected is in the development of Assisted Publishing.

Before it wasn't practical or economical to produce small quantities of books. High set up costs for traditional lithographic printing meant production runs of less than several thousand copies were prohibitively expensive.

Digital printing and print-on-demand technologies now mean books can be produced economically in short runs from 1 to 2,500 copies. Print runs of 100 or 200 copies are becoming increasingly common.

Technological developments now give writers the opportunity to by-pass the conventional publishing model (manuscript submission, literary agent and publishing house) and get their books published without losing control over their work, or suffering the disappointment of constant rejection.

The conventional model puts the publisher in control. Publishing houses are effectively king makers, choosing the authors they want and making them famous. The result is a few rich and successful writers, with the vast majority of literary creations turned down, overlooked and ignored.

Some might argue this ensures only the best fiction is published, as agents and publishers weed out weaker writers. Unfortunately this simply isn't true.

Publishing houses today are not looking for good writing; they are only interested in whether it is commercial or not. That means whether it can sell in large quantities. This is a selective measure which results in excellent writing being rejected simply because it doesn't conform to a mass-market formula.

Have you ever wondered why there are so many books in the bookshops that have similar themes, or why successful writers always seem to write to the same template? The answer is simple - that's what publishers demand because that is what sells to the mass market. And the mass market, by its very nature, is fashion or trend-based. That's why so many *Harry Potter*, *Da Vinci Code* and *Twilight* clones have turned up in recent years. There's a band-wagon that everyone tries to jumponto until the next commercial fad comes along.

It's interesting to speculate, if Emily Brontë, Ernest Hemmingway, Charles Dickens, James Joyce, or any other classic writers were alive today and submitting manuscripts to a literary agent or publishing house, they would almost certainly be rejected. Not because their manuscripts weren't well written, but because they would be considered non-commercial in today's market place.

Believe it or not, but one enterprising newspaper changed the character names and locations of one of the great classical novels and submitted it to publishers for consideration. It got rejected. No publisher recognised it for the classic that it was, but all rejected it because it was considered 'non-commercial'.

What of all the books that don't conform to this commercial mass market formula? What happens to them? Until now they were largely ignored and seldom came to be published. Yet many titles are viable in smaller quantities. They would sell and would be of interest to discerning readers, niche markets, local communities and so on. Some could even go on to become best-sellers.

Assisted Publishing has arisen because writers of all genres need help getting their books published. They need professional support but don't want to give up their rights to their work.

With Assisted Publishing, the writer gets professional support and assistance throughout the entire process of book production, publishing and marketing.

Assisted Publishing combines the benefits of both the publishing house and self-publishing routes, but with reduced economic risk and no loss of rights or control.

The key points about Assisted Publishing are:

- The Assisted Publishing company provides the ISBN, bar code and organises the legal deposit. They are your publisher but they do not own the rights to your work.

- You retain all rights to your work. The Copyright entry in your book will say all rights belong to the author (not the publisher) and copies cannot be produced without the author's permission.
- You get a fixed-price quotation for the services you require (proof-reading, editing, cover design, promotional material, marketing, etc). You are not limited to a standard package that you are forced to follow - you choose what you need and pay only for the services you use.
- You get a fixed price for producing an agreed number of books, and you choose the number of books that you want (50, 100, 250, 500, 1000, etc.).
- You decide your own selling price.
- You control the future success of your book - you get help and advice, but ultimately all decisions are yours.

Assisted Publishing gives you the best of all worlds, professional help to get your book into a print-ready format, economical printing and binding costs, retention of copyright and all selling rights, assistance with marketing and selling your book, low investment in book stocks and high share of your book's sales receipts.

If you've gone to the trouble of writing a book but haven't been able to get it published, why not give the Assisted Publishing route a try? Produce a hundred copies of your book for local sale. You will then be a published author with a published book to your credit. This will improve the chances of subsequent books being of interest to publishers.

If you think you've written a best-seller but can't find a publisher, don't despair. Use the Assisted Publishing route to get your book into the market place. Sell it successfully in your local area, or online. Then go back to the publisher with a success story. Let them see that your book really works. They may see you in a different light.

XV. Self-Publishing: The Good, the Bad and the Ugly

Writers considering the self-publishing route should ask the following questions of their potential self-publishing partner:

Are you retaining the copyright to your work? Check carefully, if the answer is Yes it's OK to proceed. If the answer is no, consider what you are doing very carefully and proceed with caution.

How much are you being asked to pay? Make sure you know the total amount; check to see if there are any add-ons or optional extras that you really need (e.g. editing, proof-reading, cover design, typesetting). If you need extras make sure you have prices for them.

Are you being offered editorial advice? If not, why not? If you are, how much is it costing?

Are you being offered a proof reading service? If not, why not? If you are, how much is costing?

Will you get a proof copy of your book before it is printed? It is important that you see a physical copy of the text and cover before it goes to print. How else can you check everything is OK? Remember a computer screen image is not the same as a physical copy.

What arrangements are being made for cover design? Are you being offered a choice of a template or a bespoke design? A template design can save cost; a bespoke design offers you complete control over the design of your cover.

Are you being offered the option to laminate the cover? If you are, what does it cost? Laminating makes the cover more durable. It is not necessary on smaller quantities, but would be desirable if you intend selling your book through retail outlets who are inclined to stick labels on the covers.

Are there illustrations, photographs or archived documents in your book? If so, what arrangements are being made to scan and print them? Are they integrated into the text or collated together in a separate section? Are there any additional costs for scanning or integrating illustrations/photographs?

Are you incorporating colour into your book? If so what printing arrangements are being made and what is it going to cost? Make sure you see a printed proof before the main print run takes place. Check the colour reproduction carefully before giving the go-ahead to print.

Is there a charge for delivery? Is it included in the price, or is it extra?

Will your books be shrink-wrapped and packed in cartons? Shrink-wrapping is essential to stop books absorbing moisture during storage. Are there extra charges for this?

Are you being given a detailed breakdown of costs for each service you require? If not, why not? Ideally you should get a quotation detailing the price you are being charged for:
   ◆ Pre-press activities - editing, proof-reading, cover design, typesetting
   ◆ Publishing - ISBN, bar code, legal deposit, copyright assistance
   ◆ Printing, binding and reprinting
   ◆ Shrink-wrapping
   ◆ Packing
   ◆ Delivery

Are you being forced down a package route? If so consider whether this is really giving you value for money.

Are you being offered a choice of book sizes (A5, Royal, Demi, A6, B and C formats etc.), or are you being restricted to just one or two sizes? Books don't need to come in just one size; having a variety of sizes to choose from increases your options when it comes to pricing and marketing your books.

Are you being offered a choice of font types and sizes? The type and size of font affects the page count, and page count affects cost and appearance. If you want more pages you need to use a bigger font size; if you want fewer pages you need to use a smaller font size. Serif fonts are generally used for fiction, sans serif are often preferred for non-fiction.

Are you being offered a choice of different paper stocks to print your book on? The choice of paper can have a big impact on the appearance of your book. White bond works best for non-fiction, bookwove looks best for general fiction, heavier paper is necessary for childrens' books, coated paper for photographs and illustrations.

If you want an audio version of your book, is this possible? The appeal of a childrens book can be enhanced if you are able to offer a complimentary CD. Check to see if your self-publishing partner can offer this service; if so at what cost?

Are you being offered a choice of binding types? Perfect bound is ideal for paperback books; Wire-O is best for cook books and manuals that people like to fold-flat; saddle-stitched is the answer for smaller booklets of up to 80 pages; case bound is ideal for hard back books.

How many copies of your book are you actually getting for your money? This is important. If you don't have a stock of books to sell how are you ever going to get your money back? I suggest a minimum of 100 copies and a maximum of 500 copies is appropriate for a first-time author. Any less than 100 copies and you have no chance of getting your investment back. Any more than 500 copies and you run the risk of being left with a big pile of unsold books in your garage. Remember you can always reprint if you sell out of copies - so don't take too many at the first run.

How much will it cost if you want to reprint your book? Find this out before you print the first run. It's important to know what a reprint will cost before you hand over your manuscript and a print-ready file is produced. You don't want to go looking for a reprint, find it is prohibitively expensive and have to start all over again getting print-ready files produced.

Are you being offered a listing on Amazon, Barnes and Noble, etc. in place of physical books? Are you being told this means your book is available for sale world-wide? A listing on these websites does no harm, but how is your book going to stand out amongst the hundreds of thousands of other books that are for sale on them? The reality is you are not going to sell many of your books on these websites, not unless you first become a best-seller. So don't hold your breath waiting for this approach to get you your money back. You really need books to sell; that is the best way to recoup your investment.

Are you being told your book will be on display in a leading bookshop? If you are, ask where and for how long? The answer is probably somewhere in Central London for 10 weeks maximum. How many of your potential readers do you think will go book-shopping in Central London? Surely it makes better sense to display your books in Irish bookshops.

What help will you get marketing and selling your book? Can your self-publishing partner provide flyers, posters, business cards, invitation cards? Are they offering to publicise your book to the media? Are they offering a library marketing service? Do they have their own on-line catalogue? Are they offering an order fulfilment service? What are the costs associated with these marketing activities?

If you sell the book yourself, how much of the net sales price (after discount) do you retain? The answer should be all of it. If it's not, or if you have to buy a copy of your own book in order to sell it, then beware.

What does it cost you if your self-publishing partner sells a copy of your book? Are they taking a commission or offering you a royalty? If they take a commission, what is the rate? I suggest 30% is acceptable. If they are paying you a royalty, what is the rate? To equate to a commission of 30% you should receive 70% royalty, any less than 70% and you are paying more than a bookshop would charge to stock and display your book on their shelves.

How much do you have to pay your self-publishing partner if a bookshop decides to stock your book? Remember a bookshop will expect at least 30% discount; so if you have to pay your self-publishing partner as well there is very little left for you.

How many books will you have to sell to get your money back? This really is the acid test. Divide the total cost by the retail price of your book (allow for an average 20% discounts). The result is the number of books you need to sell to get your money back. Are you getting enough stock (actual physical copies) to allow you to sell this many books?

Having successfuly self-published several books himself, David Jones offers the following words of encouragement to anyone considering self-publishing, or even better Assisted

Publishing: "I believe everyone has the right to be published. If you ask the questions listed above and you get the right answers, then there really is no reason why this route can't prove as successful for you as it has for me and many other authors all over the world."

XVI. ISBN and Legal Deposits

ISBN - The International Standard Book Number (ISBN) is a unique 13-digit number which identifies each particular book. The number is divided into shorter groups that identify the publisher, country or language that the book is published in, the title, edition number, etc.

All commercially published books have an ISBN. They also have a bar code representation of the ISBN which can be read by a scanner. Book distributors, retailers and libraries use the ISBN and bar code for reference, stock control, ordering, logistics management and sales check out.

The ISBN agency for Ireland and the UK is administered by Nielsen's. Their address is:

Nielsen ISBN Agency, 3rd Floor Midas House, 62 Goldsworth Road, Woking, GU21 6LQ, England.

> Tel: Int+44 870 777 8712
> Fax: Int+44 870 777 8714
> E-mail: isbn.agency@nielsen.com
> Website: www.isbn.nielsenbookdata.co.uk

Nielsen's requirements for issuing an ISBN are as follows:

- ISBNs are issued to publishers and each ISBN allocation contains a publisher identifier code. Products bearing an ISBN from that allocation are considered to be 'published by' the person or organisation so identified.

- A publisher is anyone who is making work available to the public. "The Publisher is generally the person or body who takes the financial risk in making a product available."

- As a general rule, only books qualify for ISBNs but there are exceptions - e.g. CDs, downloads, audio-books, etc. that have a textual and/or instructional content, i.e. not purely for entertainment.

- Journals published with a frequency of no more than once a year may qualify for ISBNs. Publishers of serials, periodicals, quarterly journals, etc., should apply for International Standard

Serial Numbers (ISSN).

- ISBNs are only available in blocks - minimum of ten which cost stg£107.18. It is not possible to obtain a single ISBN.
- ISBNs are not transferable.

Unless you intend publishing a lot of titles, it's probably not worth buying your own ISBN. Find an Assisted Publishing or authors services provider who will supply you with an ISBN, register your book with Nielsen's, help with copyright issues, legal deposit, etc.

Legal Deposit - There is a legal requirement in Ireland and Northern Ireland (as there is throughout the UK) that a person or group submit copies of their publications to a repository, usually a library. This is known as a legal deposit.

In the Republic of Ireland, the Copyright and Related Rights Act 2000 specifies that one copy of every book published is to be delivered to the National Library of Ireland, the Library of Trinity College, Dublin, the library of the University of Limerick, the library of Dublin City University, and the British Library. Four copies are to be delivered to the National University of Ireland for distribution to its constituent universities. Within twelve months of publication a copy is to be delivered to the Bodleian Library, Cambridge University Library, the National Library of Scotland and the National Library of Wales.

In the United Kingdom, including Northern Ireland, the Legal Deposit Libraries Act 2003 restates the Copyright Act 1911, that one copy of every book published must be sent to the British Library; five other libraries (Bodleian Library at the University of Oxford, Cambridge University Library, National Library of Scotland, the Library of Trinity College, Dublin and the National Library of Wales) are entitled to request a free copy within one year of publication. The convention for most publishers however, is to deposit their books with all 13 libraries, without waiting for a request to be made.

Trinity College Dublin benefits from legal deposit legislation in both the Republic of Ireland and the United Kingdom.

The publisher of the book, or the self-publisher if you are doing it yourself, is responsible for the ISBN, bar code and legal deposit.

XVII. Short Stories and Essays

In today's busy world where no one seems to have time for anything anymore, the short story may be poised to make a comeback. Technology at least appears to be on its side.

Short stories are very popular in the USA. Although they have been somewhat spurned by UK and Irish publishers, the fact that we tend to follow what happens in America, probably means we may well have a resurgence of short stories in the next few years.

Writing short stories requires the same level of discipline and attention to detail as a novel. It might seem a less daunting task because you only have to write under 5,000 words compared to the average novel of about 100,000 words. However many writers find it more difficult to write a short story because the plot, length and number of characters are limited. Most writers will have no problem churning out pages on a subject they are passionate about; but the short story writer and essayist, in order to keep the word count down, needs to combine the functions of author and editor.

Short stories usually involve one event: a chance encounter, a weekend away, a journey, a particular crime or rescue, a walk or visit to a relation, etc. They include a limited number of characters: a romantic couple, a small group of friends, a protagonist and his or her foe, a few fellow travellers, a pop group, sports team, a collection of neighbours or family members, etc. They usually take place over a short period of time: a weekend, an hour or two on the train, fifteen minutes of danger, a sports match or race, and so on.

Short stories also tend to have an anticipatable ending. They are read in one sitting. So from the very beginning, the end is usually in sight. Having said that, some short story writers, like Saki - the pen name of Hector Hugh Munro - excelled at introducing a twist at the end.

They can be character led or incident led; either way they need to move along at pace, with not too much detail about scenery or setting.

Suitable topics for short stories include:
- ◆ Romance
- ◆ Adultery
- ◆ Childhood memories
- ◆ Friendship
- ◆ 'Day in the life' stories
- ◆ Crime
- ◆ Obituaries and tributes
- ◆ Moralising
- ◆ Emotion
- ◆ Satire
- ◆ Redemption
- ◆ Contests
- ◆ Revenge
- ◆ Daily reflections
- ◆ Humour
- ◆ Historical events
- ◆ Real life drama
- ◆ Argument or conflict
- ◆ Heroism
- ◆ Acts of kindness and generosity, etc.

Short stories can be published singly in magazines or newspapers; or in collections as a book of short stories by one or more writers.

Women's magazines, *Ireland's Own* and specialist magazines like *The Stinging Fly* offer opportunities for first-time writers to get their short stories published.

They are also the basis of many writing competitions.

Essays are similar to short stories but contain fewer words, perhaps less than 2,000. They can be about anything but are usually non-fiction. They provide a great opening for writers of all sorts, and a good opportunity for first-time writers to get their work published in journals and magazines.

Radio is another medium that short story writers and

essayists can explore. The *Sunday Miscellany* programme has been broadcasting every Sunday on RTÉ Radio 1 for over four decades. According to the programme's website: "Reportage, appreciations, memory pieces, poetry, travel writing and personal accounts of events and happenings are all the stuff of Sunday Miscellany".

See the RTÉ website - www.rte.ie/radio1/sundaymiscellany - where you can also download submission guidelines.

XVIII. Writing for Children

The market for children's and teenage literature has increased significantly in the last five years. Harry Potter has been responsible for much of this increase. This has encouraged many writers to try to find the winning formula, and publishers to look for the next J.K. Rowling.

If you want to write for children, it's important to remember that they come in differing age groups, with differing reading abilities. Stories for 5 and 6 year olds will be of no interest to 10 and 11 year olds. Similarly teenage fiction is quite different and requires more complex plots and deeper characters.

The cardinal rule when writing for young people, is don't underestimate their knowledge, intelligence or reading ability. Don't write down to them, don't over-simplify and don't be old-fashioned.

Children live in the real world, just like adults. They communicate extensively with each other. They are up to date with technology and are aware of what is going on in the world around them. Their world is not sweetness and light; they have problems, worries and cares just like the rest of us. They also have vivid imaginations which need to be stimulated if your writing is to grab their attention.

Characters are important in children's stories. They can be human, animal or imaginary. Children don't respond well to complex settings and detailed descriptions of scenery. They prefer characterisation and animation.

It is especially important that young readers can identify with the characters in your story. You can write a mythical story or a fantasy, but your characters must have a personality and they need feelings, fears and issues to contend with.

Children's fiction varies in length, depending on the age of the reader.

For young readers under the age of 8, books range from 1,000 to 5,000 words. For 9 to 12 year olds, 20,000 to 40,000 words is appropriate.

There's also a large market for children's non-fiction - not just school books, but more general fun-based books. Young people are always keen to acquire knowledge, especially about exciting, interesting topics like history, science, geology, dinosaurs and so on. To succeed they have to be fast-moving, punchy and packed with unusual and interesting facts.

Many children's books are illustrated, but as a writer you don't need to worry about that. Stick to your story. You can worry about the illustrations later or get someone else to do it for you.

One area that is growing rapidly is encouraging children to produce books themselves as a classroom project. Each child contributes a page towards a consolidated book. Many schools see this as both a creative project for the class, and a fund raising exercise, since books can be sold to parents, family friends and in the wider community.

Subjects that are suitable for this kind of book project include:
- What pupils did on their school holidays
- Recipes submitted by pupils' grannies
- Art work produced by the pupils
- Short stories (1 or 2 pages) written by the pupils
- Field trips and school days out
- The school garden
- Nature walks, etc.

XIX. Poetry

Poetry is an art form that few understand; writing poetry is a passion that few people dare to undertake. Or so we are lead to believe.

There is no real definition of what distinguishes poetry from prose. Coleridge defined poetry as "the right words in the right order". Another definition of poetry is "maximal meaning in minimal wording".

Poems are like songs. They may rhyme, but this is not a condition. Many, perhaps most, poems are non-rhyming. They have a tempo or rhythm though, and are usually presented in verses which have a similar or repetitive pattern.

Poetry is often more focused on what it sounds like, rather than how it reads.

Prose on the other hand is more akin to the normal language of everyday speech. It is structured into paragraphs, and follows the standard rules of grammar, sentencing, clauses, punctuation, capitalisation and so on.

The market for poetry, and the consequent opportunities for getting published, has diminished over recent years. There may be many reasons for this. The popularity of song-writing and the prevalence of recorded music may be one. Lyrics are after all very similar to poetry.

If you're a poet and you want to get published then the same general guidelines apply as if you were a writer of books or short stories.

You can submit your poems individually to magazines and poetry journals. Poetry groups offer good support and opportunities to publish together in a joint anthology.

If you are thinking of publishing your own anthology you will probably need forty plus poems, depending on their length.

Poetry publishers and poetry journals are included in the listings in **Section II**.

XX. An Ghaeilge

D'éirigh leis an nGaeilge fanacht ar an saol ó ré na gCloch Oghaim go dtí an Ré Dhigiteach agus rian doscriosta a fhágáil ar chultúr agus ar thraidisiúin liteartha na ndaoine.

Cé gur tháinig meath ar an teanga labhartha ó lár na naoú haoise déag, tharla Athbheochan Ghaelach ag tús na fichiú aoise ina choinne sin. Chabhraigh sé seo, ar a laghad, leis an teanga a choimeád beo ina bhfoirmeacha liteartha, go háirithe an béaloideas agus an seanchas. Rinneadh iarrachtaí ag an bpointe seo, forbairt a dhéanamh ar an iriseoireacht agus ar an nualitríocht, iarrachtaí ar éirigh leo den chuid is mó.

Ba scríbhneoir próis é Máirtín Ó Cadhain (1906-1970) a bhfuiltear tar éis a chuid saothair, atá dlús agus castacht ag baint leis, a chur i gcomparáid le shaothar James Joyce. Ba úrscéalaí den scoth é Liam Ó Flaithearta (1896-1984) a scríobh scéalta gearra chomh maith agus a bhfuil saothair scríofa as Gaeilge agus as Béarla aige. San áireamh i liosta na bhfilí cáiliúla, tá Seán Ó Ríordáin (1907-1977) agus an liriceoir agus scoláire, Máire Mhac an tSaoi (1922).

Tháinig líon mór scríbhneoirí cáiliúla as na Blascaodaí, atá suite amach ó chósta Chiarraí, san áireamh tá Peig Sayers, a rinneadh a dírbheathaisnéis a deachtú chuig a mac, Mícheál agus ar foilsíodh sa bhliain 1936 í. Aithnítear gur saothar clasaiceach liteartha é saothar Thiomáis Ó Criomhthain, *An tOileánach*, chomh maith le *Fiche Bliain ag Fás*, le Muiris Ó Súilleabháin.

Tá Gaeilge á labhairt go forleathan ar fud na hÉireann agus ar fud Tuaisceart na hÉireann. Tá beogacht liteartha agus cultúrtha ag baint le saol na Gaeilge. Is í an Ghaeilge céad teanga oifigiúil na hÉireann agus tá stádas bainte amach aici mar theanga oifigiúil de chuid an Aontais Eorpaigh chomh maith. Tá aitheantas bainte amach ag an teanga chomh maith faoi fhorálacha *Chomhaontú Aoine an Chéasta*, 1998, trínar bunaíodh comhlacht trasteorann ar a dtugtar *Foras na Gaeilge* chun an teanga a chur chun cinn ar fud an oileáin. Tá grúpaí Gaeilge gníomhacha i dTuaisceart Mheiriceá, agus i gcathracha sa

Bhreatain agus san Astráil.

Tá an Ghaeilge réidh anois, mar mheán cumarsáide liteartha agus labhartha, chun leas a bhaint as an aois dhigiteach. Tá rogha ann comhéadan Gaeilge a úsáid ar an-chuid de na príomhtháirgí bogearraí ríomhairí a bhfuiltear ag baint úsáid forleathan astu. San áireamh sna táirgí sin tá Google, Microsoft Windows, Mozilla Firefox agus OpenOffice.

Tá an Ghaeilge le feiceáil go forleathan ar an nGréasán Domhanda, rud atá tábhachtach más rud é go bhfuil an Ghaeilge chun teacht slán go fadtéarmach. Ní haon bhac é an Tíreolaíocht a thuilleadh maidir le cumarsáid agus maidir le smaointe a tharchur. Tá fianaise ann anois gur féidir linn a chreidiúint go dtiocfaidh meas nua, leis an ré nua seo, ar na nithe stairiúla sin atá mar chuid dár n-oidhreacht le fada an lá.

San áireamh i **Rannóg II** den lámhleabhar seo, tá liostaí d'Fhoilsitheoirí Gaeilge agus de sholáthraí seirbhísí eile.

An Scríbhneoir

Foilsitheoireacht chuidithe
d'údair, do scríbhneoirí agus d'fhilí

An tseirbhís is fearr

Na praghsanna is ísle

Déantóirí Leabhair Iontacha

Deimhniú Seirbhíse a bhfuil na nithe
seo a leanas san áireamh ann:

- Tuilleadh leabhar le haghaidh do chuid airgid
- Tairiscintí agus meastacháin saincheaptha
- Coimeádann an t-údar cearta cóipchirt

Tabhair cuairt ar an Suíomh Gréasáin:

www.AnScribhneoir.ie

XXI. Newspapers and Magazines

There are hundreds of newspapers, magazines and journals published in Ireland - see the listings in **Section II**

Most rely to some extent on freelance contributors. They therefore represent a fertile opportunity for budding writers to see their words in print.

There are several ways to go about getting your writing into a newspaper or magazine.

The simplest way is via the 'Letters to the Editor' section. You can send a letter about anything to the Editor. Whether they publish it or not is entirely their decision.

If you have an idea (for example a gardening column), you can write to the Features Editor setting out your idea and enclosing some sample articles.

The main opportunities where freelance work is accepted by newspapers and magazines include:
- Local news
- Health and well-being
- Sport reviews
- Entertainment reviews
- Local history
- Real life stories
- Personal experiences.

You can submit news stories or opinion to the news desk, news editor or features editor, and ask that it be considered for publication.

Many publications, particularly women's magazines, accept short stories. If you have a short story send it to the editor and ask that it be considered for publication.

Don't forget when you are writing to a newspaper or magazine to always include your name, address and contact details.

Don't expect to always get paid for your work; many newspapers and magazines accept work on an unpaid basis only.

XXII. The World Wide Web

The Internet has been in existence for over 40 years. It's only in the last 20 years though that it has become publicly available. Even in that short space of time it has undergone a number of evolutions. The most significant development in recent years has been the emergence of broadband as a web transmission device. This has lead to an explosion in sites that specialise in file sharing. Audio-visual material, which was previously slow to download, can now be viewed with relative ease.

Nowadays you can even create your own personal TV channel by uploading your home videos to sites like YouTube. You can then choose to make this available to a vast community of nearly two billion internet users; or make it an invitation-only event. Just imagine - you could be the Director of your own TV channel!

The Web is a medium that can be read, viewed and listened to, but it can also be shared. It is first and foremost an interactive medium. The most exciting opportunity it affords is the ability to build communities and create networks of contacts.

Finances shouldn't be an issue since many of the software and online tools are free. Of course if you want to spend some money, there are plenty of people out there who will be only too happy to take it from you. As you become more comfortable with the medium, and hopefully more successful, you may want to enhance your web presence with professional design and/or software. But all you need when starting out is a computer with access to the Internet. Your local library will facilitate you if all else fails.

All this has implications for publishing. For authors, writers and poets it may even have implications for how we write. Previously you had no choice but to go through the publishing mill before unleashing your work on an unsuspecting audience. You then awaited the public reaction - where you might be hailed, savaged or ignored! An internet-savvy author now has other options at his or her disposal. There are almost 2 billion people out there now for you to target with your work.

There are a few important considerations however. Web publishing is no different to any other form of publishing. It contains all the usual legal requirements and obligations. Anything you put up on the Web can be read, by anybody. Even if you start to have second thoughts after a day or two and decide to remove certain material, that's no guarantee that it will not have already been accessed, read, copied and possibly syndicated.

Every day search engine robots trawl the Web looking for new content which is stored in their vast databases. The Wayback Machine at www.archive.org provides free access to researchers, historians, scholars, and the general public to search its vast digital library of text, images, audio, video and archived web pages. Its mission is to preserve digital data and artefacts in just the same way as a library or museum.

It used to be the cloak of anonymity that held the greatest attraction for some web users. It afforded endless potential for mischief, which can be fun but can also have unfortunate and unintended consequences. In the early days of the Web, legislators were probably taken aback by its phenomenal growth, but they are catching up.

In 2009 a US court forced Google to reveal the identity of a blogger who made disparaging remarks about a woman who worked as a model. As we write, Google itself is engaged in a high profile dispute with the government of The People's Republic of China over internet censorship. At the same time the company's CEO, Eric Schmidt, recently earned the dismay of civil rights campaigners and privacy advocates on his home turf when he commented: "If you have something that you don't want anyone to know, maybe you shouldn't be doing it in the first place".

It is likely that arguments like these will flare for some time as the issues themselves come under scrutiny. At what point does the demand for privacy itself become a form of censorship? Also, doesn't free exchange of opinion require a certain level of decorum and respect for others, even those whose opinions you do not like?

A few sensible precautions should ensure that you don't become the next high profile casualty of some lawsuit or crackdown. Unless of course you're someone who likes to fight your corner by courting controversy. The Web is, after all, a great bastion of free speech and long may it continue in that vein.

The World Wide Web offers writers, authors and poets the opportunity to broadcast their words for free, and market and sell their work for profit.

Internet services that are there to help you promote and sell your work include:

- ◆ A website
- ◆ Online sales facilities (also known as E-Commerce)
- ◆ A blog
- ◆ A mini-blog
- ◆ Social networking sites
- ◆ E-books
- ◆ E-zines.

XXIII. Websites and E-Commerce

A website is a collection of related web pages, grouped into a single domain, that link to each other and to pages in other websites. It has a specific address or domain, beginning with www (World Wide Web), followed by an identifier (john smith), and a top-level domain which is supposed to indicate the nature of the website - institution, government, business, etc. This is often more of a convention than a rule however.

Some of the more common top-level domains include:
.ie - country level domain used by Irish websites
.co.uk - United Kingdom commercial website
.com - most commonly used domain name indicating a commercial website

Other top-level domains currently in use include:
.info - short for information
.org - short for organisation
.net - short for network
.tel - short for telecommunications
.tv - actually the country level domain for the island nation of Tuvalu but also favoured by broadcasters for obvious reasons.

Web addresses are purchased and registered with Domain Name Registrars, which are usually companies that also offer web hosting and other services. Each address is unique and can occur only once. Thus there can only be one www.johnsmith.com. But there could also be www.johnsmith.ie, www.johnsmith.org and so on, each pointing to a different website or to the same location. If you find that the domain name you want is already taken you might be able to register it using a different top-level domain (e.g. using .ie instead of .com). Also, there is nothing to stop you from having several registered domain names pointing to your website.

One point to bear in mind, legislation in Ireland is stricter than elsewhere. Before you can register a 'dot ie' site you usually need to have the same name registered as a business name or company at the Companies Registration Office - go to www.cro.ie to find out how to register a business name.

The advantage of a website is that it gives you somewhere to hang out your stall. It's like having a shop window on the Internet. You can use it to promote your work, to sell your books, to present information about yourself, your characters, or to announce readings, book signings and other events that you have planned.

A website is made up of pages that are interlinked. The pages of your website may also link to other external sites. Some external websites may also link to you.

A navigational structure that is clear and accessible is an essential part of good web design. Visitors to your site need to know where they are, how they got there and where they should be going next. Otherwise they might leave. On almost all websites you will find a Home Page; an About Me/About Us page; a News page (this could also be a blog); a Catalogue page for your products and/or services; and a Contact Me/Us page.

You can register a web address at any one of a number of service sites, of which there are many. Examples include:

www.123-reg.co.uk
www.blacknight.com
www.godaddy.com

Registration costs vary. You can get some domain names for less than €10 per annum, but sought-after domain names (sometimes referred to as premium domains) can be much more expensive. However, once you have registered your domain it belongs to you for as long as you continue paying the annual subscription.

To operate on the Internet, a website needs to be hosted. Hosting means that the pages reside on a remote server, from which the pages can be accessed and downloaded over the

Internet. Companies that act as Domain Name Registrars usually offer hosting as an additional service. It's worth shopping around however. Bear in mind that you are not obliged to host your website, with the same service provider with whom you registered your domain. You might find that some companies offer very cheap rates for domain name registration but that their hosting services are not up to the standard required for your website.

Also, there are plenty of free hosting solutions you can avail of, which are perfectly adequate for blogging or for more basic websites. Among the more popular free hosting options include:

Wordpress - very popular with bloggers and website builders. You'd be surprised at how many websites are really just blogs in disguise.

Get your free blog at www.wordpress.com

Blogger - Also a very good blogging tool. It's largely a matter of preference which is better - Blogger or Wordpress? But Blogger is owned by Google and integrates well with other Google packages - Picasa, YouTube, Docs, etc.

To get started visit www.blogger.com

Google Sites - launched by Google in 2008. Takes some getting used to but well worth checking out if you are serious about getting online. Allows you to create websites from pre-built templates or customise your own designs.

Find out how on http://sites.google.com/

Joomla - an open source content management system platform for publishing on the World Wide Web and intranets. Open source, in case you don't know, is web jargon that generally means 'free'!

Find it at www.joomla.org

E-Commerce websites are those which facilitate the buying and selling of products or services online - you don't even have to leave your chair. They typically include online catalogues and shopping carts with payment facilities combined. All this sounds very technical but anyone with a website or blog can provide facilities to allow their readers and visitors to buy their books, merchandise, etc., and pay for them online in one transaction.

The simplest way to do this is to sign up for a PayPal account at www.paypal.com. Once there, navigate to the Merchant Tools section and follow the instructions for creating your own personalised version of the familiar PayPal button. It is a widely recognised logo, and seen as a safe and secure way to transfer money over the Internet. You will receive an e-mail informing you when someone buys a book so you can organise shipping to them.

There are also specialised online shops that list books - Amazon, Barnes & Noble, Ingram, Abe Books are among the largest. Most bookshops also have online sites.

As a writer it would obviously be very helpful to have your books listed on these sites. Listing on Amazon, Barnes & Noble, etc. is open to any book that has an ISBN and barcode. Listing on a bookshop's site is subject to the bookshop's discretion in exactly the same way as deciding to stock a book in the shop itself.

All books with an ISBN are also listed on Nielsen's (see **Chapter XVI. ISBN and Legal Deposits**). Bookshops all over the world use Nielsen's to find and order books for their customers. Having your book listed on Nielsen's is therefore important if you want people to be able to find it.

Your publisher, if you have one, will look after listing your book on all the popular online catalogues.

Looking for information about writing or publishing?
Check out **www.WritingandPublishing.info**
A free information service for writers, authors, poets and anyone interested in books or publishing

XXIV. Blogs and Blogging

Let's begin with a definition of Blogging. Blog is short for Web Log. It's basically an online diary or scrapbook that anyone with access to the Internet can view. Blogs are active or living websites. They are regularly updated with postings - perhaps weekly, daily, maybe even hourly.

To blog is to post text, images, podcasts, videos onto the same place on the Internet daily, weekly, or with some degree of frequency. The frequency of posting is up to the blogger.

Bloggers are online diarists writing about any subject of their choosing. All they are really doing is posting their thoughts, opinions or news onto a web page, which is open to anyone to access. It's a bit like sitting in a radio or TV studio, broadcasting to the world and hoping someone is listening or watching. Bloggers can write or post about anything they like; their cat, their favourite recipes, their holidays, or their political philosophy.

Most blogs also allow feedback from readers. Anyone is free to submit a comment for posting but the owner of the blog has control over which comments get posted and can remove comments deemed inappropriate. This is important, not just to protect against the offensive or obscene, but also because some comments posted to blogs come under the category of spam.

Blogs can also be linked to other blogs and websites in a kind of referral system. It goes something like this, if you enjoyed reading my blog then why not take a look at these ones too?

Blog posts and comments can also be syndicated through RSS feeds. RSS is usually translated as Really Simple Syndication but some prefer Rich Site Summary. It is, in effect, a format for delivering regularly changing web content, and is ideally suited to blogs and blogging. You can follow other people's blogs by subscribing to an RSS feed. They can follow your blog by the same mechanism. You can even use RSS on your own blog or website to 'aggregate and distribute' content from other sources.

Blogs are meant to be interactive and strive to build up their own online community of readers and subscribers, more often focused at a particular interest group.

Blogs are often used as daily diaries about someone's personal life. Many people who are travelling post to a blog rather than sending postcards or e-mails. Their friends and family can log in and keep track of their daily travels and submit their news for posting. "Hi everyone, 50 days down, 30 more to go. Love to you all, Passepartout."

Blogs can present political views, or social commentaries. The best bloggers are often trained professional writers, people who write because it's their passion, and politically inclined individuals who need a pulpit for their ideas. On the other hand, some bloggers have found that it leads to other things and have built careers in other media on the strength of their blogging credentials.

Blogs are also becoming marketing tools for big business; marketers and PR firms can't resist the opportunity to tell the world why we should all buy their particular brand of baked beans.

For a writer, blogs offer three great opportunities:

- A platform to write and share your ideas; an online 'Speakers Corner' if you like.
- A forum to promote and sell your work.
- A way of building a readership base while creating a network of contacts.

XXV. Social Media

Blogging is just one aspect of what is increasingly being referred to as Social Media. If the term 'blogging' is more familiar to you, that is probably just because it has been around a bit longer. The technology is constantly evolving, producing new fads and buzzwords along the way. Areas converge then break-off in new directions, becoming harder to pin down to anything specific.

Social Networking is another buzz word that is often heard but what does it mean? The World Wide Web could well be described as a vast social network. Networking through dating and matchmaking services has been around since the advent of the Web - or so we're told by the people who use them! It is often forgotten that Facebook started out in this way. It probably doesn't cross the minds of the 400 million active users worldwide today.

If Facebook was a country it would be the fifth largest in the world. Apologies if you've heard that one before but it's actually one of those nuggets of statistical information that is very revealing when you stop to think about it. In fact, social networking sites are very much like countries. The one thing that all countries have in common is that their citizens are different; they do not submit to homogenisation; they form clusters; they choose who to associate with, and seek out those in whom they recognise a shared sense of values, interests, beliefs, etc. Because of the World Wide Web we are all becoming more and more like citizens of the world - webizens if you like.

Social networking is based on a structure that allows people to both express their individuality and meet people with similar interests. This structure typically includes having profiles, friends, blog posts, widgets, and usually something unique to that particular social networking website - such as the ability to 'poke' people on Facebook or high-five someone on Hi5.

Profile. This is where you tell the world about yourself.

Profiles contain basic information, like where you live and how old you are, and personality questions, like who's your favourite actor? and what's your favourite book? Social networks dedicated to a special theme like music or movies might ask questions related to that theme.

Friends, Followers, etc. Friends or followers are trusted members of the site that are allowed to post comments on your profile or send you private messages. You can also keep tabs on how your friends are using social networking, such as when they post a new picture or update their profile. Friends are the heart and soul of social networking. Not all social networks refer to them as 'friends' - LinkedIn refers to them as 'connections', but all social networks have a way to designate members as trusted.

Groups. Most social networks use groups to help you find people with similar interests or engage in discussions on certain topics. A group can be anything from your family, your football team or church congregation, to people who like horror stories, fans of the Beatles, or people who investigate reports of UFOs. They are both a way to connect with like-minded people and a way to identify your interests. Sometimes groups are called by other names, such as the 'networks' on Facebook.

Discussions. A primary focus of groups is to create interaction between users in the form of discussions. Most social networking websites support discussion boards for the groups, and many also allow members of the group to post pictures, music, video clips, and other gossip related to the group.

Blogs. Another feature of some social networks is the ability to create your own blog entries. While not as feature-rich as blog hosts like Wordpress or Blogger, (see **Chapter XXIII. Websites and E-Commerce**) blogging through a social network is perfect for keeping people informed on what you are up to.

Widgets. A popular way of letting your personality shine through is by gracing your social networking profile with web widgets (smiley faces and so on). Many social networks allow a variety of widgets, and you can usually find interesting widgets located on widget galleries.

For a writer or poet, social media offers the opportunity to broadcast your work, chat with your readers and build a community of followers.

XXVI. Micro-blogs and Twitter

Whereas a blog is full scale text, a micro-blog is a quick note or update of only a few sentences. Micro-blogging is a bit like text messaging on a mobile phone - short and to the point: 'I'm at the shops, do you want anything?'

The difference is a text message is directed to one person at a time; whereas a micro-blog is available for anyone to read.

Micro-blogging is a feature of social networks like Facebook where subscribers can update their status, but it has become best known because of Twitter.

Twitter has taken the world by storm. Every second person seems to be doing it; but what is it? Twitter is a web-based service that allows anyone to sign up as a user and have a unique identity. They can then post short messages called Tweets (up to 140 characters) which are available to anyone in the Twitter universe to read in real time. Subscribers can also become followers of each other which means their Tweets are available to be read at a later time, a bit like a message minder service.

Twittering is obviously quick and to the point. It can be used to post gossip, news or commentary, as well as advertise and promote anything. It is a great way for people (families, groups of friends, etc) to keep in touch. It is also very useful to co-ordinate activities across a range of people; for example, companies can use it to broadcast a message to their sales team, tour guides can post dates and times of events to their group, theatres and cinemas can send a Tweet about a forthcoming event to people on their mailing list, and so on. Short stories have even been built up sequentially in short segments, one 140 character Tweet at a time.

Twitter is a great place for keeping people informed on what you are up to without the need to spend a lot of time writing an entire blog post on the subject. You just say what you need to say and leave it at that.

Twitter has become an accepted tool for social media marketing. It was used very effectively by Barack Obama's campaign during the 2008 US Presidential Election. History may well view this as the event which heralded the arrival of the social media age; where the role of the citizen journalist came to the fore in helping to shape a country's political make-up. Experienced politicians were made to look pedestrian and amateur, because they didn't really understand the impact which technology, in the hands of the grassroots, could have.

In summary, micro-blogs like Twitter are used by everyone, from magazines to movie stars, as a quick way to connect with an audience. Some celebrities, like Stephen Fry, have become even more celebrated as 'twitterers'.

For a writer, Twitter and other forms of social media are great ways to promote yourself. Far from being a fad, "Follow me on Twitter," is likely to be the most used phrase of everyone who wants to be successful.

XXVII. Writer's Blog

'To blog or not to blog?' that is the question a certain famous dramatist of the 16th century might be asking himself if he was plying his trade today.

Shakespeare wrote plays, probably for much the same reasons that Mozart wrote operas. It wasn't just because that was where their respective talents lay. These were also the popular artistic media of the time in which they lived. It's the same as cinema was for the 20th Century, or Rock and Roll represented to the post-war generation. People will always flock to the platform that has potential to reach the widest mass audience. Some will emerge as heroes, some as villains, others will belong to the ranks of the unheard.

The World Wide Web is the 21st century's equivalent of William Caxton's moveable type. Just as Caxton's printing presses heralded a new era of literacy and exchange of ideas that had revolutionary consequences, the same is happening today, right before our eyes. Today's reformer, seeking to emulate Martin Luther, doesn't have to nail a thesis to the church door. Posting it online will gain far greater impact and a much wider audience.

The reasons why people blog are manifold, but the simplest explanation is probably the obvious, *because they can*.

Bloggers, it has been claimed, are the newest and most popular 'authentic' voice on the Internet.

If you have aspirations to be a writer, if you have something to say, why not give blogging a try? Creating your own blog is easy. There really is no obstacle or impediment to you joining the community of bloggers, micro-bloggers and online publishers.

Open your mind to new technologies and new possibilities. It used to be that the only way to get your novel, your collection of short stories or your anthology of poems out to a public audience was to get it published as a book. That's not the case anymore. Think of the Internet as a publishing opportunity; create your own blog and get writing.

XXVIII. Electronic Publishing

Electronic or e-publishing, sometimes called digital publishing, though still in its infancy, will change the future of book publishing. E-books are electronically published books; e-zines are electronically published magazines and journals.

E-publishing allows books, magazines and journals (as well as manuals, reports, brochures, catalogues and specifications) in screen readable formats to be downloaded via the Internet onto computers and hand-held devices. The reader can store them, read them on their screen or print them on a local printer to be read in hard copy format.

E-books can be ordered online from an online bookstore, and downloaded direct to a PC or laptop. They can also be downloaded to special electronic book readers like the Amazon Kindle, the Sony E-reader, or the new Apple iPad.

At the time of writing e-books account for less than one per cent of total book sales. Bear in mind though that the market for English language books is worth $50 billion dollars annually and you can see how significant the market for e-books has already become. It is estimated that e-book sales double in value very year, so it won't be too long before they rival or eclipse sales of hard copy books.

It's early days, and most e-books are still read on PCs and laptops, but that is changing as advances in hand-held devices offer more facilities and screens get bigger. The day when you will be able to comfortably read a novel on your mobile phone or iPod isn't far away.

The economics of publishing via the Internet are completely different to traditional hardcopy publishing. Books can be downloaded without incurring any distribution costs, and the vast majority of any revenue generated is retained by the author.

The obvious problem is that e-publishing sets no standards; any old rubbish can be published and offered for sale. To counter this, e-publishing companies will offer much the same services as traditional hard copy publishers (they may even be the same companies). They will give readers a level of confidence that the e-book they publish will at least will be well written and readable.

What does all this mean for writers? E-publishing offers every writer a platform to get their work published, and if their work is any good to build up a readership following. Whilst it might not pay to go it completely alone, there is no doubt that a whole new campus of self-published or assisted published writers will spring up on the Internet. Their aim shouldn't necessarily be to conquer the world, but to at least build up a base of loyal readers.

Specialist books, niche genres and local interest books are particularly suited to this way of publishing.

The music industry offers many parallels as to what will probably happen in the book sector. Big publishers, like big record labels, will no longer control the sector. Niche and specialist publishers will thrive. Book shops, like record stores, will leave the High Street and shopping centres and move online. Authors (fiction, non-fiction and poetry), like musicians, will publish an increasing amount of work online.

Creativity will flourish as the traditional constraints imposed by commercial publishing are swept away. Discerning readers will demand high quality. As a consequence, a new sub-industry of freelance cover designers, typesetters, editors, web-designers, and marketers will emerge to support a growing band of independent authors.

Exciting times would appear to be ahead for all of us.

Section II

Directory

LISTINGS:

Note regarding dialing codes:

Area code prefixes provided in these directory listings assume local dialing.

The international dialing code for Éire-Ireland (also known as The Republic of Ireland) is 00353. Drop the first zero of the area code when dialing from outside Éire-Ireland.

The international dialing code for Northern Ireland, when dialing from outside the United Kingdom is 0044. The area code for Northern Ireland, when dialing within the United Kingdom is 028. When dialling Northern Ireland from Éire-Ireland there is no international dialing code but the area code becomes 048 (not 028).

A. Note from the Editors

A. Nóta ó na hEagarthóirí

We have tried to make these listings as complete and as comprehensive as possible. They contain the most up-to-date information available to us at the time of going to press. Like all things new though, they are open to future inclusion by organisations that may have been missed, and to amendment should any information be incorrect.

Entries and updates for future handbooks are welcome from publishers, agents, festival committees and event managers, as well as writers groups, book shops, distributors and anyone connected with the literary sector in Ireland or Northern Ireland.

Use the Submission Form at the back of this book or contact the editorial team at: editors@TAFPublishing.com.

Tá iarracht déanta againn a chinntiú gur lámhleabhar cuimsitheach atá sa lámhleabhar seo, chomh fada agus is féidir. Is éard atá ann ná an t-eolas is reatha atá ar fáil dúinn agus an lámhleabhar á chur i gcló. Mar is gnách maidir le rudaí nua, áfach, féadfar eagraíochtaí nár aimsíodh a chur san áireamh ann agus é a leasú más rud é go bhfuil eolas míchruinn le fáil ann.

Tá fáilte roimh iontrálacha agus roimh eolas nuashonraithe do lámhleabhair eile amach anseo, ag teacht ó fhoilsitheoirí, ó ghníomhairí, ó choistí féilte agus ó bhainisteoirí imeachtaí, chomh maith le grúpaí scríbhneoirí, siopaí leabhair, dáileoirí agus aon duine atá baint acu leis an earnáil liteartha in Éirinn nó i dTuaisceart na hÉireann.

Téigh i dteagmháil leis an bhfoireann eagarthóireachta ag eagarthóirí@tafpublishing.com.

David Jones
Oscar Duggan
April/*Aibreán* 2010

B. Writing Groups

COUNTY CARLOW

Carlow Writers Co-op
Meets every two weeks in Teach Dolmen, Carlow at 7pm on Fridays.
Contact John in Carlow Central Library, Carlow. E-mail:
carlowwriterscoop@gmail.com

Carlow Writers Group
Meets every second Tuesday in Carlow Central Library in Tullow Street.
For further information contact the Arts Officer, Carlow County Council,
Athy Road, Carlow. Tel: 059 9136206

COUNTY CAVAN

Cootehill Writers Group
Station Road, Cootehill, Co. Cavan. Contact: Kay Phelan. Tel: 049 5552321.

Meath/Cavan Lit Lab
4 Gardenrath Road, Lower Kells, Co. Meath.

COUNTY CORK

Great Island Writers Group, Cobh
Contact: Thelma Mills, 021 4816611, 086 1655025. Meets every Saturday
at 10.30am in Cobh library.

Middleton Writers Group
Courtyard Craft and Exhibition Centre, Main Street, Middleton, Cork.
Contact Michael O'Connor. Tel: 087 6743137. Meets in Courtyard Craft and
Exhibition Centre on 1st Thursday of the month at 8pm.

West Cork Writers Group
Skibbereen. Contact: Maggie Cahill. Tel: 087 2167182. E-mail:
info@westcorkwriters.com. Website: www.westcorkwriters.com.

COUNTY DONEGAL

Letterkenny Writers Group
Gallagher's Hotel, Letterkenny. Contact Brian Smeaton. Meets in Hotel on first Monday of every month.

COUNTY DUBLIN

Balbriggan Writers Group
Balbriggan Library, George's Square, Balbriggan, Co. Dublin. Contact: Jane Carroll, Co-ordinator / Assumpta Hickey, Senior Librarian. Tel: 01 8704401. Fax: 01 8411128. E-mail: bablbrigganlibrary@fingalcoco.ie. Website: www.fingalcoco.ie/library. Weekly writers' workshop, Thursdays 7.30pm.

Ballymun Writers Group
Ballymun ICA, 19 Coolrua Drive, Beaumont, Dublin 9. Contact Mary Bolton.

Bayside Writers Group
Dublin 13. Contact: John O'Malley. Tel: 087 7542321. E-mail: johnomalley1@gmail.com. Meets: last Friday of month at Bayside Community Centre.

Charleville Mall Writers Forum
Charleville Library, Dublin 3. Tel: 01 8370494. Contact Janet/Sean Flynn. Meets every Thursday at 7pm.

CIE Writers Group
E-mail: ciewriters@gmail.com

Clondalkin Village Writers
Tel: 01 621 6422. Meets in Lucan Library fortnightly on a Saturday. Under 18s only.

Coolock Chapter and Verse Writers Group
Tel: 01 8477781. Meets in Coolock Library on the first Thursday of the month.

Dalkey Library Adult Literary Scheme (ALS) Writing Group
Meets in Dalkey Library. Tel: 086 3063178

Dalkey Writers Workshop
Dalkey Library. Contact Billy Hutchinson, Chairman. Tel: 086 2569212. E-mail: dalkeywriters@gmail.com. Meets alternate Thursdays 6-8pm. Friendly, constructive group meets every fortnight in Dalkey, Co. Dublin. We workshop short stories, novels, poetry, memoirs, articles, plays for stage, radio and screen. If you are interested in joining us please contact us via e-mail.

Dolebusters Writers Group
Adelaide Road, Dublin 2. Contact: George Ferguson. Tel: 01 4941201. Meets every Wednesday at 2pm in the Presbyterian Church, Adelaide Road, Dublin 2.

Donaghmede Adult Writers Group
Tel: 01 8482833. Meets on the first Thursday of every month at 6.30pm in Donaghmede Library.

Eblana Writers Group
E-mail: info@eblana-writers.com. Website: www.eblana-writers.com.

Kevin Street Creative Writing Group
Tel: 085 1609906. Meets every Thursday from 2.30pm to 4pm. Kevin Street Library, Dublin 8.

KLEAR Writers Group
Kilbarrack, Dublin 5. Contact Siobhán Hand, 01 8671845.

Knocklyon Writing Group
Knocklyon. Contact: Kathryn Crowley. E-mail: cpd@iol.ie. Meets every second Tuesday in the Community School in Knocklyon.

Lucan Creative Writers Group
E-mail: lucanwriters@aol.com. Website: www.lucanwriters.ie.

Macro Writers
Capel Street, Dublin 1. Contact: Bry. Tel: 086 3247662. Meets last Wednesday of month.

Merrion Writers Group
Balbriggan. Tel: 01 8411128. E-mail: balbrigganlibrary@fingalcoco.ie. Meets every Thursday at 7pm in Balbriggan library.

The Phoenix Writers Group
Castleknock. Contact: Carol Thuilier. Tel: 086 0834455. E-mail: PhoenixinFingal@gmail.com. Meets every Wednesday at 8pm in the function room of the Bell Pub, Castleknock.

PS Writers Group
Contact: Audrey Kaufman. Tel: 01 677 1930. Meets: St Andrews Resource Centre, 114 Pearse Street, Dublin 2. Fridays, 10am-12 noon

Rathgar Blacksheep Arts Writers Group
Contact James Conway. Tel: 086 4025578. E-mail: neilkenealy@gmail.com

Rathmines Writers Workshop
Rathgar Village. Contact: James Conway. Tel: 086 4025578. E-mail: rathmines_ww@gmail.com. General meetings are held every second Thursday. Prose only meetings on Mondays. 7.30pm to 10pm, Christ Church, Rathgar Village.

Ringsend Writers Group
Tel: 01 2838624. Meets at CYMS (Opposite Library), St Patricks Villas, Ringsend. Wednesdays, 10am -12 noon

The Scribblers Corner
Tel: 01 8490568. Meets Tuesdays in Sailing Club @ 8.30pm, 46 Shenick Avenue, Skerries.

Skerries Writers Group
Meets: St Andrews Resource Centre, Friday, 10am - 12 noon
Contact: 01 2855613

Swords Writers Group
Contact: Geraldine Walsh, Lead Facilitator. E-mail: info@swordswriters.ie. Website: www.swordswriters.ie. Meets alternate Wednesdays in Hawthorn Hotel, Swords at 7.30pm. Swords Writers Group is made up of poets, novelists, short-story writers, screen writers and journalists who use the peer support of the group to learn about and develop our craft. We aspire to support one and other, whether published or unpublished, through honest and fair criticism and provide encouragement, motivation and inspiration to all of our members. We encourage both competition entries and publication submissions and to date the members of the group have achieved various publication credentials online and in print. Swords Writers is developing and expanding every day. It is our hope to organise events that will aim to bring Creative Writing to the forefront of our community.

Trinity Writers Group
Donaghmede. Meets at Donaghmede Library, alternate Thursdays at 7pm

Village Writers
Ballybrack. Tel: 01 2825037. Meets in Ballinacor House, Church Road, Ballybrack

Virginia House Creative Writers Group
Tallaght. Meets every Friday in the Meeting Room of RUA RED, South Dublin Arts Centre, Civic Square, Tallaght, Dublin 24

The Wednesday Group
Phibsboro. Meets every Monday in Brian Boru, Phibsboro. 9pm

The Valentine Writers Group
35 Finsbury Park, Dublin 14. Tel: 01 2988101. Meets alternate Wednesdays at 8.30pm in members' homes.

Wiser Writing Group
Trinity College, College Green, Dublin 2. E-mail: wiser@tcd.ie

COUNTY KERRY

The Arcadians
Killarney. Contacts: Mabel Counihan 064 32379, Cynthia O'Sullivan, 064 34925

Clann na Farraige
Kenmare. Contact: Eileen Connolly. Tel: 064 42095. E-mail: eileenconnolly@eircom.net

Fia Rua Writers Group
Killarney. Contact: Margaret O' Shea. Tel: 064 54077

The Knibs Writers Group
Killorglin. Contact: Mick Jones. E-mail: mick@knibs.ie. Website: www.knibs.ie. Meets Thursday mornings in Killorglin Library. 11.00am to 12.30pm.

Listowel Writers Group
Seanchaí Literary and Cultural Centre. Contacts: Cara or Kathy, 068 22212. E-mail: info@kerrywritersmuseum.com. Website: www.kerrywritersmuseum.com.

Tralee Scribblers
Hartys Bar, Castle Street. Contact: Noel King. Tel: 066 21786/29934. Meets
Tuesdays 8pm (except July and August).

COUNTY KILDARE

Celbridge Writers Group
Contact: Donal Cogan. Tel: 045 8863660.

Maynooth Gateway Writers Group
Contact: Kate Dempsey. E-mail: kate_dempsey@hotmail.com. Meets on the
first Thursday of the month.

COUNTY KILKENNY

Bennettsbridge Writers Group
Contact: Eileen Lynch. Tel: 056 61154. Meets Community Hall,
Bennettsbridge. Wednesdays, 8.15pm.

Clogh Writers Group
E-mail: webgroup@clogh.com. Website: www.clogh.com. Meets
Wednesday evenings in the Clogh Family Resource Centre.

COUNTY LONGFORD

The Ballymahon Writers Group
Nally's Pub, Ballymahon, Co. Longford. Contact: Anne Skelly. Tel: 044
9357464. E-mail: annettecol@eircom.net.

Granard Writers Group
Rath Mhuire Resource Centre, Granard, Co. Longford. Contact: Sr Maeve
Brady or Jacqui Kennedy. Tel: 043 6686309. E-mail:
rathmhuire2@eircom.net. Meets every three weeks on Monday afternoons
from 3 to 5pm.

Goldsmith Writers Group
Ballymahon. Contact: Anne Collins, Glebe, Colehill, Co. Longford. Tel: 044
9357464. E-mail: annettecol@eircom.net. Meets every third Tuesday at
8.30pm in Nally's Pub, Ballymahon.

Lanesborough Writers Group
Contact: Margaret Nohilly, Rathcline Road, Lanesboro, Co. Longford. Tel: 043 3321224

The Longford Writers Group
Longford Branch Library, Longford. Contact: Anne Skelly. Tel: 044 9357464. E-mail: annettecol@eircom.net

COUNTY LOUTH

Dundalk Writers' Circle
Contact: Garrett Molloy. Tel: 042 21444. Meets Hotel Imperial, alternate Thursdays 8pm.

Lifestyle Development Group
Drogheda. Contact: Brian Clarke. Tel: 041 43209. Meets Wednesdays at 10.30am.

COUNTY MAYO

Castlebar Writers Group
c/o Mongeys Opticians, Ellison Street, Castlebar, Co. Mayo. Contact: Iarla Mongey. Tel: 094 24115. Meets Castlebar Library on Wednesdays at 8.30pm.

Kiltimagh Writers Group (Pen & Ink)
Website: www.kiltimaghwriters.com. Meets alternate Tuesdays in the Town Hall, Kiltimagh.

Westport Writers Group
Contact: Mary McCombs. Tel: 098 25241. Meets Monday evenings, Heneghans Pub, Bridge Street, Westport.

Mayo Writers Block
Claremorris. Contact: John Corless. Tel: 087 9843900. Website: www.mayowriters.org. Meets 2nd and 4th Wednesday of each month in The Mayo Writers' Block, IRD Building, Ballyhaunis Road, Claremorris.

COUNTY MEATH

Boyne Writers Groups
Trim. Contact: Michael Farry, Secretary. E-mail: editor@boynewriters.com.
Tel: 086 8283314. Meets alternate Thursdays in the Castle Arch Hotel,
Summerhill Road, Trim, Co. Meath.

Meath/Cavan Lit Lab
4 Gardenrath Road, Lower Kells, Co. Meath.

The Meath Writers' Circle
Trim. Contact: Tommy Murray. Tel: 046 31747. E-mail:
tommymurray06@eircom.net. Meets: First Thursday of every month in the
Trim Castle Hotel, Castle Street, Trim.

The Small Impact Writers Group
Navan. Contact: Edel Gillick. Tel: 085 7068047. Meets every Wednesday at
11.30am in Navan Library.

COUNTY OFFALY

The Tullamore Poetry Group
Contact: Vincent Wynter, Carrigdhoun, Clonmynch Road, Tullamore, Co.
Offaly. Tel: 057 9321297. Meets monthly at 11.00am Saturday mornings in
Kelly's Pub, Harbour Street, Tullamore.

COUNTY ROSCOMMON

Tulsk Writers Groups
Contact: Lora O'Brien, Cruachan Ai Heritage Centre, Tulsk, Co. Roscommon.
Tel: 071 9639268. E-mail: cruachanai@gmail.com. Blog:
www.cruachanai.blogspot.com. Meets on Wednesday mornings from 10am
to 12 noon.

COUNTY TIPPERARY

Clonmel Writers Group
Cluain Meala Writers Group. Clonmel. Tel: 052 27877. E-mail:
reception@southtipparts.com. Website: www.southtipparts.com. Meets in
South Tipperary Arts Centre, Clonmel.

COUNTY WEXFORD

The Gorey Writers Group
Contact Sarah Daulten at: daultenquaile@eircom.net. Meets in The Plaza, Pearse Street, Gorey, Co. Wexford on the second Tuesday of each month.

COUNTY WICKLOW

Wicklow Writers Group
Meeting place: Kilmantin Arts, Wicklow Town. Upcoming events and activities are posted on the group's blog - www.wicklowwriters.blogspot.com

NORTHERN IRELAND

ARDS Writing Group
Newtownards, Co. Down. Contact: Moyra Donaldson. Tel: 028 9181 4210. Meets: Tuesday evenings from 7.30 - 10pm at Ards Art Centre, Town Hall, Conway Square, Newtownards, Co. Down. BT23 4DB

Bann Balladeers
Banbridge, Co. Down. Contact: Doreen McBride. Tel: 028 406892275

Derry Women Writers
Women's Centre, 24 Pump Street, Derry BT48 7DB. Contact Linda Morgan. Tel: 028 71267672.

Flowerfield Writers Group
Flowerfield Arts Centre, 185 Coleraine Road, Portstewart, BT55 7HU. Tel: 028 7083 1400. E-mail: info@flowerfield.org.

Gilford Writers
Co. Down. Contact: Joan Gaffney. Tel: 028 38799912. Meets at Craigavon School on Tuesdays and Thursdays, 8-9.30pm.

Story Finders - Belleek
Unit 2, Craft Village, Belleek, Co. Fermanagh, BT93 3FX. Tel: 028 6865 9701

Story Finders - Castlederg
Derg Valley Healthy Living Centre, 5-7Parkview Road, Castlederg, Co. Tyrone. Tel: 028 8167 0764. E-mail: castle_dergstoryfinders@yahoo.co.uk

Story Finders - Craigavon
Community Network Craigavon, 22 Church Street, Portadown. Co. Armagh.
BT62 3LQ. E-mail: craigavon.storyfinders@hotmail.co.uk

Story Finders - Dervock
13 Travers Place, Dervock, Ballymoney, Co. Antrim. BT53 8BX. E-mail:
storyfinders.dervock@hotmail.com

Story Finders - Gilford
Gilford Together Resource Centre, 36 Dunbarton Street, Gilford, Craigavon.
BT63 6HJ. Tel: 028 38831414. E-mail: gilfordstoryfinders@hotmail.co.uk

Story Finders - Limavady
63 Irish Green Street, Limavady, Londonderry BT49 9AA. Tel: 028
77764429. E-mail: limavadystoryfinders@google-mail.com

Story Finders - Newry
Ballybot House, 28 Cornmarket, Newry, Co. Down. Tel: 028 30261022. E-
mail: newrystoryfinders@yahoo.co.uk

Warrenpoint Writers Group
Co. Down. Warrenpoint Library, Summerhill. Contact: Felicity Taylor. Tel:
028 41774337.
Meets every fortnight from 10am-12 noon.

C. Literary Organisations

Arts Council / An Chomhairle Ealaíon
70 Merrion Square, Dublin 2. Tel: 01 618 0296. E-mail:
sarah.bannan@artscouncil.ie. Website: www.artscouncil.ie. Contact: Sarah
Bannan, Head of Literature. The national development agency for the arts
in Ireland.

Arts Council of Northern Ireland
77, Malone Road, Belfast BT9 AQ. Tel: 028 90285200. E-mail:
info@artscouncil-ni.org. Website: www.artscouncil-ni.org. Contact Damian
Smyth, Literature Officer. The development agency for the arts in Northern
Ireland.

Clár na Leabhar Gaeilge
Ráth Chairn, Athboy, Co. Meath. Teil: 046 9430419. Facs: 046 9430420.
Ríomhphost: leabhar@forasnagaeilge.ie. Suíomh Gréasáin: www.gaeilge.ie.
Misean: Scríbhneoireacht, Foilsitheoireacht agus Léitheoireacht na Gaeilge
a chothú. Bunaíodh Bord na Leabhar Gaeilge i 1952 chun foilsitheoireacht
na Gaeilge a chur chun cinn. Ag tús 2008, aistríodh feidhmeanna Bhord na
Leabhar Gaeilge go Foras na Gaeilge. Déantar na feidhmeanna sin a
chomhlíonadh anois faoin ainm Clár na Leabhar Gaeilge.

The Dublin Writers Museum
18 Parnell Square, Dublin 1. Tel: 01 8722077. Fax: 01 872 2231. E-mail:
writers@dublintourism.ie. Website: www.writersmuseum.com. Open
Monday to Saturday, 10am - 5pm; Sundays and Public Holidays, 11am to
5pm. Last admission 4.15pm daily. Museum includes collection and
displays in Irish literature, and the lives and works of individual Irish
writers.

Fighting Words
Behan Square, Russell Street, Dublin 1. Tel: 01 8944576. E-mail:
info@fightingwords.ie. Website: www.fightingwords.ie. A creative writing
centre, established by Roddy Doyle and Sean Love. Helps students of all
ages to develop their writing skills and to explore their love of writing.
Fighting Words is located very close to Croke Park.

Irish Writers' Centre
19 Parnell Square, Dublin 1. Tel: 01 8721302. E-mail:
info@writerscentre.ie. Website: www.writerscentre.ie.

Irish Writers' Union/Comhar na Scribhneor

19 Parnell Square, Dublin 1. Tel: 01 8721302. E-mail: iwu@ireland-writers.com. Website: www.ireland-writers.com. Represents the collective interests of writers.

The Irish Copyright Licensing Agency

25, Denzille Lane, Dublin 2. Contact: Samantha Holman, Executive Director. Tel: 01 6624211. Fax: 01 662 4213. E-mail: info@icla.ie. Website: www.icla.ie. Licenses schools and other users of copyright material to copy extracts of such material, and distributes the money collected to the authors and publishers whose works have been copied. Founded 1992.

James Joyce Centre

35 North Great George's Street, Dublin 1. Tel: 01 878 8547. E-mail: info@jamesjoyce.ie. Website: www.jamesjoyce.ie. The James Joyce Centre is dedicated to promoting an understanding of the life and works of James Joyce.

Limerick Writers Centre

12 Barrington Street, Limerick, Co. Limerick. Tel: 087 299 6409. Website: www.limerickwriterscentre.wordpress.com. The Limerick Writers Centre is a not-for-profit organisation that supports, promotes and records the creative spark of Limerick writers. It provides an accessible venue where all writers can meet with a creative or educational purpose. They also aim to create outreach programmes in schools and communities to foster a spirit of creative invention. The Centre also serves to promote great writers through festivals and publication, to promote Limerick's creative excellence in the greater world.

The Munster Literature Centre

Frank O'Connor House, 84 Douglas Street, Cork. Contact: Patrick Cotter, Artistic Director. Tel: 021 4312955. E-mail: info@munsterlit.ie. Website: www.munsterlit.ie. Founded in 1993, the Munster Literature Centre (Tigh Litríochta) is a not-for-profit arts organisation dedicated to the promotion and celebration of literature, especially that of Munster. To this end, we organise festivals, workshops, readings and competitions.

Poetry Ireland / Éigse Éireann

2 Proud's Lane, Off St Stephen's Green, Dublin 2. Contact: Joseph Woods , Director. Tel: 01 4789974. Fax: 01 4780205. E-mail: info@poetryireland.ie. Website: www.poetryireland.ie. Poetry Ireland/Éigse Éireann is the national organisation for poetry in Ireland. We serve all 32 counties and receive support from The Arts Council of Ireland/An Chomhairle Ealaíon

and The Arts Council of Northern Ireland. Useful resources for all poets with an excellent guide to upcoming poetry events and news from the world of Irish poetry.

Publishing Ireland
Guinness Enterprise Centre, Taylor's Lane, Dublin 8. Tel: 01 415 1210. E-mail: info@publishingireland.com. Website: www.publishingireland.com. Association for book publishers in Ireland and Northern Ireland.

The Seamus Heaney Centre for Poetry
The School of English, Queens University, Belfast. BT7 1NN. Tel: 028 90971070. Website: www.qub.ac.uk/heaneycentre

Seanchaí
Kerry Literary and Cultural Centre, 24 The Square, Listowel, Co. Kerry. Tel: 068 22212. E-mail: info@kerrywritersmuseum.com. Website: www.kerrywritersmuseum.com. The Seanchaí is a visitor attraction in the Heritage Town of Listowel which presents the works of the great Kerry writers in a unique audio-visual experience. Located in a 19th century Georgian residence in Listowel's magnificent Square, the Centre features five of County Kerry's most esteemed writers - John B. Keane, Bryan MacMahon, George Fitzmaurice, Brendan Kennelly and Maurice Walsh.

The Western Writers Centre - Ionad Scríbhneoirí Chaitlín Maude
Galway. The only writers' centre west of the Shannon. Tel: 087 2178138. E-mail: westernwriters@eircom.net. Website: www.twwc.ie. All the latest literary news and events from the West coast of Ireland on this lively and well-maintained blog.

D. Writing and Poetry Journals

Albedo One
Website: www.albedo1.com. Publishes stories of Irish and international authors of Science Fiction, Fantasy and Horror. Published two to three times a year.

Books Ireland
11 Newgrove Avenue, Dublin 4. Tel: 01 269 2185. Fax: 01 269 2185. E-mail: booksi@eircom.net. Magazine is published monthly from February to June and from September to December (9 a year). It has appeared without a break since 1976. It lists and reviews only Irish-interest or Irish-origin books. Subscribers include publishers, booksellers, Irish studies groups, libraries, collectors, journalists and writers in 31 countries. Submission Guidelines: Short articles (1,000 - 1,500 words) on Irish-interest books, interviews with writers, publishers etc. Most of our articles are commissioned, and it would be wise to check subject matter first with the Features Editor.

Crannóg Magazine
Galway Language Centre, Bridge Mills, Galway. Website: www.crannogmagazine.com. Galway-based literature magazine published three times a year in spring, summer and autumn. Publishes prose and poetry. Submission Guidelines: Closing dates for submissions are: January 1, May 1 and September 1.

Cyphers
3 Selskar Terrace, Ranelagh, Dublin 6. Website: www.cyphersmagazine.org. Ireland's longest running literary magazine Cyphers was founded in 1975. Publishes poetry, prose, graphics and reviews by many distinguished writers, translators and artists. The magazine publishes three editions per year.

Dublin Quarterly
Unit 14, Base Enterprise Centre, Ladyswell Road, Mulhuddart, Dublin 15, Ireland. Tel: 01 4404020. Website: www.dublinquarterly.com

The Dublin Review
P.O. Box 7948, Dublin 1. A quarterly magazine of essays, criticism, fiction and reportage. Website: www.thedublinreview.com

Enounce
Website: www.everywritersresource.com/enounce. Online publication of

poetry, audio poetry, and artwork. Interested in creating a new environment of reading and listening on the web.

Icarus Magazine

E-mail: editor@icarusmag.com. Website: www.icarusmag.com. Published three times throughout the academic year. Poetry, prose, drama and essays on literary themes and creative work by staff, students and alumni of Trinity College. Submission to: submissions@icarusmag.com.

Ireland's Own Magazine

Channing House, Rowe Street, Wexford. Tel: 053 9140140. E-mail: irelands.own@peoplenews.ie. Contact: Phil Murphy, Monthly Editor; Sean Nolan, Weekly Editor. Ireland's Own is a weekly family magazine published without a break since 1902. 64 full colour pages each week, including a special pull-out section for younger readers.
Submissions: By post to: Phil Murphy.
Unsolicited manuscripts accepted? Yes - Historical, Romantic, Biography/Autobiography, Short Fiction - maximum of 2,000 words. Also articles of general Irish interest and historical interest; profiles and biographies of Irish people of historical interest - 800/900 words.

Irish Pages

The Linen Hall Library, 17 Donegal Square, North Belfast. BT1 5GB. Editor: Chris Agee. Tel: 028 90434800. E-mail: editor@irishpages.org, gaeilge@irishpages.org. Website: www.irishpages.org.
A biannual journal, edited in Belfast and publishing, in equal measure, writing from Ireland and overseas. Its policy is to publish poetry, short fiction, essays, creative non-fiction, memoir, essay reviews, nature-writing, translated work, literary journalism, and other autobiographical, historical, religious and scientific writing of literary distinction. There are no standard reviews or narrowly academic articles. Irish Language and Ulster Scots writing are published in the original, with English translations or glosses.
The sole criteria for inclusion in the journal are the distinction of the writing and the integrity of the individual voice. Equal editorial attention is given to established, emergent and new writers. IRISH PAGES does not associate itself with any prize, award, competition, "best-of" ranking selection, fundraising initiative, or other literary promotion that vitiates against the independence of taste and judgment.
Unsolicited manuscripts accepted? Yes. Only postal submissions (with stamps, coupons or cash for return postage, though no self-addressed envelope is needed). We advise all potential contributors to read carefully the ABOUT section of our website and, if possible, to familiarise themselves

with a copy of the journal. No more than eight poems or two prose pieces should be submitted at one time, or within any six-month period. The Editors aim to respond within eight months. If work is accepted, an electronic copy may be requested. Phone queries regarding the submission process are accepted. The Editors occasionally commission non-fiction work (only). Submissions, in both Irish and English, should be sent to the relevant editor at the address above.

Moloch
Website: www.moloch.ie. Moloch is an Irish based e-journal of art and writing. Tying different art forms together in new and refreshing ways, Moloch aspires to allow artists and writers to find inspiration in each other and, in doing so, add new dimensions to each others work.

Poetry Ireland Review
No. 2 Proud's Lane, Off St Stephen's Green, Dublin 2. Tel: 01 478 9974. E-mail: info@poetryireland.ie. Website: www.poetryireland.ie. Poetry Ireland Review is published quarterly. We welcome unsolicited submissions of poems, and proposals for articles and reviews, from Ireland and abroad, in Irish or English.
Guidelines for Poetry Submissions:
- Send a maximum of six poems
- Keep a hard copy of each submission
- Poems should be original, and previously unpublished
- Poems should be typed, with the author's name on each sheet
- If a poem continues over more than one page, clearly indicate stanza breaks between pages
- A stamped self-addressed envelope should be enclosed to facilitate return. Submissions not accompanied by SAEs will not be returned
- Include an e-mail address with your posted submission if you only need notification of the editor's decision and don't need your work returned. The paperwork will be recycled in due course
- Overseas submissions should be accompanied by International Reply Coupons, or with an e-mail address (see above)
- There are no restrictions on style or subject, but Poetry Ireland strongly dislikes poems advocating sexism or racism.

The Editor normally replies within 6 months or earlier; this timeframe may vary with the volume of submissions at any given time. Poets will receive a copy of the issue in which their work appears plus a payment for their contribution.

The Sacred Heart Messenger
Morrigan Book Company, Killala, Co. Mayo. Tel: 096 32555. E-mail: morriganbooks@online.ie. Publishes non-fiction, general Irish interest, biography, history, folklore and mythology.
Unsolicited manuscripts accepted? No.

Shamrock Haiku Journal
Website: www.freewebs.com/irishhaiku. A quarterly web journal. Submissions are accepted at any time but most issues are thematic, so publication of any accepted material may be delayed.

Some Blind Alleys
Editor: Greg Baxter. Tel: 01 8176343. E-mail: editor@someblindalleys.com. Website: www.someblindalleys.com. An online journal of contemporary Irish writing and visual art, based in Dublin. Some Blind Alleys publishes high-quality essays, short stories and translations, as well as graphic essays and stories, short film and animation.

Southword Editions
Frank O'Connor House, 84 Douglas Street, Cork. Contact: Patrick Cotter, Artistic Director. Tel: 021 4312955. E-mail: info@munsterlit.ie. Website: www.munsterlit.ie. A biannual journal of poetry collections and short stories. We actively seek to support new and emerging writers and are assisted in our efforts through funding from Cork City Council, Cork County Council and the Arts Council of Ireland. Through our specialist festival and awards we have a special interest in encouraging the short story form.

The Stinging Fly
PO Box 6016, Dublin 8. Website: www.stingingfly.org. E-mail: stingingfly@gmail.com Contact: Declan Meade Publisher/Editor. Promotes the best of Irish and international writing with a strong emphasis on new writing, and particular interest in the short story form. The main objective is to provide a forum for the very best new Irish and international writing. Three issues of the magazine are published each year. It is available through selected bookstores and from the magazine's website.
Unsolicited manuscripts accepted? Short stories and poetry accepted from January to March each year. No e-mail submissions. See website for guidelines.

Verbal Magazine
The Verbal Arts Centre, Stable Lane and Mall Wall, Bishop Street Within, Derry/Londonderry, BT48 6PU. E-mail: editor@verbalartscentre.co.uk. Website: www.verbalon.com/magazine. Monthly magazine produced by

Derry's Verbal Arts Centre. It includes book reviews, new writing, features, and youth pages. Have your work reviewed, or submit your short stories and poems. Verbal covers most genres - popular and literary fiction, non-fiction, children's, graphic novels.

E. Book Publishers

A. & A. Farmar Ltd
78 Ranelagh Village, Dublin 6, Ireland. Tel: 01 4963625. E-mail:
afarmar@iol.ie. Website: www.aafarmar.ie. Specialists in writing and
producing books for companies and other organisations. Clients include the
RCPI, Findlaters, Heitons, Concern, St Luke's Hospital. Publisher of books -
Politics/Current Affairs, History, Biography/Autobiography, Business and
Finance. We do not publish fiction or poetry.
Unsolicited manuscripts accepted? Yes. Please contact Anna Farmar before
submitting any manuscript.

Abbey Press
Courtenay Hill, Newry, County Down, Northern Ireland, BT34 2ED. Irish
Poetry and Prose.

The Academia Press
E-mail: info@theacademiapress.com. Website:
www.theacademiapress.com. Publishing services for academic, education
and professional books, research papers and thesis.

Appletree Press Ltd
14 Howard Street South, Belfast BT7 1AP. E-mail: reception@appletree.ie.
Website: www.appletree.ie. Publishes gift books, biography, cookery,
guidebooks, history, Irish interest, literary criticism, music, photography,
social studies, sport, and travel.

Arlen House
PO Box 222, Galway. E-mail: arlenhouse@ireland.com. Feminist and
academic titles.

Ashfield Press
30 Linden Grove, Blackrock, Co. Dublin. Tel: 01 2889808. E-mail:
susan.waine@ashfieldpress.ie. Website: www.ashfieldpress.ie. Publishes
Irish-interest non-fiction.
Unsolicited manuscripts accepted? Yes.

Associated Editions
33 Melrose Avenue, Fairview, Dublin3. Tel: 01 857 2997. E-mail:
info@associatededitions.ie. Website: www.associatededitions.ie. Publishes
well written and beautifully designed books, highly illustrated, on a variety
of subjects including Architecture, Art, Art History, Artists Books, Children's
Books, Design, Limited Editions, Music and Social History.

Attic Press
See Cork University Press

Atrium
See Cork University Press

Avatar Media
2 Rye River Park, Dun Carraig, Leixlip, Co. Kildare. Tel: 01 4433284. E-mail: gdawed@avataronline.net. Italy: 06 83 39 82 85 France: 09 70 44 45 45. Contact: Gilbert Dawed.

BEC Publishing
Blackrock Education Centre, Kill Avenue, Dun Laoghaire, Co. Dublin. Tel: 01 2365013 / 01 2365044. Contact: Carrie Fonseca, Executive Manager. E-mail: carrie@blackrockec.ie or becbooks@blackrockec.ie. Website: www.blackrockec.ie.
Unsolicited manuscripts accepted? Yes. Blackrock Education Centre has a particular interest in training materials for children with special education needs and their teachers. Publisher of books - Education, Computers, Computer Teaching Manuals, Educational Games for the Classroom, Learning Support Materials.

Best Guides
Old Chapel, Bandon, Co. Cork. Tel: 023 8841329

Binnacle Press
Kinsale, Co. Cork. E-mail: info@binnaclepress.com. Website: www.binnaclepress.com. Contact: Deborah Lysaght. Fiction and poetry.
Unsolicited manuscripts accepted? Send covering letter, synopsis (no more than 300 words), and short biography.

Blackhall Publishing
Lonsdale House, Avoca Avenue, Blackrock, Co. Dublin. Tel: 01 2785090. E-mail: info@blackhallpublishing.com. Website: www.blackhallpublishing.com. Contact: Gerard O'Connor, Managing Director. Publisher of books - Politics/Current Affairs; Business and Finance; Lifestyles; Self-Help; Education; Law; Social Studies; Nursing. Unsolicited manuscripts accepted? Yes. Please see our website for information on submitting work.
Imprints: **Lonsdale Publishing**

Black Mountain Press
PO Box 9, Ballyclare, Co. Antrim BT39 OJW.

Blackstaff Press Ltd
4c Heron Wharf, Sydenham Bus Park, Belfast BT3 9LE. Tel: 028 9045 5006. Fax: 028 9046 6237. E-mail: info@blackstaffpress.com. Website: www.blackstaffpress.com. Publishes in a wide range of categories, including adult fiction, sport, biography, history, humour, natural history, cookery, travel and poetry.

Blackwater Press
1 Great Denmark Street, Dublin 1. Managing Director - John O'Connor. Tel: 086 2569681. E-mail: jloconnor@eircom.net. Imprint of **Folens Publishers**.

Brandon/Mount Eagle Publications
Coleen, Dingle, Co. Kerry. Tel: 066 915 1234. E-mail: info@brandonbooks.com. Website: www.brandonbooks.com. Publisher of quality fiction and non-fiction, biography, current affairs.

Brookside
See New Island Books

Campus Publishing
31 The Bailey, Circular Road, Galway. Tel: 091 524662

Carysfort Press
58 Woodfield, Scholarstown Road, Rathfarnham, Dublin 16. E-mail: info@carysfortpress.com. Website: www.carysfortpress.com. Publishes books on Drama, Literary Criticism, Music, and the Arts and Humanities.

Celtic Press
Goldenbridge Industrial Estate, Dublin 8. Tel: 01 453 0328. E-mail: celticpress@gmail.com. Website: www.celticpublications.com.

Chartered Accountants Ireland
Chartered Accountants House, 47-49 Pearse Street, Dublin 2. Tel: 01 6680842. Northern Ireland Office: The Linenhall, 32-38 Linenhall Street, Belfast BT2 8BG. Tel: 028 9032 1600. Publishing division of Chartered Accountants Ireland publishes titles in taxation, law, business and management.

Childnames.net
27 Villarea Park, Glenageary, Co. Dublin. Tel:087 9369888. E-mail: info@childnames.net. Website: www.Childnames.net. Publisher of colour-illustrated storybooks for little people on popular baby names, with the facts on each name for big people.

Children's Books Ireland
17 North Great Georges Street, Dublin 1. Contact: Jenny Murray. Tel: 01-8727475 / 01 8727476. E-mail: info@childrensbooksireland.ie. Website: www.childrensbooksireland.ie.

The Childrens Story Press
E-mail: info@thechildrens-storypress.com. Website: thechildrens-storypress.com. Illustrated book and CD publishing.

Church of Ireland Publishing
RCB Library, Braemor Park, Churchtown, Dublin 14. Tel: 01 4923979. Website: www.cip.ireland.anglican.org. Theological publications.

CJ Fallon
Ground Floor, Block B, Liffey Valley Office Campus, Dublin 22. Tel: 01 6166400. E-mail: info@cjfallon.ie. Website: www.cjfallon.ie. Publishes educational textbooks.

Clódhanna Teoranta
13 Paráid na Díge, Corcaigh.

Cló Chaisil
Ríomhphost: carico@eircom.net

Cló Iar Chonnachta Teo
Indreabhan, Conamara, Co. na Gaillimhe. Teil: 091 593307. Ríomhphost: cic@iol.ie. Suíomh Gréasáin: www.cic.ie. Foilsíonn leabhair Gaeilge den úrscéalta, gearrscéalta, drámaí, filíocht, agus stair.

Cló Mhaigh Eo
Droimnín, Clár Chlainne Mhuris, Co. Mhaigh Eo. Teil: 094 9371744 Facs: 094 937 1744. Ríomhphost: colman@leabhar.com. Suíomh Gréasáin: www.leabhar.com. Foilsíonn Cló Mhaigh Eo leabhair Ghaeilge do pháistí agus do dhaoine óga. Foilsímid úrscéalta grafacha i nGaeilge freisin a bhfuil tóir idirnáisiúnta orthu.

Coisceim
Tig Bhríde, 91 Bóthar Bhinn Éadair, Binn Éadair, Baile Átha Cliath 13. Teil: 01 8322509. Facs: 01 8320131. Suíomh Gréasáin: www.coisceim.ie.

Cois Life
62 Páirc na Rós, Ascaill na Cille, Dún Laoghaire, Co. Bhaile Átha Cliath. Teil:

01 8322509. Ríomhphost: eolas@coislife.ie. Suíomh Gréasáin:
www.coislife.ie. Literary and academic Irish-language publishers.

The Collins Press

West Link Park, Doughcloyne, Wilton, Cork. Tel: 021 4347717. E-mail:
enquiries@collinspress.ie. Website: www.collinspress.ie. Publisher of
books - Politics/Current Affairs; Business and Finance; Lifestyles; Self-
Help; Education; Law; Social Studies; Nursing. Politics/Current Affairs;
History; Biography/Autobiography; Sport; Gardening; DIY; Technical;
Computers; Photography.

Unsolicited manuscripts accepted? Yes, in the categories we publish.
WRITERS SHOULD VISIT OUR WEBSITE TO GET AN IDEA OF THE TYPES
OF BOOKS WE PUBLISH. We do not publish poetry, short stories, drama or
literary criticism and are discontinuing adult fiction and children's fiction.
Your submission package should include the following:

- A cover letter
- A self-addressed, stamped envelope large enough to return your
work. Even if you do not want your work returned, please enclose a
letter-sized envelope for our response
- A one-page (250 words) synopsis giving an overview of the entire
book. For non-fiction, please include a table of contents. If applicable,
subheads should be included that explain the content at a greater level
of detail
- A CV that includes an outline of any past publishing or writing
experience
- Either a complete manuscript or at least three sample chapters. These
do not have to be in chronological order. Selected chapters should
include what best represents your work's basic idea, its quality and
distinctive features.

Prepare the material carefully. If the manuscript is full of typographical or
grammatical errors, the reviewer's attention will be diverted from the
content. Whether submitting sample chapters or a complete work, please
advise us of the word count for the complete work.

The package should be addressed to: Mr Con Collins, The Collins Press,
West Link Park, Doughcloyne, Wilton, Cork, Ireland. Please allow a period
of eight to twelve weeks for a response from us regarding your submission.

Colourpoint Books

Colourpoint House, Jubilee Business Park, Jubilee Road, Newtownards, Co.
Down. BT23 4YH. Tel: 028 9182 6339. E-mail: info@colourpoint.co.uk.
Website: www.colourpoint.co.uk. Publishes books of Irish interest, local
history, transport, education, fiction.

Unsolicited manuscripts accepted? Send synopsis, sample chapter/section and details of experience/qualifications.
Imprints: **Plover Fiction**.

The Columba Press/The Columba Bookservice Ltd

55a Spruce Avenue, Stillorgan Industrial Park, Blackrock, Co. Dublin. Tel: 01 2942556. Website: www.columba.ie.
Contacts:

Seán O Boyle, Publisher	Tel: ext: 207	E-mail: sean@columba.ie
Cecilia West	Tel: ext: 208	E-mail: west@columba.ie
Michael Brennan	Tel: ext: 211	E-mail: michael@columba.ie
Trish Lowth	Tel: ext: 201	E-mail: trish@columba.ie

Publisher - Books: Religious/Spiritual.
Unsolicited manuscripts accepted? Yes, Scripts on religious topics.
Preferrably samples and outlines at first. Send hard copy or e-mail sean@columba.ie.
Imprints: **Currach Press**

Cork University Press

Youngline Industrial Park, Pouladuff, Togher, Cork. Tel: 021 4902980. E-mail: corkuniversitypress@ucc.ie. Publishes Irish literature, history, cultural studies, medieval studies, English literature, musicology, poetry, translations.
Imprints: **Atrium** and **Attic Press** publish books by and about women, particularly social comment, women's studies, reference guides and handbooks.

Cottage Publications

Laurel Cottage, 15 Ballyhay Road, Donaghadee, Co. Down BT21 0NG. Tel: 028 9188 8033. E-mail: info@cottage-publications.com. Website: www.cottage-publications.com. Publishes illustrated local books and prints of Ireland and England.
Imprints: **Laurel Cottages**

Currach Press

See The Columba Press

De Barra Publishing

Suite 18, Information Age Park, Ennis, Co. Clare. Tel: 065 6833066.
Website: www.projectbubbles.com. Publisher of early year's education and pre-school products and services.

Dedalus Press
13 Moyclare Road, Baldoyle, Dublin 13. Tel: 01 8392034. Website: www.dedaluspress.com. Publishing contemporary poetry from Ireland, and poetry in translation from around the world.

Doire Press
Aille Inverin, Co. Galway. E-mail: doirepress@gmail.com. Contact: Lisa Frank

Edmund Burke Publishing
27 Priory Drive, Blackrock, Co. Dublin. Tel: 01 2882159. E-mail: deburca@indigo.ie. Website: www.deburcararebooks.com. Publishes historical, topographical and limited edition books relating to Ireland.

The Educational Company of Ireland
Ballymount Road, Dublin 12. Tel: 01 450 0611. E-mail: info@edco.ie. Website: www.edco.ie. Publishers of educational textbooks for primary and post primary schools in Ireland, in English and Irish language.

Epicure Press
See Georgina Campbell Guides

Fahy Publishing Ltd
129 Delwood Close, Castleknock, Dublin 15. Tel: 01 8205230 / 086 2269330. E-mail: info@fahypublishing.com. Website: www.fahypublishing.com. Contact: Frank Fahy, Managing Director. Publishing and editorial services; literary agency representing authors of general fiction and children's fiction; publisher of *The Educational Resources Guide* for Teachers. Special interest in Children's books (9-12 years) and young adult. No picture books or poetry books considered. Unsolicited manuscripts accepted? No; initial contact by e-mail or letter required before submitting manuscript.

First Law
Merchant's Court, Merchants Quay, Dublin 8. Contact: Bart D. Daly Managing Director. Tel: 01 6790370. Fax: 01 6790057. E-mail: bartdaly@firstlaw.ie. Website: www.firstlaw.ie.
Unsolicited manuscripts accepted? No. Contact office first. Publish Law related books, journals, magazines and other specialist publications.

Fish Publishing
Durrus, Bantry, Co. Cork. E-mail: info@fishpublishing.com. Website: www.fishpublishing.com. Contact: Clem Cairns. Publishing Crime, Thriller,

Science Fiction, Fantasy, Horror, Humour, Satire, Chick Lit, Lads' Lit, Historical, Romantic, Erotic.

Flyleaf Press
4 Spencer Villas, Glenageary, Co. Dublin. Tel: 01 2845906. E-mail: books@flyleaf.ie. Website: www.flyleaf.ie. Publisher of family history and genealogy titles.

Folens Publishers
Hibernian Industrial Estate, Greenhills Road, Dublin 24. Tel: 01 4137200. E-mail: info@folens.ie. Website: www.folens.ie. Publishes educational books in English and Irish.
Imprints: **Blackwater**. Publishes general non-fiction, Irish interest and children's fiction.

Four Courts Press
7 Malpas Street, Dublin 8. Tel: 01 4534668. Website: www.fourcourtspress.ie. E-mail: info@fourcourtspress.ie. Contact: Martin Healy, Publisher; Martin Fanning, Senior Editor; Anthony Tierney, Marketing and Sales Manager. Publisher of books about Politics/Current Affairs; History; Biography/Autobiography; Religious/Spiritual; Education Unsolicited manuscripts accepted? No, contact first by telephone or e-mail.

Futa Fata
An Spideal, Co. na Gaillimhe. Teil: 091 504612. Ríomhphost: eolas@futafata.com. Suíomh Gréasáin: www.futafata.com. Foilsitheoir leabhar agus lipéad ceoil atá lonnaithe sa Spidéal, i nGaeltacht Chonamara, ar chósta thiar na hÉireann

Glór na nGael
Suíomh Gréasáin: www.glornangael.ie

The Gallery Press
Loughcrew, Oldcastle, Co. Meath. Tel: 049 854 1779. E-mail: gallery@indigo.ie. Website: www.gallerypress.com. Publishers of contemporary Irish poetry, drama and prose.

Georgina Campbell Guides
Epicure Press, PO Box 6173, Dublin 13. Tel: 01 839 5972. E-mail: info@ireland-guide.com. Website: www.ireland-guide.com. Contact: Georgina Campbell, Editor.
Unsolicited manuscripts accepted? No, but would accept detailed proposals, preferably e-mailed. Publisher of books and magazines (Irish

food, travel and hospitality only); Online publisher of Cookery; Sport; Gardening; DIY; Technical; Computers; Photography; Food and Travel, Hospitality (Irish interest)
Imprints: **Epicure Press**

Gill & Macmillan Ltd

10 Hume Avenue, Park West, Dublin 12. Tel: 01 500 9506. E-mail: ftobin@gillmacmillan.ie. Website: www.gillmacmillan.ie. Contact: Fergal Tobin, Publishing Director. Publisher of books - True Crime; Politics/Current Affairs; History; Biography/Autobiography; Business and Finance; Fashion; Cookery; Sport; Nature; Self-Help; Education; Computers. Unsolicited manuscripts accepted? - Yes.
Imprints: **Newleaf, Rí Ra**.

The Goldsmith Press Ltd

Great Connell, Newbridge, Co. Kildare. Tel: 045 433613. Irish interest. Unsolicited manuscripts accepted? No.

Guildhall Press

Unit 15, Rath Mor Business Park, Bligh's Lane, Derry. BT48 0LZ Northern Ireland. Tel: 028 71 364413. E-mail: info@ghpress.com. Website: www.ghpress.com. Contact: Paul Hippseley, Managing Editor. Publisher of books - Crime, Thriller, Politics/Current Affairs, Academic, Social Issues, History, Biography/Autobiography, Satire, Sport, Education, Photography, Science Fiction, Fantasy, Humour, Children, Young Adult, Satire, Chick Lit, Lads' Lit, Historical, Romantic. General print and design services, proof-reading and editorial services. Web Design, Visual Art Design. Unsolicited manuscripts accepted? Yes, see website for instructions.

An Gúm

7 Merrion Square, Dublin 2. E-mail: angum@forasnagaeilge.ie. Website: www.forasnagaeilge.ie. Irish language publisher of children's books, school textbooks, dictionaries, music and general readers for adults. Unsolicited manuscripts accepted? Yes. Also welcomes first and second level school textbooks for translation into Irish.

Hag's Head Press

62 Main Street, Apt. 3, Clongriffin, Dublin 1. Tel: 087 6591491. Website: www.hagsheadpress.com. Contact: Marsha Swan. Publisher of books. Crime, Politics/Current Affairs, History, Biography/Autobiography, Humour, Satire, Photography. Unsolicited manuscripts accepted? Yes, e-mail synopsis and sample chapters to Marsha Swan, info@hagsheadpress.com. Fiction and non-fiction welcome, no poetry or drama

Hachette Books Ireland

8 Castlecourt Centre, Castleknock, Dublin 15. Tel: 01 824 6288. E-mail: submissions@hbgi.ie. Website: www.hachette.ie. Contact: Ciara Doorley, Senior Editor. Hachette Books Ireland is the Irish publishing division of Hachette UK. Hachette UK is the largest and one of the most diversified book publishers in the UK. The Group is made up of several publishing companies and imprints including **Headline Publishing Group, Hodder & Stoughton, John Murray, Orion Publishing Group, Octopus Publishing Group, Little Brown Book Group, Hodder Education Group** and **Hachette Children's Books**. Publisher of books. Non-Fiction: Crime, Politics/Current Affairs, History, Biography/Autobiography, Business and Finance, Humour, Satire, Lifestyles, Fashion, Cookery, Sport, Religious/Spiritual, Self-Help. Fiction: Historical, Romantic Crime, Thriller, Science Fiction, Chick Lit, Lads' Lit.

Unsolicited manuscripts accepted? No.

Fiction: We accept submissions from agents and previously published authors. Please send the opening chapters (approx. 100 pages), a detailed synopsis and autobiographical note to below address or by e-mail to submissions@hbgi.ie.

Non-fiction: Please send opening sample chapters (approx. 100 pages), a detailed proposal, autobiographical note, along with a chapter outline to the below address or by e-mail to submissions@hbgi.ie. Submissions: Hachette Books Ireland, 8 Castlecourt Centre, Castleknock, Dublin 15.

Hardpressed Poetry

Shanbally Road, Annacotty, Co. Limerick. A small press which publishes poetry that you won't often find in your local bookshop.

The History Press, Ireland

119 Lower Baggot Street, Dublin 2. Tel: 01 244 9470. Website: www.thehistorypress.ie. Publisher of local and general history books.

The History Publisher

E-mail: info@thehistorypublisher.com. Website: www.thehistorypublisher.com. Publishing services for historians, history societies, biographers and family memoirs.

Hodder Headline Ireland

See entry under Hachette Books

IFP Media

31 Deansgrange Road, Blackrock Co. Dublin. Tel: 01 2893305. E-mail: info@ifpmedia.com. Website: www.ifpmedia.com.

Institute of Public Administration

Vergemount Hall, Clonskeagh, Dublin 6. Tel: 01 240 3767. E-mail: info@ipa.ie. Website: www.ipa.ie. Publishes books dealing with public administration and related subject areas; Administration, a quarterly academic journal; Administration Yearbook and Diary and research reports.

Irish Academic Press

2 Brookside, Dundrum Road, Dublin 14. Tel: 01 298 9937. E-mail: lisa.hyde@iap.ie. Website: www.iap.ie. Contact: Lisa Hyde, Editor. Publisher of books - Politics/Current Affairs, History, Biography/Autobiography, arts, cinema, society.
Unsolicited manuscripts accepted? Yes. We consider non-fiction manuscripts of an academic and general trade nature on history, politics, arts, theatre and film, literature and society regarding the island of Ireland. Please contact via e-mail requesting book proposal form.
Imprints: **Valentine Mitchel Publishers**

Jillbeck Books

E-mail: info@jillbeckbooks.com. Website: www.jillbeckbooks.com.

Kestrel Books

Ballydoreen, Killiskey, Ashford, Wicklow. Tel: 0404 49113

Kids' Own Publishing

Carrigeens, Ballinfull, Co. Sligo. Tel: 071 9124945. Website: www.kidsown.ie. Publishes work by children.

Lapwing Poetry

1 Ballysillan Drive, Belfast. BT14 8HQ. E-mail: lapwing.poetry@ntlworld.com. Website: www.lapwingpoetry.com.

Laurel Cottages

See Cottage Publications

Leabhar Breac

Breacán Tta, Indreabhán, Co. na Gaillimhe. Website: www.leabharbreac.com

Learning Ireland

Clarence Street, Dun Laoghaire, Co. Dublin. Tel: 01 2844738. Website: www.learningireland.ie

Liberties Press
Guinness Enterprise Centre, Taylor's Lane, Dublin 8. Tel: 01 4151286. E-mail: info@libertiespress.com. Website: www.libertiespress.com. Contact: Seán O'Keeffe, Editorial Director. Publisher of books - Crime, Politics/Current Affairs, History, Biography/Autobiography, Business and Finance, Humour, Satire, Lifestyles, Fashion, Cookery, Sport, Nature, Religious/Spiritual, Self-Help, Education, Gardening, DIY, Technical, Computers, Photography
Unsolicited manuscripts accepted? Yes. Please send a summary of the main themes dealt with in the book, and three sample chapters to: Submissions, Liberties Press, Guinness Enterprise Centre, Taylor's Lane, Dublin 8. Text should be printed on one side of the page only, with the line spacing set at 1.5 or higher. Liberties Press also commissions work from authors and would encourage people to submit ideas for books as well as samples of completed manuscripts. If you would like your manuscript returned, please enclose a stamped, self-addressed envelope with it. (Submissions from the UK and elsewhere should be accompanied by an international postal voucher.) Otherwise, replies to correspondence will generally be made by e-mail. Liberties Press will do its best to deal with submissions within one month of receipt. Please note that we receive many manuscripts and are unable to offer advice on how those that we feel are not suitable for publication should be amended, nor to suggest which other publishers to send work to.

The Liffey Press Ltd
10 Main Street, Raheny, Dublin 5. Tel: 01 8511458. E-mail: theliffeypress@gmail.com. Website: www.theliffeypress.com. Contact: David Givens. Publisher of high quality non-fiction titles - Crime, Politics/Current Affairs, History, Biography/Autobiography, Business and Finance, Lifestyles, Religious/Spiritual, Self-Help, Education.
Unsolicited manuscripts accepted? Yes. Prefer manuscripts to be sent electronically. More information on submissions can be found on our website

The Lilliput Press
62 Sitric Road, Dublin 7. Tel: 01 6711647. E-mail: info@lilliputpress.ie. Website: www.lilliputpress.ie. Publishes Irish history, contemporary culture, philosophy, biography, literature/essays, Joyce, literary fiction and nature/environment.

Londubh Books
18 Casimir Avenue, Harold's Cross, Dublin 6W. Tel: 01 4903495. E-mail: jo@londubh.ie. Website: www.londubh.ie. Contact: Jo O'Donoghue, Publisher.

Lonsdale Publishing
See Blackhall Publishing

Lyn Publications
Kells Business Park, Kells, Co. Meath. Tel: 046 41923

Management Briefs
30 The Palms, Clonskeagh, Dublin 14. Tel: 01 2788 980. Website:
www.managementbriefs.com. Publishes short easy-to-read books for busy
managers across a range of topics.

Marino Books
See Mercier Press.

Maverick House Publishers
Unit 19, Dunboyne Business Park, Dunboyne, Co. Meath. Tel: 01 825 5717.
E-mail: info@maverickhouse.com. Website: www.maverickhouse.com.

Mentor Books Ltd
43 Furze Road, Sandyford Industrial Estate, Dublin 18. Tel: 01 295 2112. E-
mail: admin@mentorbooks.ie. Website: www.mentorbooks.ie. Contact:
Daniel McCarthy, Managing Director. Publisher of books.
Fiction: Crime; Thriller; Humour; Satire; Historical; Romantic.
Non-Fiction: Crime; Politics/Current Affairs; History;
Biography/Autobiography; Business and Finance; Humour; Satire;
Lifestyles; Sport; Nature; Religious/Spiritual; Self-Help; Education;
Photography.
Unsolicited manuscripts accepted? No.

Mercier Press
Unit 3B, Oak House, Bessboro Road, Blackrock, Cork. Tel: 021 4614700. E-
mail: info@mercierpress.ie. Website: www.mercierpress.ie. Contact: Patrick
Crowley, Sales and Marketing Manager - pr@mercierpress.ie. Mercier Press
is Ireland's oldest independent publishing house, based in Cork. It was
founded in 1944 by Captain Seán and Mary Feehan. We publish primarily
for the Irish market and as such our list focuses on Irish interest non-
fiction. Publisher - Books: Crime; Politics/Current Affairs; History;
Biography/Autobiography; Business and Finance; Humour; Satire;
Lifestyles; Fashion; Cookery; Sport; Nature; Religious/Spiritual; Self-Help;
Education; Gardening; DIY; Technical; Computers; Photography.
Unsolicited manuscripts accepted? Yes. Mercier Press welcomes unsolicited
submissions from authors and illustrators. We are currently seeking mainly
History, Biography/Memoir, Politics/Current Affairs, Sport, Lifestyle and

Cookery, Folklore and Humour. While we do publish some fiction, children's and poetry our output in these areas is very limited and will remain so.

Non- Fiction Submissions: Please send a Cover Letter (not more than 1 page or 500 words), an Author CV (including a 200 word bio) and a Synopsis (not more than 2 pages or 1500 words) to us by e-mail (commissioning@mercierpress.ie). If you must send your submission by post note that WE DO NOT RETURN SUBMITTED MATERIAL WITHOUT PAID IRISH POSTAGE. Material is submitted at your own risk; please do not send your only copy. Allow 6-8 weeks for a response.

Fiction Submissions: Please send a Cover Letter (of not more than 1 page or 500 words), an Author CV (including a 200 word bio) and 3 sequential sample chapters (preferably 1, 2 and 3) of the text to us by e-mail (commissioning@mercierpress.ie). Material is submitted at your own risk; please do not send your only copy. Allow 6-8 weeks for a response.

Imprints: **Marino Books**

Merlin Publishing (Merlin Publishing and Wolfhound Press)

Newmarket Hall, St Luke's Avenue, Cork Street, Dublin 8. Tel: 01 4535866. E-mail: publishing@merlin.ie. Website: www.merlinwolfhound.com. Contact: Chenile Keogh, Managing Director/Publisher. Merlin is one of the leading non-fiction publishers in Ireland. We specialise in Biography, True Crime and Lifestyle books.

Unsolicited manuscripts accepted? Yes: Please submit your proposal by e-mail. Include a complete synopsis (two pages max) along with a sample chapter.

Imprints: **Wolfhound Press**

Messenger Publications

37 Lower Leeson Street, Dublin 2. Tel: 01 6767491. E-mail: manager@messenger.ie. Website: www.messenger.ie. Contact: Triona McKee, Marketing and General Manager.

Móinín

Loch Reasca, Ballyvaughan, Co. Clare, Ireland. Tel: 065 7077256 or 086 2118074. Fax: 065 7077256. E-mail: moinin@eircom.net. Website: www.moinin.ie. Publishers of children's, teenage and adult fiction in English and Irish. Foilsitheoirí leabhar do pháistí, dhéagóirí agus léitheoirí fásta.

Music Ireland

Sraheens, Achill Sound, Achill Island, Co. Mayo. Tel: 098 20790 / 086 2300222. E-mail: info@greatirishballads.com. Website:

www.greatirishballads.com. Publishes books of Irish music, from ballads to traditional music.

National Library of Ireland
Kildare Street, Dublin 2. Tel: 01 6030200. E-mail: info@nli.ie. Website: www.nli.ie. Publishes books, a range of reproduction prints, education packs and postcards of images from the Library's graphic collections.

New Century Publishing
Suite 9, Unit 8, Blanchardstown Corporate Park, Dublin 15. Tel: 01 8855222. Website: www.newcenturypublishing.com.

New Island Books
2 Brookside, Dundrum Road, Dublin 14. Tel: 01 2983411. E-mail: elaina.oneill@newisland.ie. Websites: www.newisland.ie / www.littleisland.ie. Contact: Elaina O'Neill Publishing Assistant for New Island and Little Island. Publisher of books - Politics/Current Affairs, History, Biography/Autobiography, Humour, and Satire. New Island specialises in fiction, poetry, and non-fiction, including biography, memoir, current affairs and history.
Unsolicited manuscripts accepted? Yes, submissions by post only - synopsis and first 3 chapters or 50 pages.
Imprints: **Brookside**, **Little Island**.
Little Island publishes non-illustrated fiction for older children and teenagers. Unsolicited manuscripts accepted? Yes, submissions by e-mail only to elaina.oneill@littleisland.ie - synopsis and first 3 chapters or 50 pages.

Newleaf
Imprint of **Gill & Macmillan Ltd**.

National Gallery of Ireland
Merrion Square West, Dublin 2. Tel: 01 6615133. Website: www.nationalgallery.ie

Nonsuch Publishing
119 Lower Baggot Street. Dublin 2. Tel: 01 2449470. Website: www.nonsuchireland.com

Oak Tree Press
19 Rutland Street, Cork. Tel: 021 431 3496. E-mail: info@oaktreepress.com. Website: oaktreepress.com. Publishes business and professional books.

The O'Brien Press Ltd
12 Terenure Road East, Rathgar, Dublin 6. Tel: 01-4923333. E-mail: books@obrien.ie. Website: www.obrien.ie. Contact: Michael O'Brien, Publisher. Mary Webb, Editorial Director. Publishes Crime, Politics/Current Affairs, History, Biography/Autobiography, Business and Finance, Humour, Cookery, Sport, Nature, Gardening, Adult Fiction, Academic.
Unsolicited manuscripts accepted? Yes. No poetry. Send copies only - unsolicited manuscripts not returned. Should your submission be 1000 words or less then you may submit your work in its entirety. Please number all the pages of your submission appropriately. For anything in excess of this length (for example a children's novel) a synopsis and 2 or 3 sample chapters is more than adequate. We will only accept submissions/proposals/artwork, etc., via the post. Please do not e-mail your work to us. Please allow a minimum of 8/10 weeks response time. As the number of unsolicited manuscripts requiring review by our editorial team can be quite high, sometimes this process can take longer. At The O'Brien Press, we are very conscious of the environment and recycle as much paper as we possibly can. We would therefore encourage you not to use excess paper clips, staples, folders, etc.

Off We Go Publishing
74 Salmon Weir, Annacotty, Co. Limerick. E-mail: avril@offwego.ie. Website: www.offwego.ie.

Onstream Publications Ltd
Currabaha, Cloghroe, Blarney, Co. Cork. Tel: 021 438 5798. E-mail: info@onstream.ie. Website: www.onstream.ie. Contact: Roz Crowley. Publisher - Books: Business and Finance; Cookery, Wine, General Health. Unsolicited manuscripts accepted? No.

Passion Publishing
27 North Great Georges Street, Dublin 1. Tel: 01 8788536

Past Exam Papers
E-mail: exampastpapers@gmail.com. Website: www.pastexampapers.ie. Publishes junior and leaving cert past papers.

Penguin Ireland
25 St Stephens Green, Dublin 2. Tel: 01 6617695. Website: www.penguin.ie. E-mail: info@penguin.ie. Commercial and literary fiction and non-fiction. See website for submission guidelines.

Phaeton Publishing Limited

28 Leeson Park, Dublin 6, Tel: 01 4981893. E-mail: phaeton@iol.ie. Contact: John O'Dwyer, Director.
Fiction: Crime, Thriller, Fantasy, Humour, Children, Satire, Historical, Romantic.

Non-fiction: History, Biography/Autobiography, Satire, Lifestyles, Fashion, Cookery, Nature, Self-Help, Education, Gardening, DIY, Photography, Other Specialist Publications.
Unsolicited manuscripts accepted? Send synopsis and sample chapter (and SAE if return desired).

Pillar Press

Ladywell, Thomastown, Co. Kilkenny. Tel: 056 772 4987. E-mail: info@pillarpress.ie. Website: www.pillarpress.ie.

Plover Fiction

See Colourpoint Books

Poolbeg Press Ltd

123 Grange Hill, Baldoyle Industrial Estate, Dublin 13. Tel: 01 8321477. E-mail: info@poolbeg.com. Website: www.poolbeg.com. Publishes popular fiction, non-fiction, current affairs. See website for submission guidelines.

Prism

See Royal Irish Academy

Púca Press

River Lane, Dingle, Co. Kerry. Bóthar an Phúca, Daingean Uí Chúis, Co. Chiarraí. Tel: 086 0662904. E-mail: lieb@pucapress.com. Website: www.pucapress.com

Rathdown

See Wordwell Publishing

Relay Books

Tyone, Nenagh, Co. Tipperary. Tel: 067 31734. E-mail: relaybooks@eircom.net

Redemptorist Publications

Liguori House, 75 Orwell Road, Dublin 6. Tel: 01 4922488. E-mail: info@redemptoristpublications.com. Website: www.redemptoristpublications.com.

Rí Ra
Imprint of **Gill & Macmillan Ltd**.

Royal Dublin Society
Science Section, Ballsbridge, Dublin 4. Tel: 01 240 7217. E-mail:
info@rds.ie. Website: www.rds.ie. Publishes books on the history of Irish
science.

Royal Irish Academy
Academy House 19 Dawson Street, Dublin 2. Tel: 01 6380917. Website:
www.ria.ie. Contact: Helena King, Acting Managing Editor of Publications.
01 6762346. (Note: please use the above as contact for 2010; Managing
Editor Ruth Hegarty is currently on leave). We publish as Royal Irish
Academy but also have a new imprint - **Prism** - for our more recent
publications aimed at a general readership. The Royal Irish Academy is
Ireland's oldest academic publisher. The Academy works in partnership
with other institutions to stimulate debate and spark interest in research.
In addition, the RIA continues to publish six scholarly journals, landmark
series and monographs. In recent years, the RIA has produced a number of
publications under a new imprint - **Prism** - aimed at disseminating
scholarship to a more general readership. Publisher - Books, Other
Specialist Publications: Politics/Current Affairs, History,
Biography/Autobiography, Education, Archaeology, Science.
Unsolicited manuscripts accepted? Yes. We accept non-fiction manuscripts;
generally academic in nature. In hardcopy, please type double-spaced.
Send for the attention of the Managing Editor of Publications, in electronic
format, saved as an MS Word document. Send to publications@ria.ie.
Authors will be asked to complete a Publication Proposal Form for
consideration by the Academy's Publication Committee.
Imprints: **Prism**

An Sagart
Teil: 066 9150000 Ríomhphost: pof@ansagart.ie nó caroline@ansagart.ie.
Suíomh Gréasáin: www.ansagart.ie. Béaloideas, Beathaisnéis, Drámaíocht,
Filíocht, Irisí, Léirmheas agus Stair na Litríochta, Prós, Spioradáltacht agus
Diagacht.

Salmon Poetry
Knockeven, Cliffs of Moher. Co. Clare. Tel: 065 7081941. E-mail:
info@salmonpoetry.com. Website: www.salmonpoetry.com. Publisher of
Irish and international poetry.

Scotus Press
PO Box 9498, Dublin 6. E-mail: info@scotuspress.com
Website: www.scotuspress.com.

Shanway Press
1-3 Eia Street, Belfast, BT14 6BT. Tel: 028 90222070. E-mail:
info@shanway.com. Website: www.shanway.com. Contact: Michael
McKernon. Publisher - Books and Magazines - Politics/Current Affairs,
History, Heritage Biography/Autobiography, Humour, Education,
Photography, Poetry. Shanway is one of Ireland's foremost publishers of
ecclesiastical and historical books, as well as producing high quality
illustrated books and films.
Unsolicited manuscripts accepted? Yes, submissions e-mailed to
info@shanway.com will be looked at.

Silver Angel Publishing
35 Granary Hall, Mount Oval Village, Rochestown, Co. Cork. Tel: 021
4366897. Website: www.silverangelpublishing.com. E-mail:
info@oliveobrien.com. Contact: Olive O'Brien Author. Publisher - Children
Books.
Unsolicited manuscripts accepted? No

An tSnáthaid Mhór
20 Gairdíní Ashley, Bóthar Lansdúin, Bóthar Aontroma, Béal Feirste, BT15
4DN. Ríomhphost: andrewwhitson@hotmail.com. Suíomh Gréasáin:
www.antsnathaidmhor.com

Southword Publishing
The Munster Literature Centre, Frank O'Connor House, 84 Douglas Street,
Cork. Tel: 021 4312955. E-mail: info@munsterlit.ie. Website:
www.munsterlit.ie.

Special Stories Publishing
Unit 13, BASE Enterprise Centre, Ladyswell Road, Mulhuddart, Dublin 15.
Tel: 087 297 3333. E-mail: kate@specialstories.ie. Website:
www.specialstories.ie. Contact: Kate Gaynor, Managing Director. Specialises
in books for children that address a range of health, social and educational
issues in a child-friendly and focused way.
Unsolicited manuscripts accepted? Yes. Send by post to Kate Gaynor,
Managing Director.

Summer Palace Press
Kilcar, Co. Donegal. E-mail: cladnageeragh@eircom.net

St Paul Publications
23 St Mels Terrace, Athlone, Co. Westmeath. Tel: 090 275124

TAF Publishing
c/o 52 Cardiffsbridge Avenue, Finglas, Dublin 11. Tel: 01 8569566 / 087 7604547. E-mail: info@tafpublishing.com. Website: www.tafpublishing.com. Contact: Oscar Duggan (General Manager). Publisher - all genres, fiction and non-fiction.
Unsolicited manuscripts accepted? Yes, new authors particularly welcome. Send synopsis and first three chapters, by post or e-mail to submissions@tafpublishing.com.

The Stinging Fly Press
PO Box 6016, Dublin 8. E-mail: stingingfly@gmail.com. Website: www.stingingfly.org. Contact: Declan Meade Publisher/Editor. Publisher - Books and Literary Magazine/Journal.
Unsolicited manuscripts accepted? Yes, short stories and poetry accepted from January to March each year. No e-mail submissions. See website for guidelines.

Wolfhound Press
See Merlin Publishing

Thomson Round Hall
43 Fitzwilliam Place, Dublin 2. Tel: 01 6625301. E-mail:info@roundhall.ie. Website: www.roundhall.thomson.com. Publishes law books and journals.

Tír Eolas
Newtownlynch, Doorus, Kinvara, Co. Galway. Tel: 091 637452. E-mail: info@tireolas.com. Website: www.tireolas.com. Publishes books and guides on ecology, archaeology, folklore and culture.

Ulster Historical Foundation
49 Malone Road, Belfast, BT9 6RY. Tel: 028 90661988. E-mail: enquiry@uhf.org.uk. Website: www.ancestryireland.com. Publisher of historical titles and family history guides relating to Ulster.

University College Dublin Press
Newman House, 86 St Stephen's Green, Dublin 2, Ireland. E-mail: ucdpress@ucd.ie. Website: www.ucdpress.ie. Contact: Barbara Mennell, Executive Editor, Tel: 01 4779812 / Noelle Moran, Assistant Editor, Tel: 01 477 9821. Publisher of academic books.
Unsolicited manuscripts accepted? Yes. Academic titles only. We accept

proposals for academic books. Proposals according to guidelines on our website can be sent by e-mail, but specimen chapters and whole manuscript should be sent as hard copy.

Valentine Mitchel Publishers
See Irish Academic Press

Veritas Publications
7/8 Lower Abbey Street, Dublin 1. Tel: 01 878 8177. E-mail: info@veritas.ie. Website: www.veritas.ie. Publishes religious education textbooks, resources such as the Irish Catholic Directory, and books on theology, spirituality, and counselling, ethical, moral and social issues.

Virtue Publishers
Lough Mogue, Dunlavin, Co. Wicklow. Tel: 045 401271

Wild Honey Press
16a Ballyman Road, Bray, Co. Wicklow, Ireland. Publishes poetry.

The Woodfield Press
17 Jamestown Square, Dublin 8. Tel: 01 454 7991. E-mail: terri.mcdonnell@ireland.com. Website: www.woodfield-press.com. Contact: Terri McDonnell. Publisher - Books: Politics/Current Affairs; Biography/Autobiography; local history; biography; women's history. Unsolicited manuscripts accepted? No. But send proposals by e-mail to terri.mcdonnell@ireland.com

Words on the Street
6 San Antonio Park, Salthill, Galway. E-mail: publisher@wordsonthestreet.com. Website: www.wordsonthestreet.com.

Wordwell Publishing
Media House, South County Business Park, Leopardstown, Dublin 18. Tel: 01 2947860 / 087 6487164. Fax: 01 2947861. E-mail: helen@wordwellbooks.com. Website: www.wordwellbooks.com. Publishes books on architecture, history and crafts, and antiquarian maps, as well as specialist archaeology books. Also publishes *History Ireland* and *Archaeology Ireland* magazines.
Imprints: **Rathdown Press** - publishes titles on health and health care, disability and related subjects

Yearbooks and Journals
E-mail: info@yearbooksandjournals.com. Website:

www.yearbooksandjournals.com. School and educational printing specialists. Produces school handbooks, homework diaries and student yearbooks.

Yes! Publications
10-12 Bishop Street, Derry / Londonderry BT48 6PW. Tel: 028 71261941 / 028 71269332. E-mail: yes@yespublications.org. Website: www.yespublications.org

Zahra Publishing
19 Railway Road, Dalkey, Co. Dublin. Tel: 01 2351394. E-mail: info@zahrapublishing.com. Website: www.zahrapublishing.com

Looking to get published?
Visit **www.WritingandPublishing.info**
A free information service for writers, authors, poets and anyone who wants to be published

F. Literary Agents

Bill Jeffrey Literary Agent
The Wordsmith's Forge, 20 Elm Court, Belfast, BT7 1DU. Tel: 028 90284163. E-mail: bill.jeffrey@hotmail.co.uk. Literary Agents: Poems and Stories...even your Songs!

Binnacle Press
Kinsale, Co. Cork. E-mail: info@binnaclepress.com. Website: www.binnaclepress.com. Contact: Deborah Lysaght. Fiction and poetry. Unsolicited manuscripts accepted? Send covering letter, synopsis (no more than 300 words), and short biography.

The Book Bureau Literary Agency
7 Duncairn Avenue, Bray, Co. Wicklow. Tel: 01 2764996. E-mail: thebookbureau@oceanfree.net. Contact: Geraldine Nichol, Managing Director. Literary Agent: Preferences are commercial women's fiction, crime/thrillers and literary fiction; also humour; satire; lifestyles; cookery; romantic; chick lit; lads' lit; autobiographies; some young adult; some non-fiction.
Unsolicited manuscripts accepted? Send preliminary letter and three sample chapters (single line spacing and 11 font). Please send along with a synopsis and short bio. We don't accept sci-fi, horror, fantasy, poetry, young children's fiction, plays or TV scripts. Return postage (International Reply Coupons only from UK and abroad), or e-mail address essential. No reading fee. Commissions: home 10%, translation 20% and USA 15%.

Causeway Literary Agency, Binnacle Press
E-mail: info@binnaclepress.com. Contact Deborah Lysaght. New agency with a particular interest in writing by Irish and Scottish authors in the commercial or literary genre. It is looking for new and established authors of fiction, including children's, and non-fiction.
Unsolicited manuscripts accepted? Send inquiry by e-mail in the first instance, containing brief synopsis, and a short author bio.

Fahy Publishing Ltd
129 Delwood Close, Castleknock, Dublin 15. Tel: 01 8205230 / 086 2269330. E-mail: info@fahypublishing.com. Website: www.fahypublishing.com. Contact: Frank Fahy Managing Director. Literary Agent, special interest in Children's books, 9-12 years and young adult. Unsolicited manuscripts accepted? No. Initial contact by e-mail or letter required before submitting manuscript. No picture books or poetry books considered.

The Feldstein Agency

123-125 Main Street, Bangor, N. Ireland BT20 4AE. Tel: 028 91472823. E-mail: paul@thefeldsteinagency.co.uk. Website: www.thefeldsteinagency.co.uk. Contact: Paul Feldstein, Director. Literary Agent, Literary Magazine/Journal, Publishing Consultant, Free-lance editorial, ghost-writing and project management. Crime Politics/Current Affairs, History, Biography/Autobiography, Humour, Satire, Lifestyles, Cookery, Sport, Photography, Thriller, Literary Fiction; General Adult Fiction.
Unsolicited manuscripts? Send synopsis only to paul@thefeldsteinagency.co.uk.

Font International Literary Agency

Hollyville House, Hollybrook Road, Clontarf, Dublin 3. Tel: 01 8532356. E-mail: info@fontlitagency.com. Website: www.fontlitagency.com. Contact: Ita O'Driscoll. Offers representation to writers of fiction and nonfiction internationally. Founded 2003. Handles book-length adult fiction and non-fiction from previously published writers (no children's, drama, sci-fi, erotic, technical or poetry).
Unsolicited manuscripts accepted? No. As an initial contact, please query our interest in your property either by e-mail or post only. Include details of writing and other media experience. SAE required. We regret that we cannot discuss queries over the phone. Commission Home 15-20%; Translation 20-25%. No reading fee. Associate: The Marsh Agency Ltd, London for translation rights.

Jonathan Williams Literary Agency

Rosney Mews, Upper Glenageary Road, Glenageary, Co. Dublin. Tel: 01 2803482. Contact: Jonathan Williams. Founded 1980. Handles general trade books: fiction, auto/biography, travel, politics, history, music, literature and criticism, gardening, cookery, sport and leisure, humour, reference, social questions, photography. Some poetry. No plays, science fiction, children's books, mind, body and spirit, computer books, theology, multimedia, motoring, aviation.
Unsolicited manuscripts accepted? Initial approach by phone or letter. UK submissions should be accompanied by Irish postage stamps or International Reply Coupons. Commission: Home 10%; US and Translation 20%. No reading fee 'unless the author wants a very fast opinion'. Overseas associates Piergiorgio Nicolazzini Literary Agency, Italy; Linda Kohn, International Literature Bureau, Holland and Germany; Antonia Kerrigan Literary Agency, Spain; Tuttle-Mori Agency Inc., Japan.

Lisa Richards Agency

108 Upper Leeson Street, Dublin 4. Tel: 01 6375000. E-mail: info@lisarichards.ie. Website: www.lisarichards.ie. Children and adult fiction and non-fiction.

Marianne Gunn O'Connor Literary Agency

Morrison Chambers, Suite 17, 32 Nassau Street, Dublin 2. Tel: 01 677 9100. E-mail: mgoclitagency@eircom.net. Contact: Marianne Gunn O'Connor. Founded 1996. Handles commercial and literary fiction, non-fiction: biography, health and children's fiction. Clients include Patrick McCabe, Cecelia Ahern, Claudia Carroll, Morag Prunty, Gisele Scanlon (Goddess Guide), Chris Binchy, Anita Notaro, Noelle Harrison, Julie Dam, Mike McCormack, Paddy McMahon, Thrity Engineer, John Lynch, Helen Falconer, Brinda Charry, Peter Murphy, Louise Douglas, Carla Gylnn, Caroline McFarlane-Watts. Interested in commercial and literary fiction, non-fiction and biography.

Unsolicited manuscripts accepted? No. Send preliminary enquiry letter plus half-page synopsis per e-mail. Commission: UK 15%; Overseas 20%; Film and TV 20%. Translation rights handled by Vicki Satlow Literary Agency, Milan.

Prizeman & Kinsella Literary Agents

Tel: 086 9883335. E-mail: info@prizemankinsella.com. Website: www.prizemankinsella.com.

Ruth Cunney Agency

5 Manor Place, Stoneybatter, Dublin 7. Tel: 01 6351963. E-mail: rcunney@indigo.ie. Agent for illustrated non-fiction and literary fiction; also interested in original work of illustrators and photographers.

Walsh Communications

75 Holywell Drive, Holywell, Swords, Co. Dublin. Tel: 086 6069313. E-mail: info@walshcommunications.ie. Website: www.walshcommunications.ie. Contact: Emma Walsh, Publishing Consultant and Literary Agent. Founded in 2006 by Emma Walsh who has over ten years experience in the Publishing industry. Walsh Communications provides creative and effective services to publishers and writers in the magazine and book industry in Ireland and the UK. The business also operates a small but highly successful literary agency. Walsh Communications Publishing Consultancy provides innovative and fresh ideas and advice to all kinds of clients in the industry from large commercial publishing companies to smaller, literary houses and from magazine and newspaper publishers to individual authors and budding writers. Services include: Book Publicity Campaigns, Author

Care and Book Tours, Publishing Industry Advice and Consultation, Creative Copywriting and Manuscript Editing and Appraisal. Walsh Communications manages a small number of exciting new writers, helping them build their writing careers and managing their literary affairs. Areas: Adult Fiction (commercial and literary), Non-Fiction and Children's Literature.

Unsolicited manuscripts accepted? Send a brief inquiry by e-mail in the first instance before sending any work. We do not accept Science Fiction, Poetry or Short Stories. No reading fee 'for clients taken on in a representative capacity'. Commission: Home 15%; US 20%.

The Writers Agent
Cardiffstown, Kilmessan, Co. Meath. Tel: 01 8569566 / 086 8826483. Website: www.thewritersagent.com. E-mail: submissions@thewritersagent.com. Contact: David Jones. Literary agent, editorial services, writing workshops and training. Interested in new and previously unpublished writers, all genres. Send initial letter, synopsis and 3 chapters by e-mail. All submissions acknowledged. Commission: Home 10%, UK, US and Overseas 20%. No reading fees.

G. Newspapers

Daily Newspapers

Belfast Telegraph
124-144 Royal Avenue, Belfast BT1
1EB
Tel: 028 90264420
E-mail: News desk -
newseditor@belfasttelegraph.co.uk.
Letters to the Editor -
writeback@belfasttelegraph.co.uk
Website:
www.belfasttelegraph.co.uk

Evening Echo
Cork Office - The City Quarter,
Lapps Quay, Cork; Dublin Office - 80
Harcourt Street, Dublin 2
Editor: Maurice Gubbins
Tel: 021 4802293
Fax: 021 4802135
E-mail: maurice.gubbins@eecho.ie
Website: www.eecho.ie

The Evening Herald
Independent House, 27 - 32 Talbot
Street, Dublin 1.
Tel: 01 705 5333. You can
freephone Letters to the Editor on
1800 733 733
E-mail: News -
hnews@independent.ie; Features -
hfeat@independent.ie;
Letters - letters@herald.ie

Financial Times
126 Lower Bagott Street, Dublin 2
Tel: 01 659 9654
Fax: 01 639 4624

Herald AM
Tel: 01 7055160

E-mail: heraldam@independent.ie
Website:
www.heraldam.blogspot.com

Irish Daily Mail
3rd Floor, Embassy House,
Ballsbridge, Dublin 4
Editor-in-Chief: Paul Field
Tel: 01 637 5800
Fax: 01 637 5833
E-mail: info@dailymail.ie
Website: www.dailymail.ie

Irish Daily Mirror
4th Floor, Park House, 191-197
North Circular Road, Dublin 7
Tel: 01 868 8615
Fax: 01 868 8612

Irish Daily Star
Independent Star Ltd, Star House,
62a Terenure Road North, Dublin
6W
Tel: 01 4901228
Fax: 01 4907425
Website: www.thestar.ie

Irish Examiner
City Quarter, Lapps Quay, Cork
Tel: 021 4272722
E-mail: editor@examiner.ie
Website: www.irishexaminer.com

The Irish Independent
Independent House, 27 - 32 Talbot
Street, Dublin 1
Tel: 01 705 5333; You may
freephone Letters to the Editor on
1800 733 733.
E-mail: Enquiries -
info@independent.ie;

Letters to the editor -
independent.letters@independent.ie
Website: www.independent.ie

The Irish News
113-117 Donegall Street, Belfast
BT1 2GE
Editor: Noel Doran
Tel: 028 9032 2226
Fax: 028 9033 7505
Website: www.irishnews.com

Irish Racing Post
Website: www.racingpost.com

Irish Sun
News International (Ireland) Ltd,
4th Floor, Bishop's Square,
Redmonds Hill, Dublin 2
Tel: 01 479 2400
Fax: 01 479 2554

The Irish Times
The Irish Times Building, PO BOX
74, 24-28 Tara Street, Dublin 2
Editor: Geraldine Kennedy
Tel: Newsdesk 01 675 8000; Letters
to the Editor 01 675 8000.
E-mail: News -
newsdesk@irishtimes.com; Letters
to the Editor -
lettersed@irishtimes.com
Website: www.irishtimes.com

Metro Herald
3rd Floor, Embassy House, Herbert
Park Lane, Ballsbridge, Dublin 4
Editor: Chris Cowley
Tel: 01 637 5900
Fax: 01 637 5853
E-mail: info@metroherald.ie; For
press releases and news enquiries
e-mail news@metroherald.ie.
Website: www.metroherald.ie

Northern Ireland Daily Mirror
Mirror Group, 415 Hollywood Road,
Belfast, BT4 2GU
Tel: 028 9056 8078
Fax: 028 9056 8053
E-mail:
cherith.andrews@mirror.co.uk
Website: www.mirror.co.uk

The People
4th Floor, Park House, North
Circular Road, Dublin 7
Tel: 01 8688610
Fax: 01 8688612

The People (Northern Ireland)
415 Hollywood Road, Belfast, BT4
2GU
Tel: 028 9056 8078
Fax: 028 9056 8053

The Times
News International (Irl) Ltd, 4th
Floor, Bishop's Square, Redmonds
Hill, Dublin 2
Tel: 01 4792550
Fax: 01 4792554

Sunday Newspapers

Irish Daily Star Sunday
Independent Star Ltd, Star House,
62a Terenure Road North, Dublin
6W
Tel: 01 4901228
Fax: 01 4907425
Website: www.thestar.ie

Irish News of the World
News International (Ireland) Ltd,
4th Floor, Bishop's Square,
Redmonds Hill, Dublin 2
Tel: 01 479 2400
Fax: 01 479 2554

Irish Mail on Sunday
3rd Floor Embassy House,
Ballsbridge, Dublin 4
Editor: Sebastian Hamilton
Tel: 01 637 5800
Fax: 01 637 5833
E-mail: info@mailonsunday.ie
Website: www.mailonsunday.ie

The Sunday Business Post
80 Harcourt Street, Dublin 2
Tel: 01 602 6000
Fax: 01 679 6496
E-mail: sbpost@iol.ie
Website: www.sbpost.ie

The Sunday Independent
Independent House, 27 - 32 Talbot
Street, Dublin 1
Tel: 01 705 5333. You may phone
Letters to the Editor on freephone
1800 733 733
E-mail: Letters to the editor -
sunday.letters@independent.ie
Website: www.independent.ie

Sunday Life
4th Floor, Bishop's Square,
Redmonds Hill, Dublin 2
Tel: 01 479 2550
Fax: 01 479 2554

Sunday Mirror
Mirror Group, 415 Hollywood Road,
Belfast, BT4 2GU
Tel: 028 9056 8078
Fax: 028 9056 8053
E-mail:
cherith.andrews@mirror.co.uk
Website: www.mirror.co.uk

The Sunday Times
News International (Ireland) Ltd,
4th Floor, Bishop's Square,
Redmonds Hill, Dublin 2
Tel: 01 479 2555
Fax: 01 479 2554

The Sunday Tribune
27-32 Talbot Street, Dublin 1
Editor: Noirin Hegarty
Tel: 01 6314300
E-mail: nhegarty@tribune.ie
Website: www.tribune.ie

The Sunday World
The Sunday World
Tel: 01 8848900; Newsdesk - 01
884 8973
E-mail: news@sundayworld.com
Website: www.sundayworld.com

Sunday World Northern Ireland
3-5 Commercial Court, Belfast, BT1
2NB
Tel: 028 9040 8731
Fax: 028 9023 6155

Other Weekly and Community Newspapers

Alive
Catholic monthly newspaper.
Alive Group, St Mary's Priory,
Tallaght, Dublin 24
Editor: Fr Brian McKevitt OP
Tel: 01 4048187
Fax: 01 4596784
E-mail: alivepaper@gmail.com

An Phoblacht
58 Parnell Square, Dublin 1
Editor: Seán Brady
Tel: 01 8733611
Fax: 01 8721859
E-mail: editor@anphoblacht.com
Website: www.anphoblacht.com

Banter
St Patrick's College Students Union
Magazine
Published by: Foresight
Communications, 11 Sallymount
Avenue, Ranelagh, Dublin 6
Tel: 01 496 7270
Fax: 01 496 5224

Church of Ireland Gazette
3 Wallace Avenue, Lisburn, BT27
4AA, Northern Ireland
Tel: 028 9267 5743
Fax: 028 9266 7580
E-mail:
gazette@ireland.anglican.org
Website:
www.gazette.ireland.anglican.org

College Times
11 Clare Street, Dublin 2
Tel: 01 662 2266
Fax: 01 662 4981

DIT Independent
Foresight Communications, 11
Sallymount Avenue, Ranelagh,
Dublin 6
Tel: 01 496 7270
Fax: 01 496 5224

expliCIT
Cork Institute of Technology
CIT Students Union, Cork Institute
of Technology, Bishopstown, Cork
Tel: 021 493 3124
Fax: 021 454 5343

The Farming Echo
Filbeck Ltd, The Echo Newspaper
Group, Mill Park Road, Enniscorthy,
Co. Wexford
Tel: 054 332 31
Fax: 054 344 92

Farm Week
113 Donegal Street, Belfast, BT1
2GE
Tel: 028 90324 480
Fax: 028 90337 539

Foinse
An Cheathrú, Co. na Gailimhe
Teil: 091 595 520
Facs: 091 595 524
Suíomh Gréasáin: www.foinse.ie

Gaelscéal
Baile Ard, An Spidéal, Co. na
Gaillimhe, Éire.
Teil: 00353-91-897766/536201
Facs: 00353-91-567970
Ríomhphost: Nuacht -
nuacht@gaelsceal.ie; Litir chuig an
Eagarthóir - litir@gaelsceal.ie
Suíomh Gréasáin: www.gaelsceal.ie

Gay Community News
Unit 2, Scarlet Row, Essex Street
West, Dublin 8
Tel: 01 671 9076/0939
Fax: 01 671 3549
E-mail: editor@gcn.ie
Website: www.gcn.ie

Gazetta
Russian Community
55 Lower O'Connell Street, Dublin 1
Tel: 01 874 0004
Fax: 01 874 0404

The Irish Catholic
Irish Farm Centre, Bluebell, Dublin 12
Tel: 01 4276400
Fax: 01 4276450
E-mail: info@irishcatholic.ie
Website: www.irishcatholic.ie

The Irish Echo
11 Hanover Square, New York, NY
10005, USA
Editor: Ray O'Hanlon
Tel: +212 4824818
Fax: +212 4826569 or +212
4827394
E-mail: rohanlon@irishecho.com
Website: www.irishecho.com

The Irish Emigrant
Irish Emigrant Publications, Unit 4,
Business Innovation Centre, NUI
Galway, Upper Newscastle, Galway
Tel: 091-569158
Website: www.emigrant.ie

Irish Farmers Journal
Irish Farm Centre, Bluebell, Dublin 12
Editor: Matt Dempsey
Tel: 01 4199500
Fax: 01 4520876

E-mail:
mdempsey@farmersjournal.ie
Website: www.farmersjournal.ie

The Irish Field
Irish Farm Centre, Bluebell, Dublin 12
Tel: 01 4554008
E-mail: editorial@theirishfield.ie;
Irish Horse World -
horseworld@theirishfield.ie
Website: www.irish-field.ie

The Irish Post
1st Floor, 26-28 Hammersmith
Grove, London W6 7HA, England
Editor: Jon Myles
Tel: +44 20 87410649
Fax: +44 20 87413382
E-mail: jonmyles@irishpost.co.uk
Website: www.irishpost.co.uk

The Irish World
Irish World House, 934 North
Circular Road, London, NW2 7JR,
England
Tel: +44 0208 453 7800
Fax: +44 0208 208 1103
E-mail: editor@theirishworld.com
Website: www.theirishworld.com

Lifetimes
26A Phibsboro Place, Phibsboro,
Dublin 7
Tel: 01 830 6667
Fax: 01 830 6833

Lietuvis
Lithuanian Community
55 Lower O'Connell Street, Dublin 1
Tel: 01 874 0004
Fax: 01 874 0404

Medicine Weekly
Eireann Healthcare Publications, 25
Windsor Place, Dublin 2
Tel: 01 475 3300
Fax: 01 475 3311

Metro Éireann
Ireland's only multicultural weekly
34 North Frederick Street (3rd
Floor), Dublin 1
Editor: Chinedu Onyejelem
Tel: 01 8783223/01 8783441
Fax: 01 8783917
E-mail: news@metroeireann.com
Website: www.metroeireann.com

Nasz Glos
Free Polish Weekly Newspaper
64 Lower Gardiner Street, Dublin 1
Tel: 085 138 0541
Fax: 01 256 0530

The Polish Express - Polski Express
56 Lower Gardiner Street, Dublin 1
Tel: 086 888 2142
Fax: 01 675 3836

Portfolio
A monthly update on living and
working in Docklands
Unit 8 , Docklands Innovation Park,
East Wall Road, Dublin 3
Tel: 01 672 5831
E-mail: info@portfolio.ie
Website: www.portfolio.ie

Provincial Farmer
Meath Chronicle, Market Square,
Navan, Co. Meath
Tel: 046 9079600 / 9079665
Fax: 046 9023565

Sporting Press
Ireland's Greyhound Paper
Davis Road, Clonmel, Co. Tipperary
Tel: 052 22611
Fax: 052 250 18
Website: www.sportingpress.ie

Tiao Wang Magazine
Chinese Community
Salamander Lodge, 80 Sandford
Road, Ranelagh, Dublin 6
Tel: 01 497 9338

Trinity News
6 Trinity College, Dublin 2
Tel: 01 869 2335
Fax: 01 896 2556

UCC Students' Union
SuCommunications, Aontas Na Mac
Lein, Students' Union, Student
Centre, Cork
Tel: 021 4903133
Fax: 021 4903219

Ulster Farmer
Observer Newspapers (NI) Ltd, Ann
Street, Dungannon, Co. Tyrone,
BT70 1ET
Tel: 028 87 722 557
Fax: 028 87 727 334

University Record
TCD Student Publication
Students Union, House 6, Trinity
College, Dublin 2
Tel: 01 6488436
Fax: 01 6777957

Voice of the Traveller
NATC, Unit 1, Monksland Business
Park, Athlone, Co. Roscommon
Editor: Olga Curley

Tel: 090 6498016
E-mail: olga.curley@natc.ie
Website: www.natc.ie

Zycie w Irlandii (Life in Ireland)
The Polish Express Ltd, 1-2
Hawkins Street, Dublin 2
Tel: 01 675 3836

Local and Regional Newspapers

CONNAUGHT

The Connacht Sentinel
15 Market Street, Galway
Group Editor: Dave O'Connell
Tel: 091 536222
Fax: 091 567970
E-mail: dave.oconnell@ctribune.ie
Website: www.galwaynews.ie

The Connacht Tribune
15 Market Street, Galway
Group Editor: Dave O'Connell
Tel: 091 536222
Fax: 091 567970
E-mail: dave.oconnell@ctribune.ie
Website: www.galwaynews.ie

The Connaught Telegraph
Cavendish Lane, Castlebar, Co. Mayo
Tel: 094 9021711 / 9021108 / 9021043
Fax: 094 9024007
E-mail: info@con-telegraph.ie
Website: www.con-telegraph.ie

Western People
Tone Street, Ballina, Co. Mayo
Editor: James Laffey
Tel: 096 60900
Fax: 096 73458
E-mail:
james.laffey@westernpeople.ie
Website: www.westernpeople.ie

LEINSTER

Leinster Express
Dublin Road, Portlaoise, Co. Acting
Editor: Pat Somers
Tel: 057 8621666
Fax: 057 8620491
E-mail: pat@leinsterexpress.ie
Website: www.leinsterexpress.ie

Leinster Express Weekender
Dublin Road, Portlaoise, Co. Laois
Tel: 057 8621666
Fax: 057 8620491
Website: www.leinsterexpress.ie

Leinster Leader
19 South Main Street, Naas, Co.
Kildare
Editor: David O'Riordan
Tel: 045 897302
Fax: 045 871108
E-mail:
david.oriordan@leinsterleader.ie
Website: www.leinsterleader.ie

Leinster Leader Weekender
19 South Main Street, Naas, Co.
Kildare
Tel: 045 897302
Fax: 045 871108
Website: www.leinsterleader.ie

MUNSTER

Munster Express
37 The Quay, Waterford
Tel: 051 872141
E-mail: news@munster-express.ie
Website: www.munster-express.ie

The Nationalist and Munster Advertiser
Queen Street, Clonmel, Co.
Tipperary
Tel: 052 6172500
Website: www.nationalist.ie

COUNTY CARLOW

Carlow First
Head Office, 41-42 Eyre Square,
Galway
Tel: 091 530 900
Fax: 091 567 150

Carlow People
Channing House, Upper Row Street,
Co. Wexford
E-mail: peoplenews@peoplenews.ie
Website: www.carlowpeople.ie

Carlow Times
37 Dublin Street, Carlow
Tel: 059 913 7111
Fax: 059 917 6886

The Nationalist
42 Tullow Street, Carlow
Tel: 059 917 0100
Fax: 059 913 0301

COUNTY CAVAN

The Anglo Celt
Anglo Celt, Station House, Cavan,
Co. Cavan
Editor: Linda O'Reilly
Tel: 049 437 9712
E-mail: linda@anglocelt.ie
Website: www.anglocelt.ie

Cavan Post
4 Abbey Street, Cavan
Tel: 049 432 0088
Fax: 049 432 7845
Website: www.cavanpost.ie

COUNTY CLARE

The Clare Champion
Barrack Street, Ennis, Co. Clare
Editor: Austin Hobbs
Tel: 065 682 8105
Fax: 065 682 0374
E-mail: editor@clarechampion.ie
Website: www.clarechampion.ie

Clare Courier
Ballycasey Design Centre, Shannon,
Co. Clare
Tel: 061 361 643
Fax: 061 361 178

The Clare People
Mill Road, Ennis, Co. Clare
Tel: 065 689 5500
Fax: 065 689 5501

COUNTY CORK

The Avondhu
Mitchelstown Office - 18 Lower
Cork Street, Mitchelstown, Co. Cork.
Fermoy Office - 24 MacCurtain
Street, Fermoy Co. Cork.
Tel: 025 24451 / 24858
Fax: 025 84463
E-mail: info@avondhupress.ie
Website: www.avondhupress.ie

Bandon Opinion
76 South Main Street, Bandon, Co.

Cork
Tel: 023 422 88
Fax: 023 422 77

Ballincollig Today
Unit 27 Ballincollig Commercial Park,
Link Road, Ballincollig, Co. Cork
Tel: 021 487 8185
Fax: 021 487 8186

The Carrigdhoun
Wylie House, Main Street,
Carrigaline, Co. Cork
Tel: 021 437 3557
Fax: 021 437 3559

Cork and County Advertiser
Lamb Street, Clonakilty, Co. Cork
Tel: 023 349 98

Cork Independent
North Point House, North Point
Business Park, Blackpool, Cork
Tel: 021 4288566
Fax: 021 4288567
Website:
www.corkindependent.com

The Corkman
The Spa, Mallow, Co. Cork
E-mail: newsdesk@corkman.ie
Website: www.corkman.ie

Cork Weekly
Unit A3/A4, Donnybrook
Commercial Centre, Donnybrook,
Douglas, Co. Cork
Tel: 021 489 6496
Fax: 021 489 6210

Imokilly People
Castlemartyr Enterprise Centre,
Mogeely Road, Castlemartyr, Co. Cork

Tel: 021 466 7657
Fax: 021 466 7582

The Southern Star
Ilen Street, Skibbereen, Co. Cork
Tel: 028 21200
E-mail: info@southernstar.ie
Website: www.southernstar.ie

Vale Mallow Star/Weekly Observer
19 Bridge Street, Mallow, Co. Cork
Tel: 022 229 10
Fax: 022 229 59

West Cork People
7 Wolfe Tone Street, Clonakilty, Co. Cork
Tel: 023 356 98

Youghal News
Seafield, Youghal, Co. Cork
Tel: 024 93358
Fax: 024 91784

COUNTY DONEGAL

Derry People and Donegal News
St Anne's Court, High Road,
Letterkenny, Co. Donegal
Tel: 074 9121014
Fax: 074 9122881
Website: www.nwipp-newspapers.com/DN/dnhomepage.php

The Donegal Democrat
Larkin House, Oldtown Road,
Letterkenny, Co. Donegal
Editor: Michael Daly
Tel: 074 9128000
E-mail:

editorial@donegaldemocrat.com
Website: www.donegaldemocrat.ie

Donegal on Sunday (Sunday Journal)
Larkin House, Oldtown Road,
Letterkenny, Co. Donegal
Editor: Connie Duffy
Tel: 074 91 88204
Fax: 074 91 28001
E-mail:
connie.duffy@donegalonsunday.com
Website:
www.donegalonsunday.com

Donegal Peoples Press
Derry Journal Group, Larkin House,
Oldtown Road, Letterkenny, Co.
Donegal
Tel: 074 912 8000
Fax: 074 912 8001

Donegal Post
Cruagorm House, Main Street,
Donegal Town
Editor: Michael McHugh
Tel: 074 9724103
Fax: 074 9725312
E-mail: editorial@donegalpost.com
Website: www.donegalpost.com

Finn Valley Post
River House, Dry Arch Business
Park, Letterkenny, Co. Donegal
Tel: 074 911 2700
E-mail: chris@finnvalleypost.com
or marie.duffy@finnvalleypost.com
Website: www.finnvalleypost.com

Inish Times
St Mary's Road, Buncrana,
Inishowen, Co. Donegal
Tel: 074 934 1055

Fax: 074 934 1059
Website: www.inishtimes.com

Letterkenny Post
Head Office, River House, Dry Arch
Business Park, Letterkenny, Co.
Donegal
Tel: 074 919 4800
Fax: 074 911 2791
Website: www.letterkennypost.com

COUNTY DUBLIN

Blanch Gazette
Gazette Group Newspapers, Block
3a, Mill Bank Business Park, Lower
Road, Lucan, Co. Dublin
Group Editor: Kevin MacDermot
Tel: 01 6010240
Fax: 01 6010251
E-mail:
kmacdermot@gazettegroup.com
Website: www.gazettegroup.com

Blanch Informer
Unit 38, Northwood Court, Santry,
Dublin 16
Group Editor: Niall Gormley
Tel: 01 813 8786
E-mail: info@informer.ie
Website: www.informer.ie

Castleknock Gazette
Gazette Group Newspapers, Block
3a, Mill Bank Business Park, Lower
Road, Lucan, Co. Dublin
Group Editor: Kevin MacDermot
Tel: 01 6010240
Fax: 01 6010251
E-mail:
kmacdermot@gazettegroup.com
Website: www.gazettegroup.com

City-Ads Weekly
Unit 32b, Rosemount Business Park,
Ballycoolin, Dublin 11
Tel: 01 8293883
Fax: 01 6267555
Website: www.cityads.ie

City Wide News
City Wide Publications, 26a
Phibsboro Place, Phibsboro, Dublin 7
Tel: 01 830 6667
Fax: 01 830 6833

Clondalkin Gazette
Gazette Group Newspapers, Block
3a, Mill Bank Business Park, Lower
Road, Lucan, Co. Dublin
Group Editor: Kevin MacDermot
Tel: 01 6010240
Fax: 01 6010251
E-mail:
kmacdermot@gazettegroup.com
Website: www.gazettegroup.com

Community Voice
Perceptions Media and
Communications, Avon Lodge,
Church Avenue, Blanchardstown,
Dublin 15
Tel: 01 822 1432

Dublin Informer
Unit 38, Northwood Court, Santry,
Dublin 9
Group Editor: Niall Gormley
Tel: 01 813 8786
E-mail: info@informer.ie
Website: www.informer.ie

Dublin People
80 - 83 Omni Park Shopping Centre,
Santry, Dublin 9
Tel: 01 862 1611

E-mail: news@dublinpeople.com
Website: www.dublinpeople.com

The Dun Laoghaire Gazette
Gazette Group Newspapers, Block 3a, Mill Bank Business Park, Lower Road, Lucan, Co. Dublin
Group Editor: Kevin MacDermot
Tel: 01 6010240
Fax: 01 6010251
E-mail: kmacdermot@gazettegroup.com
Website: www.gazettegroup.com

Dun Loaghaire Informer
Unit 38, Northwood Court, Santry, Dublin 10
Group Editor: Niall Gormley
Tel: 01 813 8786
E-mail: info@informer.ie
Website: www.informer.ie

Dublin Mail
48 Glenview Park, Tallaght, Dublin 24
Tel: 01 459 9643 / 01 455 2832
Fax: 01 455 2832

The Dundrum Gazette
Gazette Group Newspapers, Block 3a, Mill Bank Business Park, Lower Road, Lucan, Co. Dublin
Group Editor: Kevin MacDermot
Tel: 01 6010240
Fax: 01 6010251
E-mail: kmacdermot@gazettegroup.com
Website: www.gazettegroup.com

Dundrum Informer
Unit 38, Northwood Court, Santry, Dublin 11
Group Editor: Niall Gormley
Tel: 01 813 8786

E-mail: info@informer.ie
Website: www.informer.ie

The Event Guide
InterArt Media Ltd, Regus House, Harcourt Road, Dublin 2
Tel: 01 477 3933

The Local News
Bank House, 331 South Circular Road, Dublin 8
Tel: 01 4534011
Fax: 01 4549024
E-mail: frank@localnews.ie

The Lucan Gazette
Gazette Group Newspapers, Block 3a, Mill Bank Business Park, Lower Road, Lucan, Co. Dublin
Group Editor: Kevin MacDermot
Tel: 01 6010240
Fax: 01 6010251
E-mail: kmacdermot@gazettegroup.com
Website: www.gazettegroup.com

Lucan Informer
Unit 38, Northwood Court, Santry, Dublin 12
Group Editor: Niall Gormley
Tel: 01 813 8786
E-mail: info@informer.ie
Website: www.informer.ie

The Malahide Gazette
Gazette Group Newspapers, Block 3a, Mill Bank Business Park, Lower Road, Lucan, Co. Dublin
Group Editor: Kevin MacDermot
Tel: 01 6010240
Fax: 01 6010251
E-mail: kmacdermot@gazettegroup.com
Website: www.gazettegroup.com

Northside People
West and East editions
80-83 Omni Park Shopping Centre,
Santry, Dublin 9
Tel: 01 862 1611 / 041 983 0154
Fax: 041 983 0151
Website: www.northsidepeople.ie

North County Leader Newspaper
Leader House, North Street,
Swords, Co. Dublin
Tel: 01 840 0200
Fax: 01 8400 550

Raheny Informer
Unit 38, Northwood Court, Santry,
Dublin 14
Group Editor: Niall Gormley
Tel: 01 813 8786
E-mail: info@informer.ie
Website: www.informer.ie

Rathfarnham Informer
Unit 38, Northwood Court, Santry,
Dublin 19
Group Editor: Niall Gormley
Tel: 01 813 8786
E-mail: info@informer.ie
Website: www.informer.ie

Rathmines Informer
Unit 38, Northwood Court, Santry,
Dublin 15
Group Editor: Niall Gormley
Tel: 01 813 8786
E-mail: info@informer.ie
Website: www.informer.ie

Rush and Lusk News
1 Ardgillan View, Skerries, Co.
Dublin
Tel: 01 8490629
Fax: 01 8490629
Website: www.rushandlusknews.ie

Sandyford Informer
Unit 38, Northwood Court, Santry,
Dublin 13
Group Editor: Niall Gormley
Tel: 01 813 8786
E-mail: info@informer.ie
Website: www.informer.ie

Santry Informer
Unit 38, Northwood Court, Santry,
Dublin 17
Group Editor: Niall Gormley
Tel: 01 813 8786
E-mail: info@informer.ie
Website: www.informer.ie

Skerries News
1 Ardgillan View, Skerries, Co.
Dublin
Tel: 01 8490629
Fax: 01 8490629
E-mail: editor@skerriesnews.ie
Website: www.skerriesnews.ie

South City Express
TallaghtOnline Ltd, PO Box 3430,
Tallaght, Dublin 24
Tel: 01 451 9000
Fax: 01 451 9805

Southside People
80-83 Omni Park Shopping Centre,
Santry, Dublin 9
Tel: 01 862 1611 / 041 983 0154
Fax: 041 983 0151
Website: www.southsidepeople.ie

Swords Gazette
Gazette Group Newspapers, Block
3a, Mill Bank Business Park, Lower
Road, Lucan, Co. Dublin
Group Editor: Kevin MacDermot
Tel: 01 6010240

Fax: 01 6010251
E-mail:
kmacdermot@gazettegroup.com
Website: www.gazettegroup.com

Swords Informer

Unit 38, Northwood Court, Santry,
Dublin 18
Group Editor: Niall Gormley
Tel: 01 813 8786
E-mail: info@informer.ie
Website: www.informer.ie

The Fingal Independent

Main Street, Swords, Co. Dublin
E-mail: editorial@fingal-
independent.ie
Website: www.fingal-
independent.ie

COUNTY GALWAY

Galway Advertiser

41/42 Eyre Square, Galway
Group Editor: Declan Varley
Tel: 091 530 936
E-mail:
dvarley@galwayadvertiser.ie
Website: www.advertiser.ie

Galway City Tribune

15 Market Street, Galway
Group Editor: Dave O'Connell
Tel: 091 536222
Fax: 091 567970
E-mail: dave.oconnell@ctribune.ie
Website: www.galwaynews.ie

Galway First

Head Office, 41-42 Eyre Square,
Galway
Tel: 091 530 900
Fax: 091 567 150

Galway Independent

Independent House, Galway Retail
Park, Headford Road, Galway
Tel: 091 569000
Fax: 091 569333
Website:
www.galwayindependent.com

The Tuam Herald

Dublin Road, Tuam, Co. Galway
Tel: 093 24183
Fax: 093 24478
E-mail: editor@tuamherald.ie
Website: www.tuamherald.ie

COUNTY KERRY

Kerry's Eye

Tel: 066 71 49200
Fax: 066 712 3163
E-mail: news@kerryseye.com
Website: www.kerryseye.com

The Kerryman

Denny Street, Tralee, Co. Kerry
Tel: 066 71 45500
Fax: 066 71 45572
E-mail: dmalone@kerryman.ie
Website: www.kerryman.ie

Killarney Advertiser

Woodlawn, Killarney, Co. Kerry
Tel: 064 322 15
Fax: 064 327 22

The Kingdom Newspaper

65 New Street, Killarney, Co. Kerry
Tel: 064 313 92
Fax: 064 346 09

COUNTY KILDARE

Kildare Post
Unit W5D, Toughers Business Park,
Naas, Co. Kildare
Tel: 045 879 879
Fax: 045 879 880
Website: www.kildarepost.com

Kildare Times
Unit 1, Super Valu Shopping Centre,
Fairgreen, Naas, Co. Kildare
Tel: 045 895 111

The Kildare Nationalist
Edward Street, Newbridge, Co.
Kildare
Tel: 045 432 147
Fax: 045 433 720

Liffey Champion
The Cornmill, Mill Lane, Leixlip, Co.
Kildare
Tel: 01 624 5533
Fax: 01 624 3013

COUNTY KILKENNY

Kilkenny Advertiser
63 High Street, Kilkenny
Editor: Naoise Coogan
Tel: 056 777 5404
E-mail: news@kilkennyadvertiser.ie
Website: www.advertiser.ie

Kilkenny People
34 High Street, Kilkenny
Editor: Brian Keyes
Tel: 056 7791046
Fax: 056 7723533
E-mail: editor@kilkennypeople.ie
Website: www.kilkennypeople.ie

Kilkenny People Weekender
34 High Street, Kilkenny
Tel: 056 7791046
Fax: 056 7723533
Website: www.kilkennypeople.ie

COUNTY LAOIS

The Laois Nationalist
Colliseum Lane, Portlaoise, Co.
Laois
Tel: 0502 602 65
Fax: 0502 613 99

COUNTY LEITRIM

Leitrim Observer
3 Hartley Business Park, Carrick-on-
Shannon, Co. Leitrim
Tel: 071 9620025
Website: www.leitrimobserver.ie

Leitrim Observer Weekender
3 Hartley Business Park, Carrick-on-
Shannon, Co. Leitrim
Tel: 071 9620025
Website: www.leitrimobserver.ie

Leitrim Post
Riverside Centre, Carrick-On-
Shannon, Co. Leitrim
Tel: 071 962 3210
Fax: 071 967 2014
Website: www.leitrimpost.com

COUNTY LIMERICK

Limerick Chronicle
54 O'Connell Street, Limerick
Tel: 061 214 500
Fax: 061 401 424

Limerick Independent
2 Lower Shannon Street, Limerick
Tel: 061 404 900 / 1890 258 258
Fax: 061 404 940

Limerick Leader
54 O'Connell Street, Limerick
Tel: 061 214500
Website: www.limerickleader.ie

Limerick Leader Weekender
54 O'Connell Street, Limerick
Tel: 061 214500
Website: www.limerickleader.ie

Limerick Post
97 Henry Street, Limerick City
Tel: 061 413322
Fax: 061 417684
Website: www.limerickpost.ie

COUNTY LONGFORD

Longford Leader
Leader House, Dublin Road,
Longford
Editor: Sheila Reilly
Tel: 043 3345241
E-mail: sheila.reilly@longford-leader.ie
Website: www.longfordleader.ie

Longford Leader Weekender
Leader House, Dublin Road,
Longford
Tel: 043 3345241
Website: www.longfordleader.ie

The Longford News
7 Dublin Street, Longford
Editor: Thomas Lyons
Tel: 0434 6342

Fax: 0434 1549
E-mail: news@longfordnews.ie
Website: www.longfordnews.ie

COUNTY LOUTH

Drogheda Leader
Laurence Street, Drogheda, Co.
Louth
Tel: 041 9836100 or 041 9835700
Fax: 041 9841517
E-mail: news@droghedaleader.ie
Website: www.droghedaleader.net

The Drogheda Independent
9 Shop Street, Drogheda, Co. Louth
E-mail: editorial@drogheda-independent.ie
Website: www.drogheda-independent.ie

Drogheda Independent Extra
The Drogheda Independent, 9 Shop
Street, Drogheda, Co. Louth
Tel: 041 983 8658
Fax: 041 983 4271

Drogheda Weekend
9 Shop Street, Drogheda, Co. Louth
Tel: 041 983 8658
Fax: 041 983 4271

The Dundalk Argus
Partnership Court, Park Street,
Dundalk
Tel: 042 9334632
Fax: 042 9331643
E-mail: editorial@argus.ie
Website: www.argus.ie

The Dundalk Democrat
7 Crowe Street, Dundalk, Co. Louth

Editor: Anthony Murphy
Tel: 042 9334058
Fax: 042 9334058
E-mail: editor@dundalkdemocrat.ie
Website: www.dundalkdemocrat.ie

Dundalk Extra
141 Ard Easmuinn, Dundalk, Co.
Louth
Tel: 042 933 7897
Fax: 042 933 7897

COUNTY MAYO

Mayo Advertiser
Market Square, Castlebar, Co. Mayo
Editor: Toni Bourke
Tel: 094 903 5004
Fax: 094 906 0702
E-mail: news@mayoadvertiser.ie
Website: www.advertiser.ie

Mayo Echo
Chapel Street, Castlebar, Co. Mayo
Tel: 094 9038892
Fax: 094 9250319
E-mail: editor@mayoecho.com
Website: www.mayoecho.com

The Mayo News
The Fairgreen, Westport, Co. Mayo
Tel: 098 25311
Fax: 098 26108
E-mail: info@mayonews.ie
Website: www.mayonews.ie

COUNTY MEATH

The Meath Chronicle
Market Square, Navan, Co. Meath
Editor: Ken Davis
Tel: 046 907 9600
E-mail: ken@meathchronicle.ie
Website: www.meathchronicle.ie

Meath Echo
P.O. Box 8805, Rathoath, Co. Meath
Tel: 01 825 4434

Meath Post
10 Flower Hill, Navan, Co. Meath
Tel: 046 907 2032
Fax: 046 902 8772
Website: www.meathpost.com

Meath Topic
Topic Newspapers Ltd, 6 Dominic
Street, Mullingar, Co. Westmeath
Tel: 044 488 68
Fax: 044 437 77

The Weekender Newspaper
6 Charter Buildings, Kennedy Road,
Navan, Co. Meath
Tel: 046 902 2333
Fax: 046 902 9864

COUNTY MONAGHAN

Monaghan Post
MTEK Building, Old Armagh Road,
Co. Monaghan
Tel: 047 773 00
Fax: 047 773 02
Website: www.monaghanpost.com

Northern Standard
The Diamond, Monaghan
Tel: 047 818 67
Fax: 047 840 70

COUNTY OFFALY

Offaly Express
Bridge Street, Tullamore, Co. Offaly
News Editor: Alan Walsh

Tel: 057 93 21744
Fax: 057 93 51930
E-mail: alan@offalyexpress.ie
Website: www.offalyexpress.ie

The Offaly Independent

The Mall, William Street, Tullamore,
Co. Offaly
Editor: Tadhg Carey
Tel: 057 9321403
E-mail:
editor@offalyindependent.ie
Website: www.offalyindependent.ie

Offaly Topic

Topic Newspapers Ltd, Dominic
Street, Mullingar, Co. Westmeath
Tel: 044 488 68
Fax: 044 437 77

Tullamore Tribune

William Street, Tullamore
Editor: Gerard Scully
Tel: 057 9321152
Fax: 057 9321927
E-mail: editor@tullamoretribune.ie
Website: www.tullamoretribune.ie

COUNTY ROSCOMMON

The Roscommon Champion

Abbey Street, Roscommon
Editor: Richard Canny - Editor-in-
Chief
Tel: 0906 625 051
Fax: 0906 625 053
E-mail:
editor@roscommonchampion.ie
Website:
www.roscommonchampion.ie

The Roscommon Herald

St Patrick's Street, Boyle, Co.
Roscommon
Tel: 071 966 2004
Fax: 071 966 2926

COUNTY SLIGO

Sligo Champion

Connacht House, Markievicz Road,
Sligo
E-mail: editor@sligochampion.ie
Website: www.sligochampion.ie

Sligo Post

North West Business Park,
Collooney, Co. Sligo
Tel: 071 9118456
Fax: 071 9118457
Website: www.sligopost.com

Sligo Weekender

Waterfront House, Bridge Street,
Sligo
Tel: 071 9174900
Fax: 071 9174911
E-mail:
postbag@sligoweekender.com
Website: www.sligoweekender.ie

COUNTY TIPPERARY

Midland Tribune (Birr)

Syngefield, Birr, Co. Offaly
Tel: 0509 200 03
Fax: 0509 205 88

Midland Tribune (Roscrea)

Main Street, Roscrea, Co. Tipperary
Editor: John O'Callaghan
Tel: 0505 23747

Fax: 05052 4647
E-mail: editor@midlandtribune.ie
Website: www.midlandtribune.ie

The Nenagh Guardian
13 Summerhill, Nenagh, Co.
Tipperary
Tel: 067 31214
Fax: 067 33401
E-mail:
editorial@nenaghguardian.ie
Website: www.nenaghguardian.ie

South Tipp Today
Upper Irishtown, Clonmel, Co.
Tipperary
Tel: 052 273 42
Fax: 052 291 42

The Nationalist and Tipperary Star
Friar Street, Thurles, Co. Tipperary
Editor: Michael Dundon, Editor
Tel: 0504 29107
Fax: 0504 21110
E-mail: md@tipperarystar.ie
Website: www.tipperarystar.ie

Tipperary Star Weekender
Friar Street, Thurles, Co. Tipperary
Tel: 0504 29107
Fax: 0504 21110
Website: www.tipperarystar.ie

COUNTY WATERFORD

The Dungarvan Leader
78 O'Connell Street, Dungarvan,
Waterford
Tel: 058 41203
Fax: 058 45301
E-mail:

dungarvanleader@cablesurf.com
Website:
www.dungarvanleader.com

Dungarvan Observer
Shandon, Dungarvan, Co. Waterford
Tel: 058 412 05
Fax: 058 415 59

Waterford News and Star
25 Michael Street, Waterford
Tel: 051 874951
Fax: 051 855281
E-mail: editor@waterford-
news.com
Website: www.waterford-news.com

Waterford Today
36 Mayor's Walk, Waterford City
Editor: Paddy Gallagher
Tel: 051 854135 or Mobile - 086
858 6318
Fax: 051 854140
E-mail: editor@waterford-today.ie
Website: www.waterford-today.ie

COUNTY WESTMEATH

Athlone Advertiser
Editor: Maria Daly
Tel: 090 647 0927
E-mail: news@athloneadvertiser.ie
Website: www.advertiser.ie

Athlone Observer
Jesmond Lodge, Station Road,
Athlone, Co. Westmeath
Tel: 0906 474 975
Fax: 0906 478 668

Athlone Topic
Arcade Publishers Ltd, Arcade

Buildings, Barracks Street Athlone,
Co. Westmeath
Tel: 0906 494 433
Fax: 0906 494 964

The Athlone Voice
14 Sean Costello Street, Irishtown,
Athlone, Co. Westmeath
Editor: Sean O'Domhnaill. Deputy
Editor: Deirdre Flynn
Tel: 090 642 0600
Fax: 090 642 0630
E-mail: editor@athlonevoice.ie
Website: www.athlonevoice.ie

Mullingar Advertiser
Green Bridge, Mullingar, Co.
Westmeath
Tel: 044 939 6253
E-mail: info@athloneadvertiser.ie
Website: www.advertiser.ie

The Westmeath Examiner
Blackhall Place, Mullingar, Co.
Westmeath
Editor: Ellis Ryan
Tel: 044 93 46741
E-mail:
editor@westmeathexaminer.ie
Website:
www.westmeathexaminer.ie

The Westmeath Independent
Sean Costello Street, Athlone, Co.
Westmeath
Editor: Tadhg Carey
Tel: 090 643 4300
E-mail:
tadhg.carey@westmeathindepende
nt.ie
Website:
www.westmeathindependent.ie

Westmeath Topic
6 Dominick Street, Mullingar, Co.
Westmeath
Tel: 093 48868
Fax: 093 43777
E-mail: news@westmeathtopic.com
Website: www.westmeathtopic.com

COUNTY WEXFORD

Gorey Echo News
Group Editor: Tom Mooney
E-mail: editor@theecho.ie

Gorey Guardian
Channing House, Upper Row Street,
Co. Wexford
Website: www.goreyguardian.ie

New Ross Echo
The Echo Newspaper Group, 7
North Street, New Ross, Co.
Wexford
Group Editor: Tom Mooney
Tel: 051 421 568
Fax: 051 421 811
E-mail: editor@theecho.ie

New Ross Standard
Channing House, Upper Row Street,
Co. Wexford
Tel: 053 40100
Fax: 053 40192
E-mail:
peoplenews@peoplenews.ie
Website: www.newrossstandard.ie

The Enniscorthy Echo
Slaney Place, Enniscorthy, Co.
Wexford
Group Editor: Tom Mooney
Tel: 053 92 59900

Fax: 053 92 33506/34492
E-mail: editor@theecho.ie
Website: www.enniscorthyecho.ie

The Enniscorthy Guardian
Channing House, Upper Row Street,
Co. Wexford
E-mail: peoplenews@peoplenews.ie
Website: www.enniscorthyguardian.ie

The Wexford Echo
17 Selskar Street, Wexford
Group Editor: Tom Mooney
Tel: 053 91 42948
Fax: 053 91 42935
E-mail: editor@theecho.ie
Website: www.wexfordecho.ie

Wexford People
Channing House, Upper Row Street,
Co. Wexford
E-mail: front.office@peoplenews.ie
Website: www.wexfordpeople.ie

COUNTY WICKLOW

Bray People
Channing House, Upper Row Street,
Co. Wexford
Tel: 053 401 00
Fax: 053 401 92
E-mail: Website:
www.braypeople.ie

Wicklow News
Kilcoole Enterprises Park, Kilcoole,
Co. Wicklow
Tel: 01 201 8100
Fax: 01 201 8112
Website: www.wicklownews.ie

Wicklow People
Channing House, Upper Row Street,
Co. Wexford
Tel: 053 9140100
Fax: 053 9140192
front.office@peoplenews.ie
Website: www.wicklowpeople.ie

Wicklow Times
North, South and West Editions
5 Eglinton Road, Bray, Co. Wicklow
Tel: 01 286 9111
E-mail: shay@localtimes.ie
Website:

NORTHERN IRELAND

Andersonstown News
Teach Basil, 2 Hannahstown Hill,
Belfast, BT17 0LT
Editor: Robin Livingstone
Tel: 028 9061 9000 (News Desk)
Fax: 028 9062 3885
E-mail:
r.livingstone@belfastmediagroup.com
Website: www.belfastmedia.com

Antrim Guardian
5 Railway Street, Antrim, BT41 4AE
Editor: Liam Heffron
Tel: 028 9446 2624
Fax: 028 9446 5551
E-mail:
editor@antrimguardian.co.uk
Website:
www.antrimguardian.co.uk

Antrim Times
Morton Newspapers, 22
Ballymoney Street, Ballymena, Co.
Antrim, BT41 4AY
Tel: 028 2565 3300
Fax: 028 2564 1517

Armagh Advertiser
56 Scotch Street, Armagh City, BT61
7DQ
Tel: 028 3752 2639
Fax: 028 3752 7029

Armagh Observer
Observer Newspapers (NI) Ltd, Ann
Street, Dungannon, Co. Tyrone,
BT70 1ET
Tel: 028 8772 2557
Fax: 028 8772 7334

Armagh Down Observer
Observer Newspapers (NI) Ltd, Ann
Street, Dungannon, Co. Tyrone,
BT70 1ET
Tel: 028 8772 2557
Fax: 028 8772 7334

Ballycastle Chronicle
78 Castle Street, Ballycastle, BT54
6AR
Editors: Louise Glass and Aine
McGrady
Tel: 028 2076 1282
Fax: 028 2076 1283
E-mail:
ballycastle.news@thechronicle.uk.com
Website:
www.ballycastle.thechronicle.uk.com

Ballyclare Gazette
36 The Square, Ballyclare, BT39
9BB
Editor: Neil Cobain
Tel: 028 9335 2967
Fax: 028 9335 2449
E-mail:
newsdesk@ballyclaregazette.co.uk
Website:
www.ballyclaregazette.co.uk

Ballymena Chronicle
Observer Newspapers (NI) Ltd, Ann
Street, Dungannon, Co. Tyrone,
BT70 1ET
Tel: 028 8772 2557
Fax: 028 8772 7334

Ballymena Guardian
83 Wellington Street, Ballymena,
BT43 6AD
Editor: Jim Flanagan
Tel: 028 2564 1221
Fax: 028 2565 3920
E-mail:
editor@ballymenaguardian.co.uk
Website:
www.ballymenaguardian.co.uk

Ballymena Times
22 Ballymoney Street, Ballymena,
BT43 6AL
Editor: Des Blackadder
Tel: 028 2565 3300
E-mail:
dessie.blackadder@jpress.co.uk
Website: www.ballymenatimes.com

Ballymoney Times
71 Upper New Row, Coleraine,
BT52 1EY
Tel: 028 7035 5260
Fax: 028 7035 6186

Ballymoney and Moyle Times
6 Church Street, Ballymoney, Co.
Antrim, BT536DL
Tel: 028 2766 6216
Website:
www.ballymoneytimes.co.uk

Ballymoney Chronicle
3 High Street, Ballymoney, BT53
6AH

Editors: Alan Millar and Lisa Gregg
Tel: 028 2766 2354
Fax: 028 2766 7682
E-mail:
ballymoney.news@thechronicle.uk.com
Website:
http://ballymoney.thechronicle.uk.com

Banbridge Chronicle
14 Bridge Street, Banbridge, BT32 3JS
Tel: 028 4066 2322
Fax: 028 4062 4397

Banbridge Leader
25 Bridge Street, Banbridge, Co. Down, BT32 3JL
Editor: John Hooks
Tel: 028 4066 2745
Website:
www.banbridgeleader.co.uk

Belfast News
46-56 Boucher Cresent, Belfast, BT12 6QY
Tel: 028 9068 0000
Fax: 028 9066 4420

Belfast News Letter
2 Esky Drive, Carn Industrial Estate, Craigavon BT63 5YY
Editor: Darwin Templeton
Tel: 028 3839 3939
E-mail:
darwin.templeton@jpress.co.uk
Website: www.newsletter.co.uk

Carrickfergus Advertiser
6 Market Place, Carrickfergus, BT38 7AW
Editor: David Hall

Tel: 028 9336 3651
Fax: 028 9336 3092
E-mail:
editor@carrickadvertiser.co.uk
Website:
www.carrickadvertiser.co.uk

Carrickfergus Times
Carrick Times, 19 North Street, Carrickfergus, BT38 7AQ
Tel: 028 9335 1992
Website:
www.carrickfergustimes.co.uk

Coleraine Chronicle
20 Railway Road, Coleraine, BT52 1PD
Editor: John Fillis
Tel: 028 7034 3344
Fax: 028 7032 9889
E-mail: editor@thechronicle.uk.com
Website:
www.coleraine.thechronicle.uk.com

Coleraine Northern Constitution
35 Market Street, Limavady, BT49 0ET
Editor: Jenny Church
Tel: 028 7776 2130
Fax: 028 7776 3986
E-mail:
editor@northernconstitution.co.uk
Website:
coleraine.northernconstitution.co.uk

Coleraine Times
5 Stone Row, Coleraine, Co. Londonderry BT52 1EP
Editor: David Rankin
Tel: 028 7035 7610
E-mail:
david.rankin@colerainetimes.co.uk
Website: www.colerainetimes.co.uk

Community Telegraph
124-144 Royal Avenue, Belfast, BT1
1EB
Tel: 028 9026 4074
Fax: 028 9055 4504

County Derry Post
122 Main Street, Dungiven, Co.
Derry, BT47 4LG
Tel: 028 7774 3970
Fax: 028 7774 0748

County Down Outlook (Kilkeel)
6 The Square, Kilkeel, Co. Down,
BT34 4AA
Editor: Alan McVeigh
Tel: 028 4176 9058
Fax: 028 4176 9995
E-mail: news@outlooknews.co.uk
Website: www.outlooknews.co.uk

**County Down Outlook
(Rathfriland)**
Castle Street, Rathfriland, Co. Down,
BT34 5QR
Tel: 028 4063 0781
Fax: 028 4063 1022

County Down Spectator
91 Main Street, Bangor, Co. Down,
BT20 4AF
Tel: 028 9127 0270
Fax: 028 9127 1544

Craigavon Echo
Morton Newspapers Ltd, 14 Church
Street, Portadown, Craigavon, BT62
3LQ
Tel: 028 9035 0041
Fax: 028 9035 0203

Derry News
26 Balliniska Road, Spingtown

Industrial Estate, Derry BT48 0LY
Tel: 028 7129 6600
Fax: 028 7129 6605

Dromore Leader
30A Market Street, Dromore, Co.
Down, BT25 1AW
Editor: Mark Weir
Tel: 028 9269 2217
Website: www.dromoreleader.co.uk

Down Recorder
W.Y. Crichton and Co., 2-4 Church
Street, Downpatrick, Co. Down,
BT30 6EJ
Tel: 028 4461 3711
Fax: 028 4461 4624

Dungannon Observer
Observer Newspapers NI Ltd, Ann
Street, Dungannon, Co. Tyrone,
BT70 1ET
Tel: 028 8772 2557
Fax: 028 8772 7334

East Antrim Advertiser
Morton Newspaper Group, 8 Duluce
Street, Larne, Co. Antrim, BT40 1JG
Tel: 028 2565 3303
Fax: 028 2826 0255

Fermanagh Herald
30 Belmore Street, Enniskillen, Co.
Fermanagh, BT74 6AA
Tel: 028 6632 2066
Fax: 028 6632 5521
Website: www.nwipp-
newspapers.com/FH

Fermanagh News
Observer Newspapers (NI) Ltd, Ann
Street, Dungannon, Co. Tyrone,
BT70 1ET

Tel: 028 8772 2557
Fax: 028 8772 7334

Larne Gazette
20 Main Street, Larne, BT40 1SS
Editor: John Brownlow
Tel: 028 2827 7450
Fax: 028 2826 0733
E-mail: news@larnegazette.co.uk
Website: www.larnegazette.co.uk

Larne Times
8 Dunluce Street, Larne, BT40 1JG
Tel: 028 2827 2303
Website: www.larnetimes.co.uk

Limavady Chronicle
35 Main Street, Limavady, BT49 0ET
Editor: Jenny Church
Tel: 028 7776 2130
Fax: 028 7776 3986
E-mail:
editor@northernconstitution.co.uk
Website:
www.limavady.thechronicle.uk.com

Limavady Northern Constitution
35 Market Street, Limavady, BT49 0ET
Editor: Jenny Church
Tel: 028 7776 2130
Fax: 028 7776 3986
E-mail:
editor@northernconstitution.co.uk
Website:
limavady.northernconstitution.co.uk

Londonderry Sentinel
Unit 4and5 Spencer House, Spencer Road, Waterside, Londonderry, BT476AA
Tel: 028 7134 8889

Website:
www.londonderrysentinel.co.uk

Lurgan Mail
4 High Street, Lurgan, Craigavon, BT66 8AW
Editor: Clint Aiken
Tel: 028 3832 7777
E-mail:
clint.aiken@lurganmail.co.uk
Website: www.lurganmail.co.uk

Lurgan and Portadown Examiner
Observer Newspapers (NI) Ltd, Ann Street, Dungannon, Co. Tyrone, BT70 1ET
Tel: 028 8772 2557
Fax: 028 8772 7334

Magherafelt Northern Constitution
4-6 Queen Street, Magherfelt, BT45 6AB
Editors: Ian Allen and Neil McGuckin
Tel: 028 7963 2686
Fax: 028 7963 1508
E-mail:
magherafelt.news@northernconstitution.co.uk
Website:
magherafelt.northernconstitution.co.uk

Mid Ulster Mail
52 Oldtown Street, Cookstown, Co. Tyrone BT80 8EF
Tel: 028 8676 2288
Website: www.midulstermail.co.uk

Mid-Ulster Echo
Morton Newspapers, 52 Oldtown Street, Cookstown, Co. Tyrone,

BT45 6AA
Tel: 028 8676 1364
Fax: 028 7976 4295

Mid-Ulster Observer
Observer Newspapers Ltd, Ann Street, Dungannon, Co. Tyrone, BT70 1ET
Tel: 028 8772 2557
Fax: 028 8772 7334

Mourne Observer
The Roundabout, Castlewellan Road, Newcastle, Co. Down BT33 0JX
Tel: 028 4372 2666
Fax: 028 4372 4566
E-mail: info@mourneobserver.com
Website:
www.mourneobserver.com

Newry Democrat (incorporating the Down Democrat)
45 Hill Street, Newry, Co. Down, BT34 1AF
Editor: Jackie McKeown
Tel: 028 3025 1250
Fax: 028 3025 1017
E-mail:
Jackie.McKeown@newrydemocrat.com
Website: www.newrydemocrat.com

Newry Reporter
4 Margaret Street, Newry, Co. Down, BT34 1DF
Tel: 028 3026 7633
Fax: 028 3026 3157
E-mail: editor@newryreporter.com
Website: www.newryreporter.com

Newtownabbey Times
Morton Newspapers, 2 Esky Drive,

Cam Industrial Estate, Craigavon, BT63 5YY
Tel: 028 3839 3939
Fax: 028 3832 9940

North Belfast News
Editor: Maria McCourt
Tel: 028 9058 4444 (News Desk)
E-mail:
m.mccourt@belfastmediagroup.com
Website: www.belfastmedia.com

Northwest Echo
Morton Newspapers Ltd, Spencer House Spencer Road, Waterside, Derry, BT47 6AA
Tel: 028 7134 2226
Fax: 028 7134 1175

Portadown Times
14 Church Street, Portadown, BT62 3LQ
Editor: Alistair Bushe
Tel: 028 3833 6111
Fax: 028 3935 0203
E-mail:
alistair.bushe@portadowntimes.co.uk
Website:
www.portadowntimes.co.uk

South Belfast News
Editor: Maria McCourt
Tel: 028 9060 8807 (News Desk)
E-mail:
m.mccourt@belfastmediagroup.com
Website: www.belfastmedia.com

Strabane Chronicle
15 Main Street, Strabane, Co. Tyrone, BT82 8AS
Tel: 028 7188 2100
Fax: 028 7188 3199

Strabane Weekly News
31 Abercorn Square, Strabane,
BT82 8AQ
Editor: Anna Maguire
Tel: 028 7188 6869
Fax: 028 7188 6867
E-mail:
news@strabaneweekly.co.uk
Website:
www.strabaneweekly.co.uk

The Big List
Flagship Media Group Ltd, 48-50
York Street, Belfast, BT15 1AS
Tel: 028 9031 9008
Fax: 028 9072 7800

The Democrat
Observer Newspapers NI Ltd, Ann
Street, Dungannon, Co. Tyrone,
BT70 1ET
Tel: 028 8772 2557
Fax: 028 8772 7334

The Derry Journal
22 Buncrana Road, Derry BT48 8AA
Editor: Sean McLaughlin
Tel: 028 7127 2254
E-mail:
sean.mclaughlin@derryjournal.com
Website: www.derryjournal.com

The Impartial Reporter
8-10 East Bridge Street, Enniskillen,
BT74 7BT
Tel: 028 6632 4422
E-mail:
editorial@impartialreporter.com
Website:
www.impartialreporter.com

The Lakeland Extra
William Trimble Ltd, 8-10 East

Bridge Street, Enniskillen, Co.
Fermanagh, BT74 7BT
Tel: 028 6632 4422
Fax: 028 6632 5969

The Leader
20 Railway Road, Coleraine, BT52
1PD
Editor: Louise Glass
Tel: 028 7034 3344
Fax: 028 7034 3606
E-mail: news@theleader.uk.com
Website: www.theleader.uk.com

The Lisburn Echo
12a Bow Street, Lisburn, Co.
Antrim, BT28 1BN
Tel: 028 9260 1114
Fax: 028 9260 2904

The Newtownards Chronicle
(and Co. Down Observer)
25 Frances Street, Newtownards,
Co. Down, BT23 7DT
Editor: John Savage
Tel: 028 9181 3333
Fax: 028 9182 0087
E-mail: news@ardschronicle.co.uk
Website:
www.newtownardschronicle.co.uk

Tyrone Constitution
25-27 High Street, Omagh, BT78
1BD
Editor: Wesley Atchison
Tel: 028 8224 2721
Fax: 028 8224 3549
E-mail: news@tyronecon.co.uk
Website: www.tyronecon.co.uk

Tyrone Courier (Cookstown)
23 Old Town Street, Cookstown,
BT80 8EE

Editor: Ian Greer
Tel: 028 8676 6692
Fax: 028 8676 9149
E-mail:
newsdesk@tyronecourier.uk.com
Website: www.tyronecourier.uk.com

Tyrone Courier (Dungannon)

58 Scotch Street, Dungannon, BT70 1BD
Editor: Ian Greer
Tel: Dungannon Office 028 8772 2271
Fax: Dungannon Office 028 8772 6171
E-mail:
newsdesk@tyronecourier.uk.com
Website:
www.tyronecourier.uk.com

Tyrone Times

Thomas Street, Dungannon, BT70 1HN
Tel: 028 87752801
Website: www.tyronetimes.co.uk

Ulster Gazette (Armagh)

Alpha Newspaper Group, 56 Scotch Street, Armagh, BT61 7DQ
Tel: 028 3752 2639
Fax: 028 3752 7029

Ulster Gazette (Portadown)

48-50 West Street, Portadown, BT62 3JQ
Editor: Melanie Simmons
Tel: 028 3752 2639
Fax: 028 3752 7029
E-mail:
newsdesk@ulstergazette.co.uk
Website: www.ulstergazette.co.uk

Ulster Herald

14 John Street, Omagh, Co. Tyrone, BT78 1DW
Tel: 028 8224 3444
Fax: 028 8225 5953
Website: www.nwipp-newspapers.com/UH

Ulster Star (Lisburn Today)

12A Bow Street, Lisburn, BT28 1BN
Editor: David Fletcher
Tel: 028 9267 9111
Fax: 028 9260 2904
E-mail:
david.fletcher@ulsterstar.co.uk
Website: www.lisburntoday.co.uk

H. Magazines and Periodicals

AN GHAEILGE - IRISH LANGUAGE

Feasta
Reiviú den Smaointeachas Éireannach - litríocht, eolaíocht, polaitíocht.
Seolta Phoist: 43 Na Cluainte, Trá Lí, Co. Chiarraí,
Eagarthóir: Pádraig Mac Fhearghusa
Teil: 066 7124169
Facs: 01 4785428
Ríomhphost: feasta@eircom.net
Suíomh Gréasáin: www.feasta.ie

Nós Magazine
Seolta Phoist: PO BOX 188, An tIúr / Newry BT35 5BA
Eagarthóir: Tomaí Ó Conghaile
Teil: 0775 9837019
Ríomhphost: eolas@nosmag.com
Suíomh Gréasáin:
www.nosmag.com

Saol
Nuachtiris Mhíosúil Phobal na Gaeilge
Seolta Phoist: Foras na Gaeilge, 7 Cearnóg Mhuirfean, Baile Átha Cliath 2
Eagarthóir: Colm ó Tórna
Teil: 01 8313333
Ríomhphost: saol@eircom.net

ARTS, CULTURE, MUSIC

Circa
Arts and Visual Culture
The Priory, John Street West, Dublin 8
Editor: Peter FitzGerald
Tel: 01 6401585
Website: www.recirca.com

Connected
33 Pearse Street, Dublin 2
Tel: 01 445 0595
E-mail: info@connected.ie
Website: www.connected.ie

Fiction Matters
Newsletter of the IMPAC Dublin Literary Award
Dublin City Library and Archive, 138-144 Pearse Street, Dublin 2.
Tel: 01 6744802
Fax: 01 6744879
E-mail: literaryaward@dublincity.ie
Website: www.impacdublinaward.ie

Film Ireland
Curved Street Building, Temple Bar, Dublin 2
Acting Editor: Nerea Aymerich
Tel: 01 679 6716
Fax: 01 679 6717
E-mail: news@filmireland.net
Website: www.filmireland.net

Foggy Notions
International Music Magazine
Liberty Lane Publishing, 38c Camden Row, Dublin 8
Tel: 01 4755000
E-mail: info@foggynotions.ie
Website: www.foggynotions.ie

Hot Press
Music and Current Affairs
13 Trinity Street, Dublin 2
Editor: Niall Stokes
Tel: 01 241 1500

Fax: 01 241 1538
E-mail:
contributions@hotpress.com (for submissions)
Website: www.hotpress.com

Humanism Ireland

Jointly produced by the Humanist Association of Ireland and the Humanist Association of Northern Ireland
Rose Cottage, Balrothery, Balbriggan, Co. Dublin
Assistant Editor: Ann James
Tel: 01 8413116
E-mail: anncjames@hotmail.com
Website: www.humanism.ie and www.nireland.humanist.org.uk

Ireland's Eye

6 Dominic Street, Mullingar, Co. Westmeath
Tel: 044 488 68
Fax: 044 437 77

Irish Arts Review

State Apartments, Dublin Castle, Dublin 2
Editor: John Mulcahy
Tel: 01 679 3525
Fax: 01 633 4417
E-mail:
editorial@irishartsreview.com
Website: www.irishartsreview.com

Irish Music Magazine

11 Clare Street, Dublin 2
Tel: 01 662 2266
Fax: 01 662 4981

The Journal of Music

An Spidéal, Conamara, Co. Galway
Tel: 091 558824 / 086 8241309

E-mail: toner@journalofmusic.com
Website: www.journalofmusic.com

Journal Of Music In Ireland

Edenvale, Esplanade, Bray, Co. Dublin
Tel: 01 494 1071
Fax: 01 494 1071

Midlands

Free publication published three times a year about the arts in the Midlands
Editor: Ann Egan
Published by: Laois, Offaly, Longord and Westmeath County Councils. Contact the Arts Officer.

Rap Ireland Magazine

17 Stockton Drive, Castleknock, Dublin 15
Tel: 087 989 2011

State Magazine

144 The Old Distillery, Cuckoo Lane, Dublin 7
Editorial Team: Phil Udell, Niall Byrne and John Walshe
E-mail: editorial@state.ie
Website: www.state.ie

Visual Artists News Sheet

37 North Great Georges Street, Dublin 1
Tel: 01 872 2296
Fax: 01 872 2364
E-mail: info@visualartists.ie
Website: www.visualartists.ie

BUSINESS, MANAGEMENT, PROPERTY, FINANCE

Blue Lake
Blue Lake House, Brookfield
Terrace, Blackrock, Co. Dublin
Tel: 01 487 7837
Fax: 01 487 7837
E-mail: info@bluelake.ie
Website: www.bluelake.ie

Business and Finance
Cunningham House, 130 Francis
Street, Dublin 8
Editor: John Walsh
Tel: 01 416 7800
E-mail:
john.walsh@businessandfinance.ie
Website:
www.businessandfinance.ie

Business Cork
PO Box 69, Ballinlough, Cork
Tel: 1850 502 005
Fax: 1850 502 006

Business Eye
Buckley Publications, Editorial,
Accounts and Subscription Dept, 20
King's Road, Belfast BT5 6JJ
Editor: Richard Buckley
Tel: 028 9047 4490
Fax: 028 9047 4495
E-mail: info@businesseye.co.uk
Website: www.businesseye.co.uk

Business Galway
EBI House, Galway Technology Park,
Parkmore, Golway
Tel: 1850 502 005
Fax: 1850 502 006

Business Ireland
Produced by the Dublin Chamber of
Commerce
Dublin Chamber of Commerce, 7
Clare Street, Dublin 2
Tel: 01 644 7200
Fax: 01 676 6043
E-mail: info@dublinchamber.ie
Website: www.dubchamber.ie

Business Limerick
Business Limerick Publications, 17
Mallow Street, Limerick
Tel: 061 467 518
Fax: 061 467 518

Business Plus
30 Morehampton Road, Dublin 4
Editor: Nick Mulcahy
Tel: 01 660 8400
E-mail: info@businessplus.ie
Website: www.bizplus.ie

Business Post
Direct Marketing magazine
produced by An Post
An Post, GPO, Dublin 1
Editor: Bryan Healy
Tel: 01 7058121
E-mail: business.post@anpost.ie
Website: www.anpost.ie

Business Sligo
PO Box 286, Finisklin Business
Park, Sligo
Tel: 087 986 1601
Fax: 071 918 6963

Business Travel Ireland
A12 Calmount Park, Ballymount,
Dublin 12
Tel: 01 450 2422
Fax: 01 450 2954

Business Waterford
Unit 1B Industrial Park, Cork Road,
Waterford
Tel: 1850 502 005
Fax: 1850 502 006

Corporate Ireland
Exact Media Ltd, 45 Upper Mount
Street, Dublin 2
Tel: 01 661 1660
Fax: 01 661 1632

Enterprize
Mainstream Publications, 140
Thomas Street, Portadown, Co.
Armagh, BT62 3BE
Tel: 028 3833 4272
Fax: 028 3835 1046

Finance Magazine
Fintel Publications Ltd, Fintel House
6 The Mall, Beacon Court
Sandyford, Dublin 18
Tel: 01 293 0566
Fax: 01 293 0560

Free Property Guide - Cork
Free Property Guide Ltd, 2
Rocksavage Business Centre,
Anglesea Street, Cork
Tel: 021 484 0888
Fax: 021 484 0889

Home and Property Echo
Head Office, Millpark Road,
Enniscorthy, Co. Wexford
Tel: 054 332 31
Fax: 054 335 06 / 344 92

Inside Business - Dublin City
60 Lower Baggot Street, Dublin 2
Tel: 01 602 4788
Fax: 01 602 4751

Inside Business - Dublin West
50 Anley Court, Lucan, Co. Dublin
Tel: 01 621 3670
Fax: 01 621 3670

**Inside Business - Dun Laoghaire
Rathdown**
60 Lower Baggot Street, Dublin 2
Tel: 01 602 4788
Fax: 01 602 4751

**Inside Business - Louth Newry
and Mourne**
Blackrock, Co. Louth
Tel: 042 932 2809
Fax: 042 932 2809

The Investor
Ashville Media Group, Longboat
Quay, 57-59 Sir John Rogerson's
Quay, Dublin 2
Tel: 01 432 2200
Fax: 01 672 7100

Irish Entrepreneur
Morrissey Media Ltd, M4 McConnell
Business Centre, Kerlogue, Rosslare
Road, Co. Wexford
Tel: 053 262 40
Fax: 053 475 23

Irish Marketing Journal
Mount Media Ltd, 45 Upper Mount
Street, Dublin 2
Tel: 01 661 1660
Fax: 01 661 1632
E-mail:
editor@irishmarketingjournal.ie
Website: www.adworld.ie

Irish Property Buyer
16/17 College Green, Dublin 2
Tel: 01 612 1430
Fax: 01 612 1429

Marketing
1 Albert Park, Sandycove, Co. Dublin
Editor: Michael Cullen
Tel: 01 280 7735 and 01 284 4456
Fax: 01 280 7735
E-mail: cullen@marketing.ie
Website: www.marketing.ie

PropertyWise Magazine
Ladytown Lodge, Ladytown, Naas,
Co. Kildare
Tel: 045 896 600
Fax: 045 889 756

Recruitment
Flaship Media, 48-50 York Street,
Belfast, BT15 1AS
Tel: 028 9031 9008
Fax: 028 9072 7800

Running Your Business Magazine
Firsthand Publising Ltd, 24 Terenure
Road East, Rathgar, Dublin 6
Tel: 01 4902244
Fax: 01 492 0578

Ulster Business
5B Edgewater Business Park,
Belfast Harbour Estate, Belfast, BT3
9JQ
Editor: David Elliott
Tel: 028 9078 3200
Fax: 028 9078 3210
E-mail:
davidelliott@greerpublications.com
Website: www.ulsterbusiness.com

WMB (Women Mean Business)
47 Harrington Street, Dublin 8
Managing Editor: Rosemary
Delaney
Tel: 01 4155056
E-mail:
rosemary@womenmeanbusiness.com
Website:
www.womenmeanbusiness.com

You and Your Money Magazine
Ashville Media, 57-59 Longboat
Quay, Sir John Rogerson's Quay,
Dublin 2
Editor: Brian O'Neill
Tel: 01 432 2200
E-mail: Brian.ONeill@ashville.com
Website: www.youandyourmoney.ie

CARS AND MOTORING

AA Motoring
7 Cranford Centre, Montrose, Dublin 4
Tel: 01 260 0899
Fax: 01 260 0911

Autobiz
Shangort, Knocknacarra, Golway
Tel: 091 523 292
Fax: 091 584 411

Auto Ireland Magazine
Harmonia, Rosemount House,
Dundrum Road, Dundrum, Dublin 14
Tel: 01 240 5300
Fax: 01 661 9486

Auto Trader
Paramount Court, Corrig Road,
Sandyford Industrial Estate, Dublin 18
Tel: 01 449 0600
Fax: 01 449 0606

Auto Trade Journal
Automotive Publications Ltd,
Glencree House, Lanesborough
Road, Roscommon

Tel: 0906 625 676
Fax: 0906 637 410

Auto Woman
Harmonia, Rosemount House,
Dundrum Road, Dundrum, Dublin 14
Tel: 01 240 5300
Fax: 01 661 9486

Bike Buyers Guide
Page 7 Media, 3rd Floor, Arena
House, Arena Road, Sandyford
Industrial Estate, Dublin 18
Tel: 01 240 5555
Fax: 01 240 5550

Car Buyers Guide
Page 7 Media, 3rd Floor, Arena
House, Arena Road, Sandyford
Industrial Estate, Dublin 18
Tel: 01 240 5555
Fax: 01 240 5550

CarSport Magazine
5B Edgewater Business Park,
Belfast Harbour Estate, Belfast, BT3
9JQ
Editor: Pat Burns
Tel: 028 9078 3200
Fax: 028 9078 3210
E-mail:
patburns@greerpublications.com
Website:
www.greerpublications.com

Drive Magazine
7 Cranford Centre, Montrose, Dublin 4
Tel: 01 2600899
E-mail: info@drivemagazine.ie
Website: www.drivemagazine.ie

Ireland's Motor Trader
The Ideal Centre, Prosperous, Naas,

Co. Kildare
Tel: 045 893 344
Fax: 045 893 349

Irish Car
Whelan Byrne Associates, 2
Sunbury, Kilcullen, Co. Kildare
Tel: 045 481 090

Irish Racer
5 Colvin House, Dundonald
Enterprise Park, Carrowreagh Road,
Dundonald, Belfast BT16 1QT
Tel: 028 9048 6430
Fax: 028 9048 8954
E-mail: editor@irishracer.com
Website: www.irishracer.com

Irish Vintage Scene
Ireland's only vintage magazine.
3d Deerpark Business Centre,
Oranmore, Co. Galway
Tel: 091 388805
E-mail: info@irishvintagescene.ie
Website: www.irishvintagescene.ie

Motoring Life
Ireland's longest established
Motoring magazine.
48 North Great Georges Street,
Dublin 1
Editor: Geraldine Herbert
Tel: 01 8780444
Fax: 01 878 7740
E-mail: gherbert@motoringlife.ie
Website: www.motoringlife.ie

Northern Ireland Auto Trader
James House, Dargan Crescent,
Belfast, Co. Antrim, BT3 9JP
Tel: 028 9037 0444
Fax: 028 9037 0332

Used Car Price Guide
Page 7 Media, 3rd Floor, Arena
House, Arena Road, Sandyford
Industrial Estate, Dublin 18
Tel: 01 240 5555
Fax: 01 240 5550

COMMUNITY, VOLUNTARY, HEALTH

ACRA News
The National Body for Residents
Associations
Editor: Michael Whelan
Tel: 046 9555825
E-mail: acra@iol.ie
Website: www.acra.ie

All In ... Social Inclusion
Produced by Dublin City Council
Social Inclusion Unit, Block 4 East,
Floor 1, Civic Offices, Dublin 8
Editor: Hugh Foley
Tel: 01 2223139
E-mail:
socialinclusion@dublincity.ie

Cancerwise
Eireann Healthcare Publications, 25
Windsor Place, Dublin 2
Tel: 01 475 3300
Fax: 01 475 3311

Cornerstone
Magazine of The Homeless Agency
The Homeless Agency, Parkgate
Hall, 6-9 Conyngham Road, Dublin 8
Editor: Simon Brooke
Tel: 01 7036100
Fax: 01 7036170
E-mail: homeless@dublincity.ie
Website: www.homelessagency.ie

Diabetes Ireland
Med Media Ltd, 25 Adelaide Street,
Dun Laoghaire, Co. Dublin
Tel: 01 280 3967
Fax: 01 280 7076

Diabeteswise
Eireann Healthcare Publications, 25
Windsor Place, Dublin 2
Tel: 01 475 3300
Fax: 01 475 3311

Drugnet Ireland
Newsletter of the Alcohol and Drug
Research Unit
ADRU, Health Research Board,
Knockmaun House, 42-47 Lower
Mount Street, Dublin 2
Editor: Joan Moore
Tel: 01 2345127
E-mail: adru@hrb.ie

Heartwise
Eireann Healthcare Publications, 25
Windsor Place, Dublin 2
Tel: 01 475 3300
Fax: 01 475 3311

NCBI News - incorporating The Blind Citizen (1923)
Whitworth Road, Drumcondra,
Dublin 9
Editor: Frank Callery
Tel: 01 8307033 / 087 6724097
Fax: 01 8307787
E-mail: omegapub@eircom.net
Website: www.ncbi.ie

One Family Matters
Voice, Support, Action for One
Parent Families
Cherish House, 2 Lower Pembroke
Street, Dublin 2

Editor: Hilary Fennell
Tel: 01 6629212
Fax: 01 6629096
E-mail: info@onefamily.ie
Website: www.onefamily.ie

Osteowise
Eireann Healthcare Publications, 25
Windsor Place, Dublin 2
Tel: 01 475 3300
Fax: 01 475 3311

Painwise
Eireann Healthcare Publications, 25
Windsor Place, Dublin 2
Tel: 01 475 3300
Fax: 01 475 3311

Senior Times
4 Fitzwilliam Square East, Dublin 2
Tel: 01 676 1810
Fax: 01 676 1944

Spokeout
A lifestyle magazine for the 20,000
members of the Irish Wheelchair
Association
Dyflin Media, Cunningham House,
130 Francis Street, Dublin 8
Editor: Joanna Marsden
Tel: 01 416 7900
Fax: 01 416 7901
E-mail: marsdenjoanna@gmail.com

Trefoil News
Magazine of the Irish Girl Guides.
Trefoil House, 27 Pembroke Park,
Dublin 4
Editor: Katherine Ryan
E-mail: news@irishgirlguides.ie

Youth Now
Published by City of Dublin Youth

Service Board
70 Morehampton Road,
Donnybrook, Dublin 4
Tel: 01 4321100
Fax: 01 4321199
E-mail: info@cdysb.cdvec.ie
Website: www.cdysb.ie

EDUCATION, SCIENCE AND TECHNOLOGY

Archaeology Ireland
Trintech Building, South Co. Dublin
Business Park, Dublin 18
Tel: 01 2765221
Fax: 01 2765207
Website: www.wordwellbooks.com

Click Magazine
Blue Lake House, Brookfield
Terrace, Blackrock, Co. Dublin
Tel: 01 4877837
Fax: 01 4877837

ComputerScope
Mediateam Ltd, Media House, South
County Business Park,
Leopardstown, Dublin 18
Editor: Paul Hearns
Tel: 01 2947777
Fax: 01 2947799
E-mail: paul.hearns@mediateam.ie
Website: www.techcentral.ie

Digital Ireland
Top Floor, 43B Yeats Way, Park West
Business Park, Nangor Road, Dublin 12
Tel: 01 625 1400
Fax: 01 625 1402

Education Magazine
Keelaun Ltd, 9 Maypark, Malahide

Road, Dublin 5
Tel: 01 832 9243
Fax: 01 832 9246

Eircom's Broadband Magazine
Digital Media House, 9 Baggot
Court, Dublin 2
Tel: 01 669 1750
Fax: 01 669 1769

GradIreland
Careers Directory
GTI Ireland, 77 Pembroke Square,
Upper Grand Canal Street, Dublin 4
Tel: 01 667 6291
Fax: 01 660 6623

History Ireland
PO Box 69, Bray, Co. Wicklow
Editor: Tommy Graham
Tel: 01 276 5221
Fax: 01 276 5207
E-mail: editor@historyireland.com
Website: www.historyireland.com

Irish Computer
Mediateam Ltd, Media House, South
County Business Park,
Leopardstown, Dublin 18
Editor: Cliff Hutton
Tel: 01 294 7777
Fax: 01 294 7799
E-mail: cliff.hutton@mediateam.ie
Website: www.techcentral.ie

Irish Computer Channels
Trintech Building, South County
Business Park, Leopardstown,
Dublin 18
Tel: 01 207 4288
Fax: 01 207 4299

Irish Crime Magazine
New Century Publishing, 101
Grangeway, Baldoyle Industrial
Estate, Baldoyle, Co. Dublin
Tel: 01 839 8008
Fax: 01 839 8007

Knowledge Ireland
Whitespace Publishing Group Ltd,
Top Floor, Block 43B, Yeats Way,
Park West Business Park, Nangor
Road, Dublin 12
Editor: John Kennedy
Tel: 01 6251400
Fax: 01 6251402
E-mail:
editorial@knowledgeireland.ie
Website: www.knowledgeireland.ie

PC Live!
Mediateam Ltd, Media House, South
County Business Park,
Leopardstown, Dublin 18
Editor: Niall Kitson
Tel: 01 294 7777
Fax: 01 294 7799
E-mail: niall.kitson@mediateam.ie
Website: www.techcentral.ie

Science Spin
Ireland's Science, Wildlife and
Discovery Magazine.
Joint Editors: Tom Kennedy and
Seán Duke
E-mail: tom@sciencespin.com or
sean@sciencespin.com
Website: www.sciencespin.com

Smart Company
Draws on the editorial resources of
sister titles ComputerScope, PC
Live! and Irish Computer.
Mediateam Ltd, Media House, South

County Business Park,
Leopardstown, Dublin 18
Tel: 01 294 7777
Fax: 01 294 7799
Website: www.techcentral.ie

Technology Ireland
The Plaza, East Point Business Park,
Dublin 3
Editor: Mary Sweetman
Tel: 01 727 2954
E-mail:
mary.sweetman@enterprise-ireland.com
Web: www.technologyireland.ie

ENTERTAINMENT, SHOPPING, GOING OUT

Buy and Sell
Buy and Sell House, Argyle Square,
Donnybrook, Dublin 4
Tel: 0818 434 343
Fax: 01 608 0701

Buy and Sell (NI)
Lyndon Court, Queen Street, Belfast,
Co. Antrim, BT1 6BY
Tel: 028 90530 066

Choice Magazine
Magazine of The Consumers'
Association of Ireland
43/44 Chelmsford Road, Ranelagh,
Dublin 6
Editor: Kieran Doherty
Phone: 01 4978600
E-mail: cai@consumerassociation.ie
Website: www.thecai.ie

Corklife
19 Old Court, Greenfields,

Ballincollig, Co. Cork
Tel: 021 4898858
E-mail: info@corklife.ie
Website: www.corklife.ie

Cork Now
Cork Now Productions Ltd, 4 South
Terrace, Cork
Tel: 021 484 7393
Fax: 021 484 7393

Day and Night Magazine
Independent House, 27-32 Talbot
Street, Dublin 1
Tel: 01 705 5397
Fax: 01 705 5498

The Event Guide
InterArt Media Ltd, Regus House,
Harcourt Road, Dublin 2
Tel: 01 477 3933

Free Ads Trader
Independent House, 27-32 Talbot
Street, Dublin 1
Tel: 1800 280 480
Fax: 021 489 7984

Galway Now
1A Clarenbridge Business Park,
Clarenbridge, Co. Galway
Tel: 091 777 077
Fax: 091 777 080

In Dublin Magazine
Seven Hats Media Ltd, 3rd Floor,
Arena House, Arena Road, Sandyford
Industrial Estate, Dublin 18
Tel: 01 2405555
Website: www.indublin.ie

Limerick Event Guide
101 Baker Place, Tait Square,

Limerick
Tel: 086 835 5354

Movies Plus
The Picture Works, 97 Upper
Georges Street, Dun Laoghaire, Co.
Dublin
Tel: 01 230 0558
Fax: 01 230 2759

The Red Book
Business and Shopping Guide Ltd,
Athlumney, Navan, Co. Meath
Tel: 046 902 1095
Fax: 046 902 7227

RTE Guide
RTÉ Publishing, Library Building,
First Floor, RTÉ, Donnybrook,
Dublin 4
Tel: 01 208 2919
Fax: 01 208 2092
E-mail: rteguide@rte.ie
Website: www.rteguide.ie

**S4W (Something For The
Weekend)**
P & G Publishing Ltd, 17
Donnybrook Court, Donnybrook,
Dublin 4
Tel: 01 260 3476
Fax: 01 260 3476

Star 7 Magazine
Star House, 62A Terenure Road
North, Terenure, Dublin 6W
Tel: 01 499 3400
Fax: 01 4907425

Sky Magazine
Alexandra House, Earlsfort Terrace,
Dublin 2
Tel: 01 614 7607
Fax: 01 614 7676

The Spanner
Foresight Communications, 11
Sallymount Avenue, Ranelagh,
Dublin 6
Editor: Eoin Ryan
Tel: 01 496 7270
Fax: 01 496 5224
E-mail: editor@oxygen.ie
Website: www.oxygen.ie

Totally Dublin
56 Upper Leeson Street
Dublin 4
Tel: 01 6870695
E-mail: editor@totallydublin.ie
Website: www.totallydublin.ie

TV Now!
3 Ely Place, Dublin 2
Tel: 01 676 9832
Fax: 01 480 4799

**Whazon (Waterford and
Kilkenny)**
Boardroom, The Spires, Bandon
Road, Cork
Tel: 021 484 0088

FOOD, FASHION, LIFESTYLES

All Ireland Kitchen Guide
Ashgrove House, Kill Avenue, Dun
Laoghaire, Co. Dublin
Tel: 01 272 2616
Fax: 01 272 2617

Baby and Child
7 Cranford Centre, Montrose, Dublin 4
Tel: 01 260 0899
Fax: 01 260 0911

Beautiful Irish Homes
Ashgrove House, Kill Avenue, Dun
Laoghaire, Co. Dublin
Tel: 01 272 2616
Fax: 01 272 2617

The Book of Interiors
Montauge Publications Group, 39
Fitzwilliam Street Upper, Dublin 2
Tel: 01 669 2101
Fax: 01 669 2104

Blueprint Home Plans
Oisín Publications, 4 Iona Drive,
Dublin 9
Tel: 01 830 5236
Fax: 01 830 7860
E-mail: oisinpr@iol.ie

Build Your Own House and Home
Dyflin Media, Cunningham House,
130 Francis Street, Dublin 8
Editor: Karen Hesse
Tel: 01 416 7905
Fax: 01 416 7901
E-mail: editor@houseandhome.ie
Website: www.houseandhome.ie

Bushmills Restaurant And Event Guide
Portside House, Portside Business
Centre, East Wall Road, Dublin 3
Tel: 01 836 6102
Fax: 01 836 6131

Childcare.ie Magazine
The Childcare Directory, Burnaby
Buildings, Church Road, Greystones,
Co. Wicklow
Tel: 01 201 6000
Fax: 01 201 6002
E-mail: info@childcare.ie
Website: www.childcare.ie

City and Town Magazine
Page 7 Media, 3rd Floor, Arena
House, Arena Road, Sandyford
Industrial Estate, Dublin 18
Tel: 01 240 5555
Fax: 01 240 5550

Confetti
Dyflin Publications Ltd,
Cunningham House, 130 Francis
Street, Dublin 8
Tel: 01 416 7900
Fax: 01 416 7901
E-mail: info@confetti.ie
Website: www.confetti.ie

Country Homes Ireland
Genoa House, 1A Drummartin Road,
Dublin 14
Tel: 01 296 0677

Dining in Dublin
35 Ferndale Court, Rathmichael, Co.
Dublin
Tel: 01 272 1188
Fax: 01 272 1970

The Dubliner
3 Ely Pace, Dublin 2
Editor: Nicola Reddy
Tel: 01 480 4700
E-mail: editor@thedubliner.ie
Website: www.thedubliner.ie

Dundrum Magazine
Harmonia, Rosemount House,
Dundrum Road, Dundrum, Dublin 14
Editor: Katie Byrne
Tel: 01 240 5391
Fax: 01 661 9486
E-mail: kbyrne@harmonia.ie

Easy Food Magazine
Zahra Publishing Ltd, 1st Floor, 19
Railway Road, Dalkey, Co. Dublin
Editor: Ciara McDonnell
E-mail:
editoreasyfood@zahrapublishing.com
Website: www.easyfood.ie

Easy Health and Living
Zahra Publishing Ltd, 1st Floor, 19
Railway Road, Dalkey, Co. Dublin
Editor: Emma Parkin
Tel: 01 654 4015
E-mail:
editoreasyhealth@zahrapublishing.
com
Website: www.easyhealth.ie

EasyFood
Zahra Publishing, First Floor, 19
Railway Road, Dalkey, Co. Dublin
Tel: 01 235 1408/9
Fax: 01 235 4434

Easyhealth
Zahra Publishing, 1st Floor, 19
Railway Road, Dalkey, Co. Dublin
Tel: 01 235 1408
Fax: 01 235 4434

Food and Wine Magazine
Harmonia, Rosemount House,
Dundrum Road, Dundrum, Dublin 14
Editor: Ross Golden Bannon
Tel: 01 240 5387
Fax: 01 661 9486
E-mail: ross@harmonia.ie

Food Ireland Yearbook and Directory
Tara Publishing Co. Ltd, 1-2 Poolbeg
Street, Dublin 2
Tel: 01 241 3095
Fax: 01 241 3010

Garden Heaven Magazine
BARK, 14-16 Main Street, Blackrock,
Co. Dublin
Editor: Dermot O'Neill
Tel: 01 2719600
E-mail: editorial@gardenheaven.ie

Getting Married
Mainstream Publications, 139-140
Thomas Street, Portadown, Co.
Armagh
Tel: 028 38 334 272
Fax: 028 38 351 046

Health Magazine
Crofton Hall, 22 Crofton Road, Dun
Laoghaire, Co. Dublin
Tel: 01 280 8415
Fax: 01 280 8309

Health Living and Wellbeing Magazine
Basement 2, 42 Lower Baggot
Street, Dublin 2
Tel: 01 611 0932
Fax: 01 611 0948

House Magazine
Architecture, Design, Garden Advice
9 Sandyford Office Park, Sandyford,
Dublin 18, Ireland
Tel: 01 295 8115
Fax: 01 295 9350
Website: www.architecturenow.ie

House and Home
Dyflin Media, Cunningham House,
130 Francis Street, Dublin 8
Tel: 01 416 7905
Fax: 01 416 7901

Intermezzo Magazine
Beehive Media Ltd, 7 Cranford

Centre, Montrose, Dublin 4
Tel: 01 260 1114
Fax: 01 260 0911
Website:
www.intermezzomagazine.com

Image
22 Crofton Road, Dun Laoghaire, Co. Dublin
Editor: Melanie Morris
Tel: 01 2719612
E-mail: mmorris@image.ie
Website: www.image.ie

Image Interiors Magazine
Crofton Hall, 22 Crofton Road, Dun Laoghaire, Co. Dublin
Editor: Amanda Cochrane
Tel: 01 2719602
Fax: 01 2808309
E-mail: acochrane@image.ie

Ireland's Antiques and Period Properties
20/21 South William Street, Dublin 2
Tel: 01 677 4847

Ireland's Pets
Mainstream Publications, 140 Thomas Street, Portadown, Co. Armagh, BT62 3BE
Tel: 028 38 334 272
Fax: 028 38 351 046

Irish Brides and Homes
Crannagh House, 198 Rathfarnham Road, Dublin 14
Tel: 01 4900550
Fax: 01 4906763

The Irish Garden
Mediateam Ltd, Media House, South Co. Business Park, Leopardstown,

Dublin 18
Editor: Gerry Daly
Tel: 01 2947722
E-mail:
gerry.daly@theirishgarden.ie
Website: www.garden.ie

Irish Homes Magazine
Kellar House, Staplestown Road, Carlow
Tel: 059 917 0764
Fax: 059 917 0765

Ireland's Homes Interiors and Living
Northern Address - PO Box 42, Bangor, Co. Down, BT19 7AD;
Southern Address - Ashgrove House, Kill Avenue, Dun Laoghaire, Co. Dublin
Editors: Lisa Sykes and Stuart Collins
Tel: 028 9147 3979
E-mail: editorial@ihil.net
Website: www.ihil.net

Irish Kitchens
Editor: Judith Robinson Lyttle
E-mail:
judith@bayviewpublishing.net
Website:
www.bayviewpublishing.net

Irish Kitchens and Bathrooms
Ireland's only kitchen and bathroom magazine
Dyflin Media, Cunningham House, 130 Francis Street, Dublin 8
Editor: Karen Hesse
Tel: 01 416 7905
Fax: 01 416 7901
E-mail: editor@houseandhome.ie

Irish Tatler Magazine
Rosemount House, Dundrum Road,
Dublin 16
Editor: Jessie Collins
Tel: 01 2405300
Fax: 01 6619757
E-mail: jcollins@harmonia.ie

The Irish Vegetarian
Magazine of the Vegetarian Society
of Ireland
c/o Dublin Food Co-Op, 12
Newmarket, Dublin 8
Tel: 1890 328834
E-mail: eolas@irishvegetarian.com
or vegsoc@ireland.com
Website: www.irishvegetarian.com

Irish Wedding and New Home
Cloughmore Media Gruop, 1-4
Swift's Alley, Off Francis Street,
Dublin 8
Tel: 01 416 7810
Fax: 01 416 7899

Irish Wedding Diary
10 Rathgar Road, Rathmines, Dublin 6
Tel: 01 498 3242
Fax: 01 498 3217

Kiss Magazine
Ireland's only teen magazine
3 Ely Place, Dublin 2
Tel: 01 4804700
Fax: 01 4804799
E-mail: info@kiss.ie
Website: www.kiss.ie

KT Parenting
KT Parenting magazine, 51 Allen
Park Road, Stillorgan, Co. Dublin
Tel: 01 205 6895
Fax: 01 210 0884

Life and Fitness Magazine
Borrisoleigh, Thurles, Co. Tipperary
Tel: 0504 519 45
Fax: 0504 519 45

Living Design
39 Boucher Road, Belfast BT12 6UT
Tel: 028 9066 3311
Fax: 028 9038 1915
Website: www.ulstertatler.com

Maternity
Ashville Media Group, Apollo House,
Tara Street, Dublin 2
Tel: 01 432 2200
Fax: 01 672 7100

Maternity and Infant
Longboat Quay, 57-59 Sir John
Rogerson's Quay, Dublin 2
Editor: Emily Manning
Tel: 01 432 2200
E-mail: editorial@infant.ie
Website:
www.maternityandinfant.ie

Modern Woman
Market Square, Navan, Co. Meath
Tel: 046 907 9600
Fax: 046 902 3565

Moving In Magazine
29 Charlemont Lane, Clontarf,
Dublin 3
Tel: 01 833 0560
Fax: 01 833 0826

Munster Interiors
Pembroke Publishing Ltd, Unit F5
Bymac Centre, Northwest Business
Park, Dublin 15
Tel: 01 822 4477
Fax: 01 822 4485

myDEBS
Claran, Headford, Galway
Tel: 093 366 85
Fax: 093 365 94

New Houses
Mainstream Publications, 139-140
Thomas Street, Portadown, Co.
Armagh
Tel: 028 38 334 272
Fax: 028 38 35 1046

Northern Ireland Baby Magazine
Mainstream Publications, 140
Thomas Street, Portadown, Co.
Armagh, BT62 3BE
Tel: 028 38 334 272
Fax: 028 38 351 046

**Northern Ireland Homes and
Lifestyle**
Editor: Judith Robinson Lyttle
E-mail:
judith@bayviewpublishing.net
Website:
www.bayviewpublishing.net

Northern Woman
5B Edgewater Business Park,
Belfast Harbour Estate, Belfast, BT3
9JQ
Editor: Lyn Palmer
Tel: 028 9078 3200
Fax: 028 9078 3210
E-mail:
lynpalmer@greerpublications.com
Website:
www.greerpublications.com

Off The Rails Magazine
TV Building, RTE, Donnybrook,
Dublin 4
Tel: 01 208 2880
Fax: 01 208 2092

PetCare
IFP Media Ltd, 31 Deansgrange
Road, Blackrock, Co. Dublin
Tel: 01 289 3305
Fax: 01 289 6406

Pet Life
51 Allen Park Road, Stillorgan, Co.
Dublin
Tel: 01 205 6895
Fax: 01 210 0884

Pioneer
Pioneer Total Abstinence
Association, 27 Upper Sherrard
Street, Dublin 1
Tel: 01 874 9464
Fax: 01 874 8485

Polish Lifestyle Magazine SOFA
Salamander Lodge, 80 Sandford
Road, Ranelagh, Dublin 6
Tel: 01 406 0101
Fax: 01 497 6010

Prudence
A new kind of magazine for the
thinking woman.
Cunningham House, 130 Francis
Street, Dublin 8
Tel: 01 416 7900
Fax: 01 416 7901
E-mail: annette@prudence.ie
Website: www.prudence.ie

Renovate Your House and Home
Ireland's only comprehensive guide
to renovating your home
Dyflin Media, Cunningham House,
130 Francis Street, Dublin 8
Editor: Karen Hesse
Tel: 01 416 7905
Fax: 01 416 7901

E-mail: editor@houseandhome.ie
Website: www.houseandhome.ie

Restaurant and Event Guide
Portside Media, Portside Business
Centre, East Wall Road, Dublin 3
Tel: 01 836 6102
Fax: 01 836 6131

Room
Gold Star Publications Ltd, 7
Cranford Centre, Montrose, Dublin 4
Tel: 01 260 0899
Fax: 01 260 0911

Select Architecture
Easton, Bellvue Road, Delgany, Co.
Wicklow
Tel: 01 287 3860
Fax: 01 287 1840

Select Furniture and Interiors
Easton, Bellevue Road, Delgany, Co.
Wicklow
Tel: 01 287 3860
Fax: 01 287 1840

Sláinte Magazine
CKN Publishing, 2nd Floor, 13
Upper Baggot Street, Dublin 4
Tel: 1800 812800
Email: info@slaintemagazine.ie
Website: www.slaintemagazine.ie

Social and Personal
19 Nassau Street, Dublin 2
Tel: 01 633 3993
Fax: 01 633 4353

Social and Personal Living
19 Nassau Street, Dublin 2
Tel: 01 633 3993
Fax: 01 633 4353

Social and Personal Weddings
19 Nassau Street, Dublin 2
Tel: 01 633 3993
Fax: 01 633 4353

South Belfast Life
39 Boucher Road, Belfast BT12 6UT
Tel: 028 9066 3311
Fax: 028 9038 1915
Website: www.ulstertatler.com

Spring Home / Autumn Home
John Coughlan Publishing, 12
Claremont Road, Howth, Co. Dublin
Tel: 01 832 5403
Fax: 01 832 5950

Today's Parent
Select Media Ltd, 11 Clare Street,
Dublin 2
Tel: 01 662 2266
Fax: 01 662 4981

U Magazine
Harmonia, Rosemount House,
Dundrum Road, Dundrum, Dublin 14
Tel: 01 240 5300
Fax: 01 661 9486
Editor: Jen Stevens
E-mail: jstevens@harmonia.ie

Ulster Bride
39 Boucher Road, Belfast BT12 6UT
Tel: 028 9066 3311
Fax: 028 9038 1915
Website: www.ulstertatler.com

Ulster Tatler
39 Boucher Road, Belfast BT12 6UT
Tel: 028 9066 3311
Fax: 028 9038 1915
E-mail: info@ulstertatler.com
Website: www.ulstertatler.com

Ulster Tatler Interiors
39 Boucher Road, Belfast BT12 6UT
Tel: 028 9066 3311
Fax: 028 9038 1915
Website: www.ulstertatler.com

VIP Magazine
3 Ely Place, Dublin 2
Tel: 01 6769832
Fax: 01 6788161
Website: www.vipmagazine.ie

Wedding Journal
Penton Publications Ltd, 38 Heron
Road, Sydenham Business Park,
Belfast, BT3 9LE
Tel: 028 90457 457
Fax: 028 90456 611

The White Book
Publications Group, 39 Upper
fitzwilliam Street, Dublin 2
Tel: 01 6692101
Fax: 01 6692104
E-mail: info@montaguegroup.ie
Website: www.thewhitebook.ie

Wine Ireland
CPG House, Glenageary Office Park,
Dun Laoghaire, Co. Dublin
Tel: 01 284 7777
Fax: 01 284 7584

Woman's Way
Rosemount House, Dundrum Road,
Dublin 14
Editor: Aine Toner
Tel: 01 2405318
Fax: 01 6619757
E-mail: atoner@harmonia.ie

Your Childs First Communion
10 Rathgar Road, Rathmines, Dublin 6

Tel: 01 498 3242
Fax: 01 498 3217

Your New Baby
Supplement with Woman's Way
Harmonia Ltd, Clanwilliam House,
Clanwilliam Place, Dublin 2
Tel: 01 240 5386
Fax: 01 661 9757

NEWS, CURRENT AFFAIRS, COMMENTARY

Feasta
6 Harcourt Street, Dublin 2
Tel: 01 478 3814
Fax: 01 478 5428

Focus - Action for Global Justice
Comhlámh, 2nd Floor, Ballast
House, Aston Quay, Dublin 2
Tel: 01 4783490
E-mail: info@comhlamh.org

Fortnight Magazine
11 University Road, Belfast, BT7
1NA
Tel: 028 90232 353
Fax: 028 90232 650
E-mail: rgoldsmith@fortnight.org
Website: www.fortnight.org

Ireland's Issues
30 Gardiner Place, Dublin 1
Tel: 01 873 5137
Fax: 01 873 5143
Website:
www.irelandsissuesmagazine.com

Magill Magazine
Cloughmore Media Group, 1-4
Swift's Alley, Dublin 8

Tel: 01 416 7800
Fax: 01 416 7899

New Internationalist
PO Box 8115, Dublin 15
Tel: 01 811 5970
Fax: 01 821 9907

Red Banner
A magazine of socialist ideas.
PO Box 6587, Dublin 6
E-mail: red_banner@yahoo.com
Website:
www.redbannermagazine.com

Sustainability
Making the transition to a post-oil
society.
Corrig, Sandyhill, Westport, Co.
Mayo
Tel: 087 7652953 or 087 6714075
E-mail: office@sustainability.ie
Website: www.sustainability.ie

Sustainable Ireland
The Old Coach House, 12 Main
Street, Hillsborough, Co. Down,
BT26 6AE
Tel: 028 92 688 888
Fax: 028 92 688 866

The Phoenix
44 Lr Baggot Street, Dublin 2
Tel: 01 661 1062
Fax: 01 662 4532
E-mail: editor@thephoenix.ie
Website: www.thephoenix.ie

Village Magazine
Village Communications Ltd, 44
Westland Row, Dublin 2
Tel: 01 642 5065
Fax: 01 642 5001
Website: www.villagemagazine.ie

RELIGIOUS AND SPIRITUAL

Africa
Divine World Missionaries,
Maynooth, Co. Kildare
Tel: 01 505 4467
Fax: 01 628 9184

The Brandsma Review
Catholic magazine
E-mail:
brandsmabooks@eircom.net
Website: www.brandsmareview.ie

Daystar in Africa
Divine World Missionaries,
Maynooth, Co. Kildare
Tel: 01 505 4467
Fax: 01 628 9184

Face Up Magazine
Redemptorist Publications, 75
Orwell Road, Rathgar, Dublin 6
Tel: 01 492 2488
Fax: 01 442 2949

Far East
Divine World Missionaries,
Maynooth, Co. Kildare
Tel: 01 505 4467
Fax: 01 628 9184

The Furrow
A journal for The Contemporary
Church
St Patrick's College, Maynooth, Co.
Kildare
Tel: 01 708 3741
Fax: 01 708 3908
E-mail:furrow.office@may.ie
Website: www.thefurrow.ie

Intercom
Divine World Missionaries,
Maynooth, Co. Kildare
Tel: 01 505 4467
Fax: 01 628 9184

Link Up
Divine World Missionaries,
Maynooth, Co. Kildare
Tel: 01 505 4467
Fax: 01 628 9184

Maria Legionis
Divine World Missionaries,
Maynooth, Co. Kildare
Tel: 01 505 4467
Fax: 01 628 9184

The Presbyterian Herald
Church House, Belfast, BT1 6DW
Tel: 028 90322 284
Fax: 028 90248 377

Reality Magazine
75 Orwell Road, Rathgar, Dublin 6
Tel: 01 492 2488
Fax: 01 492 2654

Religious Life Review
Dominican Publications, 42 Parnell
Square, Dublin 1
Tel: 01 872 1611
Fax: 01 873 1760

The Sacred Heart Messenger
37 Lower Leeson Street, Dublin 2
Tel: 01 6767491
E-mail: manager@messenger.ie
Website: www.messenger.ie

St Joseph's Advocate
Divine World Missionaries,
Maynooth, Co. Kildare

Tel: 01 505 4467
Fax: 01 628 9184

St Martin's Magazine
Divine World Missionaries,
Maynooth, Co. Kildare
Tel: 01 505 4467
Fax: 01 628 9184

Salesian Bulletin
Salesian College, Maynooth Road,
Celbridge, Co. Kildare
Tel: 01 627 5060
Fax: 01 630 3601

The Sheaf
23 Merrion Square North, Dublin 2
Tel: 01 676 2593
Fax: 01 676 2549

Spirituality
42 Parnell Square, Dublin 1
Tel: 01 872 1611
Fax: 01 873 1760

Studies An Irish Quarterly Review
35 Lower Leeson Street, Dublin 2
Tel: 01 676 6785
Fax: 01 676 2984
E-mail: studies@jesuit.ie
Website: www.studiesirishreview.ie

Your Destiny
Mac Communications, Taney Hall,
Eglinton Terrace, Dundrum, Dublin 14
Tel: 01 296 0000
Fax: 01 296 0383

SPORT, RECREATION, TRAVEL

Abroad Magazine
Top Floor, 75/76 Camden Street,
Dublin 2
Editor: Orla Neligan
Tel: 085 7584153
Fax: 01 4757301
E-mail:
editor@abroadmagazine.com
Website: www.abroadmagazine.com

Afloat Magazine
2 Lower Glenageary Road, Dún
Laoghaire, Co. Dublin
Tel: 01 2846161
Fax: 01 2846192
Website: www.afloat.ie

Backpacker Magazine Ireland
75-76 Camden Street, Dublin 2
Tel: 085 758 4154
Fax: 01 475 7301

Backspin Golf Magazine
Birkdle, 4 Rathmichael Manor,
Loughlinstown, Co. Dublin
Tel: 01 282 7269
Fax: 01 282 7483

Cara Magazine
Harmonia, Rosemount House,
Dundrum Road, Dundrum, Dublin 14
Tel: 01 240 5300
Fax: 01 661 9486

Discover Ireland
Spring/Summer and
Autumn/Winter issues
Tudor Journals, 74 Amiens Street,
Dublin 1
Tel: 01 855 4382
Fax: 028 90323 536

Dublin Horse Show Magazine
Goldstar Publications Ltd, 7
Cranford Centre, Montrose, Dublin 4
Tel: 01 260 0899
Fax: 01 260 0911

Connections
Dublin Airport's Passenger
Magazine
Mac Communications, Taney Hall,
Eglinton Terrace, Dundrum, Dublin 14
Tel: 01 296 0000
Fax: 01 296 0383

Emerald Rugby
32 The Slopes Ballydougan,
Craigavon, Co. Armagh N.Ireland
BT63 5NT
  or
PO Box 35, Dundalk, Ireland
Tel: 028 3834 4333
Fax: 028 3834 3454
Website: www.emeraldrugby.com

Equestrian Ireland Annual
Goldstar Publications Ltd, 7
Cranford Centre, Montrose, Dublin 4
Tel: 01 260 0899
Fax: 01 260 0911

Express It
Aer Arann In Flight Magazine
Marketing Solutions, 75 Clonard
Village, Clonard, Wexford
Tel: 053 267 89
Fax: 053 267 89

Fáilte Welcome
Mac Communications, Taney Hall,
Eglinton Terrace Dundrum, Dublin 14
Tel: 01 296 0000
Fax: 01 296 0383

Gaelic World
Official GAA Magazine
13 Abbey Lane, Abbey Farm,
Celbridge, Co. Kildare
Tel: 01 6279666
Fax: 01 6279667

Gale Sports Ulster
5 University Street, Belfast, BT7 IFY
Tel: 028 90246 624
Fax: 028 90246 936

Golf Digest Ireland
E7 Calmount Office Park,
Ballymount, Dublin 12
Tel: 01 419 9604
Fax: 01 429 3910

The Golfers Guide to Ireland
Portside Media, Portside Business
Centre, East Wall Road, Dublin 3
Tel: 01 836 6102
Fax: 01 836 6131

Gofling
Official Magazine of the Golfing
Union of Ireland
E7 Calmount Office Park,
Ballymount, Dublin 12
Tel: 01 419 9621
Fax: 01 492 3910

Golf Ireland
PO Box 8111, Swords, Dublin 12
Tel: 01 807 8122
Fax: 01 807 8203

Going Places
BES&R Media Ltd, 51 Allen Park
Road, Stillorgan, Co. Dublin
Tel: 01 205 6895
Fax: 01 210 0884

Golden Holidays for the Over 55's
Tudor Journals, 74 Amiens Street,
Dublin 1
Tel: 01 8554382
Fax: 028 9032 3163

Highball Magazine
Ashville Media Group, Apollo
House, Tara Street, Dublin 2
Tel: 01 432 2200
Fax: 01 672 7100

House Hunters in the Sun
Blendon Communications Ltd, The
Harcourt Centre Block, 3 Harcourt
Road, Dublin 2
Tel: 01 418 2222
Fax: 01 418 2234

Ireland at Your Leisure
Ashville Media, Apollo House, Tara
Street, Dublin 2
Tel: 01 432 2200
Fax: 01 672 7100

Irish Country Sports and Country Life
42 Gransha Road, Dundonald,
Belfast, BT16 2HD
Tel: 028 90483 873
Fax: 028 90480 195
E-mail:
info@countrysportsandcountrylife.com
Website:
www.countrysportsandcountrylife.com

The Irish Horse
Irish Farm Centre, Bluebell, Dublin 12
Tel: 01 419 9555
Fax: 01 450 4297

Irish Racing Yearbook
29 Lower Patrick Street, Kilkenny
Tel: 056 776 1504
Fax: 056 776 1510

Irish Rugby Review
PO Box 7992, Dun Laoghaire, Co. Dublin
Tel: 01 284 0137
Fax: 01 284 0137

Irish Runner
PO Box 1227, Dublin 8
Tel: 01 620 0089

Ireland's Equestrian
Mainstream Publications, 140 Thomas Street, Portadown, Co. Armagh, BT62 3BE
Tel: 028 3833 4272
Fax: 028 3835 1046

Ireland's Horse Review
Review Publishing, Garden Street, Ballina, Co. Mayo
Tel: 096 735 55
Fax: 096 720 77

Ireland of the Welcomes
Harmonia Ltd, Rosemount House, Dundrum Road, Dundrum, Dublin 14
Editor: Sean Carberry
Tel: 01 240 5300
E-mail: info@irelandofthewelcomes.com or scarberry@harmonia.ie
Website: www.irelandofthewelcomes.com

More Than 90 Minutes
Celtic FC Supporters Magazine
The Green Room, 137 Crushrod Avenue, Drogheda, Co. Louth
Tel: 01 494 1071

Outsider
Ireland's Outdoor Magazine
20 Fitzwilliam Street Upper, Dublin 2
Tel: 01 6432308
Fax: 01 6432306
E-mail: editor@outsider.ie
Website: www.outsider.ie

Peil
Ladies GAA
Above Board Publishing, 1st Floor, 40-41 Main Street, Arklow, Co. Wicklow
Tel: 0402 228 00
Fax: 0402 228 01

Roadrunner
1b Ring Terrace, Inchicore, Dublin 8
Tel: 01 453 0797
Fax: 01 453 3643

Seascape
Swansea Cork Ferries Magazine
Failte Publications, 32 Kilkerrin Park, Tuam Road, Galway
Tel: 091 758811
Fax: 091 758812

Sports Ireland
Cathedral Building, Middle Street, Galway
Tel: 091 569 158
Fax: 091 569 178

Sub Sea
Ireland's Diving magazine
Irish Underwater Council, 78a Patrick Street, Dun Laoghaire, Co. Dublin
Editor: Marie Grennan
Tel: 01 2844601
Fax: 01 2844602
E-mail: info@cft.ie
Website: www.cft.ie

Total Football Magazine
Midland Building, Whitla Street,
Belfast, BT15 1NH
Tel: 028 90756 112

Travel Extra
6 Sandyford Office Park, Dublin 18
Tel: 01 291 3708
Fax: 01 295 7417

Visitor Days
97 Botanic Avenue, Belfast, BT7 1JN
Tel: 028 90320 088
Fax: 028 90323 163
E-mail: info@tudorjournals.com
Website: www.tudorjournals.com

Visitors Journal
Penton House, 38 Heron Road,
Sydenham Business Park, Belfast,
BT3 9LE
Tel: 028 90457 457
Fax: 028 90456 611

Visitor Magazine
Mac Communications Ltd, Taney
Hall Eglinton Terrace, Dundrum,
Dublin 14
Tel: 01 296 0000
Fax: 01 296 0383

Walking World Ireland
PO Box 9543, Dublin 6
Tel: 01 498 2645
Fax: 01 498 3043

You Boys In Green
7 Marley Villas, Rathfarnham,
Dublin 16
Tel: 086 163 4454

TRADE AND PROFESSIONAL

About Banking
Irish Bankers Federation, Nassau
House, Nassau Street, Dublin 2
Tel: 01 671 5311
Fax: 01 679 6680

Accountancy Ireland
Chartered Accountants House, 47-
49 Pearse Street, Dublin 2
Tel: 01 637 7392
E-mail:
editor@accountancyireland.ie
Website:
www.accountancyireland.ie

Accountancy Plus
9 Ely Place, Dublin 2
Tel: 01 676 7353
Fax: 01 661 2367

**Architecture
Ireland/Architecture Now**
Official Journal of the Royal
Institute of the Architects of Ireland
9 Sandyford Office Park, Sandyford,
Dublin 18
Tel: 01 295 8115
Fax: 01 295 9350
Website: www.architecturenow.ie

**Advanced Manufacturing
Technology**
Unit 13c Wicklow Enterprise Ctr,
The Murrough, Wicklow Town, Co.
Wicklow
Tel: 0404 209 60

Ambulance
Ocean Publishing, 14 Upper
Fitzwilliam Street, Dublin 24
Tel: 01 678 5165
Fax: 01 678 5191

BSNews - Irish Building Service News
Pressline Ltd, Carraig Court,
George's Avenue, Blackrock, Co.
Dublin
Tel: 01 288 5001/2/3
Fax: 01 288 6966

Business and Commerce Newspaper
Editor: Mr. Brian J. Byrne
Tel: 01 6707177
E-mail: bjb@bac.ie
Website: www.bac.ie

Butchershop
IFP Media Ltd, 31 Deansgrange
Road, Blackrock, Co. Dublin
Tel: 01 289 3305
Fax: 01 289 6406

Catering and Licensing Review
Greer Publications, 5B Edgewater
Business Park, Belfast, BT3 9JQ
Tel: 028 90783 200
Fax: 028 90783 210

Checkout
3 Adelaide Street, Dun Laoghaire,
Co. Dublin
Tel: 01 230 0322
Fax: 01 230 0629

The Childcare Directory Ltd
Burnaby Buildings, Church Road,
Greystones, Co. Wicklow
Tel: 01 201 6000
Fax: 01 201 6002

Childrenswear In Ireland Magazine
Futura Communications Ltd, 5 Main
Street, Blackrock, Co. Dublin

Tel: 01 283 6782
Fax: 01 283 6784

CIS Report
Construction Information Services,
8 The Mall, Beacon Court,
Sandyford, Dublin 18
Tel: 01 299 9200
Fax: 01 299 9299

Commercial Interiors of Ireland
Unit F5, The Bymac Centre,
Northwest Business Park, Dublin 15
Tel: 01 822 4477
Fax: 01 822 4485

Construct Ireland
Magazine dedicated exclusively to
sustainable construction in Ireland.
Temple Media Ltd, Blackrock, PO
Box 9688, Co. Dublin
Editor: Jeff Colley
Tel: 01 2107513
Fax: 01 2107512
E-mail: info@constructireland.ie
Website: www.constructireland.ie

Construction
Dyflin Publications Ltd, 99 South
Circular Road, Dublin 8
Tel: 01 416 7923
Fax: 01 416 7901

Construction and Property News
Grattan House, Temple Road,
Blackrock, Co. Dublin
Editor: Maev Martin
Tel: 01 764 2706
Fax: 01 764 2750
Website:
www.constructionandpropertynew
s.com

Constabulary Gazette
39 Boucher Road, Belfast, Co.
Antrim, BT12 6UT
Tel: 028 9066 1091

An Consatoir
Official magazine of the Irish
Defence Forces
40/41 Main Street, Arklow, Co.
Wicklow
Tel: 0402 228 00
Fax: 0402 228 01

**Conveyancing and Property Law
Journal**
Thomson Round Hall, 43
Fitzwilliam Place, Dublin 2
Tel: 01 662 5301
Fax: 01 662 5302

Council Review
Ocean Publishing, 14 Upper
Fitzwilliam Street, Dublin 2
Tel: 01 678 5165
Fax: 01 678 5191

Credit Union News
Silchester Marketing, Dalkey
Business Centre, 17 Castle Street,
Dalkey, Co. Dublin
Tel: 01 285 9111
Fax: 01 285 7823

CU Focus
Magazine of the Irish League of
Credit Unions
ICLU, 33-41 Lower Mount Street,
Dublin 2
Tel: 01 6146700
Fax: 01 6146701
E-mail: info@creditunion.ie
Website: www.creditunion.ie

**Dairy and Food Industries
Magazine**
MJM Publications, No. 7
Ballingarrane, Cahir Road, Clonmel,
Co. Tipperary
Tel: 052 707 67
Fax: 052 239 99

Dairy Ireland
IFP Media, 31 Deansgrange Road,
Blackrock, Co. Dublin
Tel: 01 289 3305
Fax: 01 289 6406

Decision Magazine
Business magazine with controlled
circulation of 5,000 copies to senior
management of Irish corporates.
Dillon Publications Ltd, PO Box
7130, Dublin 18
Editor: Frank Dillon
Tel: 01 2179418 / 086 8241235
E-mail: frank@decisionireland.com
Website: www.decisionireland.com

Drinks Industry Ireland
Louisville Publishing Ltd,
"Louisville", Enniskerry, Co.
Wicklow
Tel: 01 204 6230
Fax: 01 204 6231

Drystock Farmer
9 Lyster Square, Portlaoise, Co.
Laois
Tel: 0502 621 20
Fax: 0502 621 21

Education Matters
Kilcolgan, Co. Galway
Tel: 091 485969
E-mail: info@educationmatters.ie
Website: www.educationmatters.ie

Emergency Services Ireland
Ocean Publishing, 14 Upper
Fitzwilliam Street, Dublin 2
Tel: 01 678 5165
Fax: 01 678 5191

**Environment and Energy
Management**
Food and Drink Business, Unit 51, Park
West Enterprise Centre, Dublin 12
Tel: 01 612 0880
Fax: 01 612 0881

Euro Food and Drink
Ashville Media Group, Apollo House,
Tara Street, Dublin 2
Tel: 01 432 2284
Fax: 01 672 7100

Euro Times
Temple House, Temple Road,
Blackrock, Co. Dublin
Tel: 01 209 1100
Fax: 01 209 1112

Export and Freight Magazine
4 Square Media, The Old Coach
House, 12 Main Street,
Hillsborough, Co. Down, BT23 6AE
Tel: 028 92 688 888
Fax: 028 92 688 866

Extraction Industry Ireland
Mainstream Publications, 139-140
Thomas Street, Portadown, Co.
Armagh
Tel: 028 38 334 272
Fax: 028 38 351 046

Farm and Plant Buyers Guide
Page 7 Media, 3rd Floor, Arena
House, Arena Road, Sandyford
Industrial Estate, Dublin 18

Tel: 01 240 5555
Fax: 01 240 5550

Fire Brigade Journal
Ocean Publishing, 14 Upper
Fitzwilliam Street, Dublin 2
Tel: 01 678 5165
Fax: 01 678 5191

Fleet Car
D'Alton Street, Claremorris, Co.
Mayo
Tel: 094 937 2819
Fax: 094 936 2814

Fleet Journal
Automotive Publications Ltd,
Glencree House, Lanesborough
Road, Roscommon
Tel: 0906 625 676
Fax: 0906 637 410

Fleet Management Magazine
D'Alton Street, Claremorris, Co.
Mayo
Tel: 094 937 2819
Fax: 094 936 2814

Food Service Ireland
Food and Drink Business, Unit 51, Park
West Enterprise Centre, Dublin 12
Tel: 01 612 0880
Fax: 01 612 0881

Food Technology and Packaging
Greer Publications Ltd, 5 Edgewater
Business Park, Belfast Harbour
Estate, Belfast, BT3 9JQ
Tel: 028 90783 200
Fax: 028 90783 210

Footwear in Ireland
Futura Communications Ltd, 5 Main

Street, Blackrock, Co. Dublin
Tel: 01 283 6782
Fax: 01 283 6784

Forage and Nutrition Guide
IFP Media, 31 Deansgrange Road,
Blackrock, Co. Dublin
Tel: 01 289 3305
Fax: 01 289 6406

Forum
Journal of the Irish College of
General Practitioners
MedMedia Group, 25 Adelaide
Street, Dun Laoghaire, Co. Dublin
Tel: 01 280 3967
Fax: 01 280 7076

Franchise Options
Mount Media Ltd, 45 Upper Mount
Street, Dublin 2
Tel: 01 661 1660
Fax: 01 661 1632
E-mail: info@franchiseoptions.ie
Website: www.franchiseoptions.ie

Futura Magazine
Futura Communications Ltd, 5 Main
Street, Blackrock, Co. Dublin
Tel: 01 283 6782
Fax: 01 283 6784

Garage Trader
5B Edgewater Business Park,
Belfast Harbour Estate, Belfast, BT3
9JQ
Editor: Pat Burns
Tel: 028 9078 3200
Fax: 028 9078 3210
E-mail:
patburns@greerpublications.com
Website:
www.greerpublications.com

Garda Review
Garda Review, Floor 5, Phibsboro
Tower, Dublin 7
Editor: Neil Ward
Tel: 01 8303533
Fax: 01 8303331
E-mail: editor@gardareview.com
Website: www.gardareview.ie

Garda Times
Ashville Media Group, 57-59
Longboat Quay, Sir John Rogerson's
Quay, Dublin 2
Tel: 01 432 2200
Fax: 01 672 7100

Garda Voice
Concept Publications Ltd, Unit B2
Riverside Business Park, New
Nangor Road, Dublin 12
Tel: 01 456 8453
Fax: 01 456 8454

Guide to Industrial Estates
Mainstream Publications, 139-140
Thomas Street, Portadown, Co.
Armagh
Tel: 028 38 334 272
Fax: 028 38 351 046

Hairdressing Career and Training
MOHH Publishing, PO Box 28 An
Post Mail Centre, Coosan, Athlone,
Co. Westmeath
Tel: 0906 477 418

Handling Network
Magazine devoted to all aspects of
the materials handling, storage and
distribution industry in Ireland
15 Putland Road, Bray, Co. Dublin
Tel: 01 286 3963
E-mail: info@handling-

network.com
Website: www.handling-
network.com

Health and Safety Review
IRN Publishing, 121-123 Ranelagh
Road, Dublin 6
Tel: 01 497 2711
Fax: 01 497 2779

Health and Safety Times
Ocean Publishing, 14 Upper
Fitzwilliam Street, Dublin 2
Tel: 01 678 5165
Fax: 01 678 5191

Health Manager
The Magazine of the Health
Management Institute of Ireland
Dyflin Media, Cunningham House,
130 Francis Street, Dublin 8
Editor: Maureen Browne
Tel: 01 416 7905
Fax: 01 416 7901
E-mail: hmieditor@dyflin.ie

Hospital Doctor
Eireann Healthcare Publications, 25
Windsor Place, Dublin 2
Tel: 01 475 3300
Fax: 01 475 3311

Hospitality Review NI
5B Edgewater Business Park,
Belfast Harbour Estate, Belfast, BT3
9BW
Editor: Emma Cowan
Tel: 028 9078 3200
Fax: 028 9078 3210
E-mail:
emma.cowan@btinternet.com
Website:
www.greerpublications.com

Hospitality Ireland
Madison Publications, 3 Adelaide
Street, Dun Laoghaire, Co. Dublin
Tel: 01 236 5880
Fax: 01 230 0325

Hotel and Catering Review
Grattan House, Temple Road,
Blackrock, Co. Dublin, Ireland
Editor: Sarah Grennan
Tel: 01 764 2704
Fax: 01 764 2750
Website:
www.hotelandcateringreview.ie

Hotel and Restaurant Times
H & R House, Carton Court,
Maynooth, Co. Kildare
Tel: 01 628 5447
Fax: 01 628 5447

House and Home
The Irish Interiors Magazine
Dyflin Publications Ltd,
Cunningham House, 130 Francis
Street, Dublin 8
Editor: Eimear Nic an Bhaird
Tel: 01 416 7900
E-mail: eimear@houseandhome.ie
Website: www.houseandhome.ie

**HR and Recruitment Ireland
Magazine**
10 Rathgar Road, Rathmines, Dublin 6
Tel: 01 498 3242
Fax: 01 498 3217

IICM Newsletter
Irish Institute of Credit
Management, c/o Denshaw House,
121 Lower Baggot Street, Dublin 2
Tel: 01 676 7822
Fax: 01 639 1122

Industrial and Manufacturing Engineer
5B Edgewater Business Park,
Belfast Harbour Estate, Belfast, BT3 9JQ
Editor: David Elliott
Tel: 028 9078 3200
Fax: 028 9078 3210
E-mail:
davidelliott@greerpublications.com
Website:
www.greerpublications.com

Industrial Relations News (IRN)
IRN Publishing, 123 Ranelagh,
Dublin 6
Tel: 01 497 2711
Fax: 01 497 2779

Inside Government
19 Irishtown Road, Ringsend,
Dublin 4
Tel: 01 231 3593
Fax: 01 667 7752

Intouch
Irish National Teacher's
Organisation, 35 Parnell Square,
Dublin 1
Tel: 01 872 9890
Fax: 01 872 2462

IPA Journal
The International Police Assocation
- Irish section
Concept Publications Ltd, Unit B2
Riverside Business Park, New
Nangor Road, Dublin 12
Tel: 01 456 8453
Fax: 01 456 8454
Website: www.ipaireland.com

IPS Magazine
International Purchasing and
Supply
12 Mountjoy Square, Dublin 1
Tel: 041 987 3213

I.P.U. Review
Journal of the Irish Pharmacy Union
Butterfield House, Butterfield
Avenue, Rathfarnham, Dublin 14
Tel: 01 4936401
Fax: 01 4936407
E-mail: ipurev@ipu.ie
Website: www.ipu.ie

Ireland's Forecourt and Convenience Retailer
Penton Publications Ltd, 38 Heron
Road, Sydenham Business Park,
Belfast, BT3 9LE
Tel: 028 9045 7457
Fax: 028 9045 6611

Ireland's Horse Trader
Mainstream Publications, 140
Thomas Street, Portadown, Co.
Armagh, BT62 3BE
Tel: 028 3833 4272
Fax: 028 3835 1 046

Ireland's Transport Journal Export and Freight
The Mill House, 12 Main Street,
Hillsborough, Co. Down, BT26 6AE
Tel: 028 9268 8888
Fax: 028 9268 8866

Irish Bodyshop Journal
Automotive Publications Ltd,
Glencree House, Lanesborough
Road, Roscommon
Tel: 0906 625 676
Fax: 0906 637 410

Irish Broker
Holyrood Publications, 136
Baldoyle Industrial Estate, Baldoyle,
Dublin 13
Tel: 01 839 5060
Fax: 01 839 5062

Irish Building Magazine
1 Windsor Mews, Summerhill
Parade, Sandycover, Co. Dublin
Tel: 01 280 6030
Fax: 01 284 632

Irish Construction Industry Magazine
Idrone Mews, 24 Idrone Lane,
Blackrock, Co. Dublin
Tel: 01 283 3233
Fax: 01 283 3044

Irish Dentist
Website: www.irishdentist.ie

Irish Electrical Review
Sky Publishing Ltd, 5 Main Street,
Blackrock, Co. Dublin
Tel: 01 283 6755
Fax: 01 283 6784

Irish Engineers Journal
IFP Media Ltd, 31 Deansgrange
Road, Blackrock, Co. Dublin
Tel: 01 289 3305
Fax: 01 289 6406

Irish Engineers Journal
IFP Media Ltd, 31 Deansgrange
Road, Blackrock, Co. Dublin
Tel: 01 289 3305
Fax: 01 289 6406

Irish Farmer's Monthly
IFP Media Ltd, 31 Deansgrange

Road, Blackrock, Co. Dublin
Tel: 01 289 3305
Fax: 01 289 6406

Irish Food
IFP Media Ltd, 31 Deansgrange
Road, Blackrock, Co. Dublin
Tel: 01 289 3305
Fax: 01 289 6406

Irish Gift Retailer
Premier Publishing, 51 Park West
Enterprise Centre, Nangor Road,
Dublin 12
Tel: 01 612 0880
Fax: 01 612 0881

Irish Hairdresser
MOHH Publishing, PO Box 28, An
Post Mail Centre, Coosan, Athlone,
Co. Westmeath
Tel: 0906 477 418

Irish Hardware
Grattan House, Temple Road,
Blackrock, Co. Dublin, Ireland
Editor: Martin Foran
Tel: 01 764 2702
Website: www.irishhardware.com

Irish Journal of Medical Science
Royal Academy of Medicine in
Ireland, 2nd Floor, International
House, 20-22 Lower Hatch Street,
Dublin 2
Tel: 01 661 1684
Fax: 01 661 6684

Irish Journal of Psychological Medicine
MedMedia Ltd, 25 Adelaide Street,
Dun Laoghaire, Co. Dublin
Tel: 01 280 3967
Fax: 01 280 7076

Irish Medical Device Manufacturing and Technology Reference / Buyers Guide
Advance Publications Ltd, Acorn House, 38 St Peters Road, Phibsboro, Dublin 7
Tel: 01 868 6640
Fax: 01 868 6651

Irish Medical Journal
Irish Medical Organisation, IMO House, 10 Fitzwilliam Place, Dublin 2
Tel: 01 676 7273
Fax: 01 661 2758

Irish Medical News
Mac Communications Ltd, Taney Hall, Eglinton Tarrace, Dundrum, Dublin 14
Tel: 01 296 0000
Fax: 01 296 0380

Irish Medical Times
Medical Publications Ireland, 24-26 Upper Ormond Quay, Dublin 7
Editor: Terence Cosgrave
Tel: 01 8176341
E-mail: editor@imt.ie
Website: www.imt.ie

Irish Motor Management
IFP Media Ltd, 31 Deansgrange Road, Blackrock, Co. Dublin
Tel: 01 289 3305
Fax: 01 289 6406

Irish Pensions
Irish Association of Pension Funds (IAPF), Suite 2, Slane House, 25 Lower Mount Street, Dublin 2
Tel: 01 661 2427
Fax: 01 662 1196

Irish Pharmacy Journal
2 Lower Glenageary Road, Dun Laoghaire, Co. Dublin
Tel: 01 284 6161
Fax: 01 284 6192

Irish Pharmacist
Eireann Healthcare Publications, 25 Windsor Place, Dublin 2
Tel: 01 475 3300
Fax: 01 475 3311

Irish Practice Nurse
Eireann Health Care Publications, 25-26 Windsor Place, Dublin 2
Tel: 01 475 3300
Fax: 01 475 3311

Irish Printer
Grattan House, Temple Road, Blackrock, Co. Dublin
Editor: Grainne Burns
Tel: 01 764 2703
Website: www.irishprinter.ie

Irish Psychiatrist
Eireann Healthcare Publications, 25 Windsor Place, Dublin 2
Tel: 01 475 3300
Fax: 01 475 3311

The Irish Skipper
Annagry, Co. Donegal
Editor: John Rafferty
Tel: 074 956 2843
E-mail: skippereditor@iol.ie
Website: www.irishskipper.net

Irish Tax Review
Irish Taxation Institute, 19 Sandymount Avenue, Dublin 4
Tel: 01 668 8222
Fax: 01 668 8387

Irish Travel Trade News
Belgrave Group Ltd, A12 Calmount
Park, Ballymount, Dublin 12
Tel: 01 450 2422
Fax: 01 450 2954

Irish Van and Truck
Whelan Byrne Associates, 2
Sunbury, Kilcullen, Co. Kildare
Tel: 045 481 090

Irish Veterinary Journal
IFP Media Ltd, 31 Deansgrange
Road, Blackrock, Co. Dublin
Tel: 01 289 3305
Fax: 01 289 6406

Iris Oifigiúil
Government Publications, Unit 20,
Lakeside Retail Park, Claremorris,
Co. Mayo
Tel.: 01 6476636
Fax: 01 6476843 or 094 9378964
E-mail: info@irisoifigiuil.ie
Website: www.irisoifigiuil.ie

Journal of the Irish Dental Association
IFP Media, 31 Deansgrange Road,
Blackrock, Co. Dublin
Tel: 01 289 3305
Fax: 01 289 7546

Keystone
Magazine for the construction and
design industry
Flagship Media, 48-50 York Street,
Belfast, BT15 1AS
Tel: 028 90319 008
Fax: 028 90727 800

Kitchen Retailer Ireland
Editor: Judith Robinson Lyttle

E-mail:
judith@bayviewpublishing.net
Website:
www.bayviewpublishing.net

Law Society Gazette
Blackhall Place, Dublin 7
Editor: Mark McDermott
Tel: 01 672 4828
Fax: 01 672 4877
E-mail: gazette@lawsociety.ie
Website: www.lawsociety.ie

Licensed and Catering News
Ulster Magazines Ltd, 8 Lowes
Industrial Estate, 31 Ballynahinch
Road Carryduff, Belfast, BT8 8EH
Tel: 028 9081 5656
Fax: 028 9081 7481

Licensing World
Grattan House, Temple Road,
Blackrock, Co. Dublin
Editor: Nigel Tynan
Tel: 01 764 2700
Fax: 01 764 2750
Website: www.licensingworld.ie

Local Authority Times
Institute of Public Administration,
57-61 Lansdowne Road,
Ballsbridge, Dublin 4
Tel: 01 240 3600
Fax: 01 668 9135

Manufacturing Ireland
Advance Publications Ltd (APL),
Acorn House, 38 St Peters Road,
Phibsboro, Dublin 7
Tel: 01 868 6640
Fax: 01 868 6651

Marine Times
Cranny Road, Inver, Co. Donegal
Editor: Mark Mc Carthy
Tel: 074 9736899 / 9732635
Fax: 074 9736958
E-mail: marinetimes@eircom.net
Website: www.marinetimes.ie

Marketing News
Quarterly Magazine of the
Marketing Institute
Mercury Media, 13 Meadow Court,
Stepaside Park, Dublin 18
Tel: 01 294 5847

Medico-Legal Journal
Round Hall Ltd, 43 Fitzwilliam
Place, Dublin 2
Tel: 01 662 5301
Fax: 01 662 5302

MIMS Ireland
Medical Publications Ireland, 24-26
Upper Ormond Quay, Dublin 7
Editor: Marie-Catherine Mousseau
Tel: 01 8176322
E-mail: marie-
catherine.mousseau@mims.ie
Website: www.imt.ie/mims

Modern Medicine
Eireann Healthcare Publications, 25
Windsor Place, Dublin 2
Tel: 01 475 3300
Fax: 01 475 3311

Mortgage Magazine
Mortgage Magazine, 5 Clarendon
Mews, Lad Lane, Dublin 2
Tel: 01 250 0050
Fax: 01 250 0087

Neighbourhood Retailer
Penton Publications Ltd, 38 Heron
Road, Sydenham Business Park,
Belfast, BT3 9LE
Tel: 028 9045 7457
Fax: 028 9045 6611

Northern Builder
Unit 22, Lisburn Enterprise Centre,
Ballinderry Road, Lisburn, Co.
Antrim, BT28 2BP
Tel: 028 9266 3390
Fax: 028 9266 6242

Northern Ireland Medicine Today
Penton Publications Ltd, 38 Heron
Road, Sydenham Business Park,
Belfast, BT3 9LE
Tel: 028 9045 7457
Fax: 028 9045 6611

Nursing in the Community
MedMedia Group, 25 Adelaide
Street, Dun Laoghaire, Co. Dublin
Tel: 01 280 3967
Fax: 01 280 7076

Off Licence Magazine
Jemma Publications Ltd, Grattan
House, Temple Road, Blackrock, Co.
Dublin
Tel: 01 764 2700
Fax: 01 764 2750

Offshore Investment
Lombard House, 10-20 Lombard
Street, Belfast, BT1 1BW
Tel: 028 9032 8777
Fax: 028 9032 8555

Painting Today
73 Iona Road, Glasnevin, Dublin 9
Tel: 01 8162941
Fax: 01 8302921

Perspective
Journal of the Royal Society of
Ulster Architects.
Ulster Journals Ltd, 39 Boucher
Road, Belfast BT12 6UT
Tel: 028 9032 3760
Fax: 028 9023 7313
E-mail:
perspective.rsua@btconnect.com
Website: www.rsua.org.uk

Plan Magazine
Quantum House, Temple Road,
Blackrock, Co. Dublin
Editor: Denise Maguire
Tel: 01 7642421
E-mail: denise@planmagazine.ie
Website: www.planmagazine.ie

Plant and Civil Engineer
4 Square Media, The Old Coach
House, 12 Main Street,
Hillsborough, Co. Down, BT26 6AE
Tel: 028 9268 8888
Fax: 028 9268 8866

Plant and Machinery Magazine
Jemma Publications Ltd, Grattan
House, Temple Road, Blackrock, Co.
Dublin
Tel: 01 7642700
Fax: 01 7642750

Plantman Magazine
1 The Green, Kingswood Heights,
Dublin 24
Tel: 01 4520898
Fax: 01 4520898

**Plumbing and Heating In
Northern Ireland**
140 Thomas Street, Portadown, Co.
Armagh, BT62 3BE

Tel: 028 3839 2000
Fax: 028 3835 1046

Primary Times
Website: www.primarytimes.net

The Property Professional
Design Room, Salamander Lodge,
Ranelagh, Dublin 6
Tel: 01 4979022
Fax: 01 4977097

The Property Valuer
38 Merrion Square, Dublin 2
Tel: 01 6611794
Fax: 01 6611797

Public Sector Times
5 Eglinton Road, Bray, Co. Wicklow
Tel: 01 2869111
E-mail: shay@localtimes.ie

Retail Grocer
Ulster Magazines Ltd, 8 Lowes
Industrial Estate, 31 Ballynahinch
Road Carryduff, Belfast, BT8 8EH
Tel: 028 9081 5656
Fax: 028 9081 7481

Retail Intelligence
Adelaide Hall, 3 Adelaide Street,
Dun Laoghaire, Co. Dublin
Tel: 01 230 0322
Fax: 01 230 0629

Retail News
Poolbeg House, 1-2 Poolbeg Street,
Dublin 2
Tel: 01 2413095
Fax: 01 2413010

Risk Manager
Rosebank Media, First Floor, 72

Tyrconnel Road, Inchicore, Dublin 8
Tel: 01 4163678
Fax: 01 4534121

Salon Ireland Magazine
Voyager House, Block H2,
Centrepoint Business Park, Oak
Road, Dublin 12
Tel: 01 4604985
Fax: 01 4097952

Seanda
Archaelogy magazine of the
National Roads Authority
NRA, St Martin's House, Waterloo
Road, Dublin 4
Website: www.nra.ie/archaeology
(PDF versions available)

SelfBuild Extend and Renovate
SelfBuild Ireland Ltd, 96 Lisburn
Road, Saintfield, Co. Down, BT24
7BP
Tel: 028 9751 0570

ShelfLife
Mediateam Ltd, Media House, South
County Business Park,
Leopardstown, Dublin 18
Editor: Fionnuala Carolan
Tel: 01 2947768
E-mail:
fionnualacarolan@mediateam.ie
Website: www.shelflife.ie

Shoptalk
Cunningham House, 130 Francis
Street, Dublin 8
Tel: 01 4167956
Fax: 01 4167901

Signal
RACO - Representative Association

of Commissioned Officers
Ashville Media Group, Appolo
House, Tara Street, Dublin2
Tel: 01 4322200
Fax: 01 6727100

Spa Ireland Magazine
Voyager House, Block H2,
Centrepoint Business Park, Oak
Road, Dublin 12
Tel: 01 4604985
Fax: 01 4097952

Specify
Northern Ireland's Construction
Magazine
5B Edgewater Business Park,
Belfast Harbour Estate, Belfast, BT3
9JQ
Editor: Emma Cowan
Tel: 028 9078 3200
Fax: 028 9078 3210
E-mail:
emma.cowan@btinternet.com
Website:
www.greerpublications.com

Stubbs Gazette
BusinessPro, 23 South Frederick
Street, Dublin 2
Tel: 01 6725939

Today's Farm
Irish Farm Centre, Bluebell, Dublin 12
Tel: 01 419 9556
Fax: 01 4504297

Today's Grocery Magazine
The Mews, Eden Road Upr, Dun
Laoghaire, Co. Dublin
Tel: 01 2809466
Fax: 01 2806896

Tyre Trade Journal
Automotive Publications Ltd,
Glencree House, Lanesborough
Road, Roscommon
Tel: 0906 625676
Fax: 0906 625636

UCD Connections
UCD University Relations Alumni
and Development, Tierney Building,
Belfield, Dublin 4
Tel: 01 7161447
Fax: 01 7161160

Ulster Architect
Jemma Publications (Northern
Ireland) Ltd, 182 Ravenhill Road,
Belfast, BT6 8EE
Tel: 028 9073 1636
Fax: 028 9045 9829

Ulster Grocer
5B Edgewater Business Park,
Belfast Harbour Estate, Belfast, BT3
9JQ
Editor: Kathy Jensen
Tel: 028 9078 3200
Fax: 028 9078 3210
E-mail:
kathyjensen@greerpublications.com
Website:
www.greerpublications.com

United News
Membership magazine of United
Dairy Farmers Ltd
5B Edgewater Business Park,
Belfast Harbour Estate, Belfast BT3
9JQ
Editor: Anne McLaughlin
Tel: 028 9078 3200
Fax: 028 9078 3210
E-mail:
anne.mclaughlin@UTDNI.co.uk

Veterinary Today
Penton Publications Ltd, 38 Heron
Road, Sydenham Business Park,
Belfast, BT3 9LE
Tel: 028 9045 7457
Fax: 028 9045 6611

VFI Update Magazine
Vintners Federation of Ireland, 25
Dawson Street, Dublin 2
Tel: 01 6705866
Fax: 01 6705866

The World of Irish Nursing
MedMedia Group, 25 Adelaide
Street, Dun Laoghaire, Co. Dublin
Tel: 01 2803967
Fax: 01 2807076

I. Writers Support Services

The Author's Friend
c/o 52 Cardiffsbridge Avenue, Finglas, Dublin 11. Tel: 01 8569566 or 087 7604547. Website: www.the authorsfriend.com. E-mail: info@theauthorsfriend.com. Contact: Oscar Duggan (General Manager). Assisted publishing service for writers of all genres - fiction, non-fiction, childrens, poetry, family memoirs, local history, community news etc. Manuscript preparation and editorial services; printing and binding options; publishing assistance including copyright protection, ISBN and legal deposit; sales, marketing and promotion of the finished product - a quality produced book.

Averill Buchanan
20 Loopland Gardens, Belfast BT6 9ED, N. Ireland. Tel:028 90503449. 07875 857278. E-mail: averill@averillbuchanan.com. Website: www.averillbuchanan.com. Editor, proofreader, writer, indexer Member of the AFEPI, SfEP and the Society of Indexers.

Beta Printing Services
Long Meadow, Moortown, Ratoath, Co. Meath. Contact: Ray Lynn. Tel: 01 8259609 / 087 2563702. E-mail: betaprintingservices@gmail.com. Specialise in producing books. Offers a design and printing service for books including brokerage services to publishers and authors.

Choice Publishing
Unit 12a, Boyne Business Park, Greenhills, Drogheda, Co. Louth. Tel: 041 9841551. Website: www.choicepublishing.ie E-mail: info@choicepublishing.ie. Website: www.choicepublishing.ie

The Creative Writer's Workshop
Kinvara, Co. Galway. Tel: 086 2523428. E-mail: creativewriting@ireland.com (writing workshops). Websites: www.TheCreativeWritersWorkshop.com. The Creative Writer's Workshop offers Residential Writing Retreats and LIVE, interactive, online workshops in memoir and fiction writing.

Documents and Manuscripts.com
E-mail: info@documentsandmanuscripts.com. Website: www.DocumentsandManuscripts.com. The online office assistant. For all your layout, design and presentation needs. Manuscript preparation and book-setting services available. Also specialise in web design, campaign management and cloud computing services.

Dominic Carroll
Ballynoe, Dunowen, Ardfield, Clonakilty, Co. Cork. Tel: 023 8840881. E-mail: dominic@iol.ie. Copy-editor, proofreader, indexer, typesetter, designer, rewriter, project manager, publisher

Eagle Eyes Editing
Contact: Mary McElroy. Tel: 087 6876204. E-mail: mcelroym@vodafone.ie. Website: www.eagleeyesediting.ie. Copywriter, rewriter and proof-reader for books, manuscripts, documents, reports, etc. Specialises in Website Content Management Services - copywriting, reviewing, cross-checking. Search Engine Optimisation (SEO) services also available.

E-book Producers.com
E-mail: info@e-bookproducers.com. Website: www.e-bookproducers.com. Electronic publishing services. Produces, markets and sells e-books.

Inkwell Writer's Workshops
Tel: 01-2765921 / 087 2835382. E-mail: info@inkwellwriters.ie. Website: www.inkwellwriters.ie. Scouts for leading Irish literary agents and publishers. Provide critiquing and editorial services.

Maighread Medbh
George's Square, Balbriggan, Co. Dublin. Tel: 01 8704401. Fax: 01 8411128. E-mail: maighreadmedbh@gmail.com. Website: www.maighreadmedbh.ie. Poet and prose writer who gives workshops in poetry and creative writing generally, for children 10+ and adults.

The Memoir Writing Club
Kinvara, Co. Galway. Tel: 086 2523428. E-mail: office@thememoirwritingclub.com. Website: www.The MemoirWritingClub.com. Encourages individuals to form memoir writing clubs in their local area, to write and share their life experiences, using The Memoir Writing Workbook as their guide.

Mitchell Design
Co. Wicklow. Contact: Shanon Mitchell-O'Bracken, Graphic Designer. E-mail: mitchell.obracken@gmail.com.

MMW DESIGN
13 Hollybank Avenue Upper, Ranelagh, Dublin 6. Contact: Martine Maguire-Weltecke, Graphic Designer / Typesetter. Tel: 01 4974720 / 087 4198849. E-mail: martine@mmw-design.com / info@academic-typesetting.com. Websites: www.mmw-design.com / www.academic-typesetting.com

Original Writing
Spade Enterprise Centre, North King Street, Smithfield, Dublin 7. Tel: 01 617 4834. E-mail: info@originalwriting.ie. Website: www.originalwriting.ie.

An Scríbhneoir
Ríomhphost: anscribhneoir@gmail.com. Suíomh Gréasáin: www.anscribhneoir.ie. Seirbhísí foilsitheoireachta cuidithe as Gaeilge don údar, do scríbhneoirí agus d'fhilí.

Signature Publishing Solutions
Milltown, Dingle, Co. Kerry. Contact: Peter Malone, editor. Tel: 066 9152377 / 086 8506870. E-mail: petermalone@eircom.net. Peter Malone has 25 years of experience in publishing and media. Editor at Brandon for several years, he subsequently edited and produced books for O'Brien, Mercier, Wolfhound, Merlin and Irish Academic Press, as well as internet publishers Guru Books. He has worked with well-known and more especially new writers. He offers authors a full range of editorial supports, from initial editorial assessment through all stages of copy-editing, design and publishing. Signature produces books, magazines, newsletters and reports for individuals, social groups, businesses and associations.

The Writers' Consultancy
The Farmhouse, Dooneen, Upper Kinsale, Co. Cork. Tel: 087 1231274. E-mail: info@writersconsultancy.ie. The Writers' Consultancy is a literary consultancy working for writers in Ireland. It provides professional critical assessment, together with market-aware editorial advice, to authors writing in English at any stage in their development.

The Writers Friend
E-mail: info@thewritersfriend.info. Website: www.thewritersfriend.info. Training and Education courses through our associated division The Writers' Study. Publishing advice for for both individual authors and collective projects, anthologies etc. Web Services for writers groups to help co-ordinate activities among your membership.

The Written Word
E-mail: thewrittenwordservices@gmail.com. Website: www.thewrittenword.ie. Ghost-writing services for clubs, associations, corporations and individuals.

J. Bookshops and Book Distributors

ONLINE BOOKSHOPS

Audiobooks.ie
Unit 9 Coolmine Ind Est, Dublin 15.
Tel: 01 4404030 and 01 8237646

books4multilinguals.com
8 Oldcourt Avenue, Dublin 24.
Tel: 01 4148374

Directebooks.com
The Rubicon Centre, CIT Campus,
Bishopstown, Co. Cork.
Contact: Gareth Cuddy, Managing
Director
Tel: 021 4928950
E-mail: info@directebooks.com
Websites: www.directebooks.com /
www.digitalpublishing.ie

Kennys Bookshop and Art Galleries
Liosbán Retail Park, Tuam Road,
Galway, Ireland.
Tel: 091 709350
Fax: 091 709351
E-mail: books@kennys.ie
Website: www.kennys.ie

Michael Doherty School Supplies Ltd
U6A Greenhills Road Industrial
Estate, Tallaght Dublin 24.
Website: www.schoolbookshop.ie

Schoolbooks.ie
Davitt Road, Inchicore, Dublin 12 .
Tel: 01 4600084
Website: www.schoolbooks.ie

Schoolbooks4u.ie
Malones Bookshop, Wicklow Town.
Tel: 0404 68150
Website: www.schoolbooks4u.ie

Special Stories Publishing
Drogheda, Co. Louth.
Tel: 087 2973333
Website: www.specialstories.ie

Totalonlinepurchase.com
Barndarrig, Kilbride, Co. Wicklow.
Tel: 087 1225200
Website:
www.totalonlinepurchase.com

COUNTY CARLOW

Wordplay
U5 Kennedy Avenue, Carlow, Co.
Carlow
Tel: 059 9139920

COUNTY CAVAN

Cavan Book Centre
Main Street, Cavan Town
Tel: 049 4362882

COUNTY CLARE

Scéal Eile Books
16 Lower Market Street, Ennis, Co.
Clare. Contact: Éibhleann Ní
Ghríofa, Gerald Griffey, Proprietors.
Tel: 065 6848648.
E-mail: scealeilebooks@gmail.com.
Website: www.scealeilebooks.ie.

COUNTY CORK

Bantry Book Shop
Bridge Street, Bantry, Co. Cork.
Tel: 027 55946

Chapter One
Main Street, Schull, Co. Cork.
Tel: 028 27606

Clonakilty Bookshop
12 Pearse Street, Clonakilty, Co.
Cork.
Tel: 023 33661

Cork Bookshop Limited
Unit 18 Douglas Village Shopping
Centre Douglas, Cork.
Tel: 021 4364122

Coughlan Laurence Book Shop
11 Rossa Street, Clonakilty, Co.
Cork.
Tel: 023 33068

Dervish
50 Cornmarket Street, Cork.
Tel: 021 4278243

Eason and Son Ltd
113/115 Patrick Street, Cork,
Tel: 021 427 0477
Fax: 021 427 2681
E-mail: cork@easons.com

Eason and Son Ltd
Unit 10/11 Ballincollig Town
Centre, Ballincollig, Co. Cork.
Tel: 021 482 6388
Fax: 021 482 6389
E-mail: ballincollig@easons.com

Eason and Son Ltd
Unit 14/15 Mahon Shopping
Centre, Mahon, Cork.
Tel: 021 4972010
Fax: 021 4972011
E-mail: mahon@easons.com

Forum Publications
23 Washington Street, Cork.
Tel: 021 4270500

Hickey's Bandon
1 South Main Street, Bandon, Co.
Cork
Tel: 023 41176

Hippo Fun
Riverpark House, Marine
Commercial Park Centre, Park Road,
Cork.
Tel: 021 4899591

Hyland's Educational Book Shop
22 Lower Cork Street,
Mitchelstown, Co. Cork.
Tel: 025 24528

J & K Schoolbooks
2 Cross Street, Cork.
Tel: 021 4274255

John Smiths Bookshop
Student Centre UCC.
Tel: 021 4902206

Kanturk Book Shop
Strand Street, Kanturk, Co. Cork.
Tel: 029 20851

Karen Millward
Coorycommane, Coomhola, Bantry,
Co. Cork.
Tel: 027 53898

Macroom Book Shop
West Square, Macroom, Co. Cork.
Tel: 026 41888

Mainly Murder Bookstore
2A Paul Street, Cork.
Tel: 021 4272413

Mercier Bookshop
18 Academy Street, Cork.
Tel: 021 4275040

Midleton Books
103 Main Street, Midleton, Co. Cork.
Tel: 021 4633063

O'Donovan's Book Shop
35 Main Street, Cork.
Tel: 028 21279

Philips Bookshop
34 Bank Place, Mallow, Co. Cork.
Tel: 022 42471

Ruiseal Liam Teo
49/50 Oliver Plunkett Street, Cork.
Tel: 021 4270981

Schull Books
Ballydehob, Co. Cork
Tel: 028 37317
E-mail: schullbooks@eircom.net
Website: www.schullbooks.net

The Shelf Bookshop
12 Georges Quay, Cork.
Tel: 021 4312264

Uneeda Bookshop
71 Oliver Plunkett Street, Cork.
Tel: 021 4270899

Walnut Books
12 Wellington Square, Cork City.
Tel: 021 4340348

Waterstone's Booksellers
69 Patrick Street, Cork.
Tel: 021 4276522

Yawl Books
Unit 6 North Main Street, Youghal,
Co. Cork.
Tel: 024 25805

DONEGAL

A Novel Idea
Castle Street, Ballyshannon, Co.
Donegal.
Tel: 071 9858124

Books and Charts
Dungloe, Co. Donegal.
Tel: 074 9522077

Books Direct
Letterkenny Shopping Centre, Port
Road, Letterkenny, Co. Donegal.
Tel: 074 9129960

Four Masters Book Shop
The Diamond, Donegal, Co. Donegal.
Tel: 074 9721526

Veritas Bookshop
13 Main Street, Letterkenny, Co.
Donegal.
Tel: 074 9124814

COUNTY DUBLIN

A Twist In The Tail Limited
Powerscourt Town Cntr, Dublin 18.
Tel: 01 6709946

Abacus Books
19 Park Villas Castleknock, Dublin
15.
Tel: 086 1944939

Alan Hanna's Bookshop
270 Rathmines Road, Dublin 6.
Tel: 01 4967398

America's Best Books
15 Dawson Street, Dublin 2.
Tel: 01 6777570

Book Worms
75 Middle Abbey Street, Dublin 1.
Tel: 01 8735772

Books Now
The Ashleaf Shopping Centre,
Dublin 12.
Tel: 01 4650346

Books On The Green
2 Seafort ave Sandymount Village,
Dublin 4.
Tel: 01 2837909

Books Unlimited
141 Blanchardstown Shopping
Centre, Dublin 15.
Tel: 01 8222182

Books Upstairs
36 College Green, Dublin 2
Tel: 01 6796687

Books Upstairs
U25 Omnipark Shopping Centre,
Dublin 9.
Tel: 01 8421210

The Campus Bookshop
University College Dublin, Belfield,
Dublin 4.
Tel: 01 2691384

Cathedral Books Ltd
4 Sackville Place, Dublin 1.
Tel: 01 8745284

Celtic Publications
Malahide, Co. Dublin.
Tel: 086 3701160

Chapters Bookstore
108/109 Middle Abbey Street,
Dublin 1.
Tel: 01 8723297

Christian Publication Centre
110 Middle Abbey Street, Dublin 1.
Tel: 01 8726754

Clarendon Medical Ltd
43 Clarendon Street, Dublin 2.
Tel: 01 6793693

De Búrca Rare Books
51 Dawson Street, Dublin 2.
Contact: Éamonn and Vivien De
Búrca (proprietors)
Tel: 01 6719609
Website:
www.deburcararebooks.com

Dubray Books
36 Grafton Street Dublin 2

Dubray Books
Dun Laoire Shopping Centre, Co.
Dublin.

Dubray Books
Blackrock Shopping Centre,
Blackrock Co. Dublin.

Dubray Books
Swan Shopping Centre, Rathmines,
Dublin 6.

Dubray Books
Stillorgan Shopping Centre, Co.
Dublin.

Dundrum Books
100 Rathgar Road, Dublin 6.
Tel: 01 4928600

Eason and Son Ltd
40 O'Connell Street Lower, Dublin 1
Tel: 01 858 3800
Fax: 01 858 3806
E-mail: info@eason.ie

Eason and Son Ltd
5 Upper Georges Street, Dun
Laoghaire Co. Dublin.
Tel: 01 280 5528
Fax: 01 284 2728
E-mail: dunlaoghaire@easons.com

Eason and Son Ltd
Blanchardstown Shopping Centre,
Dublin 15
Tel: 01 822 1117
Fax: 01 822 1153
E- mail:
blanchardstown@easons.com

Eason and Son Ltd
Busaras Central Bus Station,

Beresford Place, Dublin 1.
Tel: 01 8781149
Fax: 01 8781149
E-mail: busaras@easons.com

Eason and Son Ltd
Unit 12 14, Dundrum Town Centre,
Sandyford Road, Dublin 14.
Tel: 01 216 9160
Fax: 01 216 9161
E-mail: dundrum@easons.com

Eason and Son Ltd
Irish Life Centre Talbot Street,
Dublin 1.
Tel: 01 8727010
Fax: 01 8745487
E-mail: talbot@easons.com

Eason and Son Ltd
Liffey Valley Shopping Centre,
Clondalkin, Dublin 22.
Tel: 01 626 1040
Fax: 01 626 1083
E-mail: liffeyv@easons.com

Eason and Son Ltd
New Ashbourne Town Centre,
Killegland Court, Ashbourne Co.
Dublin.
Tel: 01 8359117
Fax: 01 8359170
Email:
ashbourne@easonfranchise.com

Eason and Son Ltd
The Square Tallaght Town Ctr Co.
Dublin.
Tel: 01 452 4855
Fax: 01 452 5590
E-mail: tallaght@easons.com

Eason and Son Ltd
Unit 115-241 The Blanchardstown
Shopping Centre, Blanchardstown,
Dublin 15
Tel: 01 8221117
Fax: 01 8221153
E-mail:
blanchardstown@easons.com

Eason and Son Ltd
Unit 2 and 5, Heuston Station
Kilmainham, Dublin 8.
Tel: 01 670 3852
Fax: 01 670 3091
E-mail: heuston@easons.com

Eason and Son Ltd
Unit g1, The Pavilion Shopping
Centre, Swords Co. Dublin.
Tel: 01 8900978
Fax: 01 8900988
E-mail: swords@easons.com

Eblana Bookshop Ltd
Dublin Industrial Estate, Dublin 11.

EFL Books and Services
Celtic Publications, Malahide, Co.
Dublin.
Tel: 01 8456860

Exchange Bookshop
34 Castle Street, Dalkey Co. Dublin.

Fred Hanna's Bookshop
1 Dawson Street, Dublin
Tel: 01 677 1255
Fax: 01 671 4330

James Fenning (A.B.A.)
12 Glenview, Rochestown Avenue,
Co. Dublin.
Tel: 01 2857855

Finchcross Books Ltd
Unit B Crag cres Clondalkin
Industrial Estate, Dublin.
Tel: 01 4577968

Frascati Books
U6 Frascati Shopping Centre,
Blackrock, Co. Dublin.
Tel: 01 2834316

The Genealogy Bookshop
3 Nassau Street, Dublin 2.
Tel: 01 6797020

Government Publications
4-5 Harcourt Road, Dublin 2.
Tel: 01 6613111

Greene's Bookshop Ltd
Unit 7, 78 Furze Road, Sandyford,
Dublin 18.

The Hodges Figgis Bookstore
56-58 Dawson Street, Dublin 2.
Tel: 01 6774754

R & A Hughes Bookseller
Nutgrove Shopping Centre,
Rathfarnham, Co. Dublin.
Tel: 01 4936633

International Books
18 Frederick Street, Dublin 2.
Tel: 01 6799375

Irish Church Missions
28 Bachelor's Walk, Dublin 1.
Tel: 01 8730829

Modern Languages Ltd
39 Westland Row, Dublin 2.
Tel: 01 6764285

Murder Ink Ltd
15 Dawson Street, Dublin 2.
Tel: 01 6777570

The National Bible Society of Ireland
41 Dawson Street, Dublin 2.
Tel: 01 6773272

The Open Book Company
Sutton Cross, Dublin 13.
Tel: 01 8324931

Rathgar Bookshop
100 Rathgar Road, Rathgar, Dublin 6.

The Royal Kilmainham Bookshop Ltd
I.M.M.A. Royal Hospital, Dublin 8.
Tel: 01 6770783

The Scholar Book Shop
Newtown Shopping Mall, Swords, Co. Dublin.
Tel: 01 8405292

School Supply Centre
Rathfarnham, Co. Dublin.
Tel: 01 4931059

Scripture Union Book and Music Centre
Talbot Street, Dublin 1.

Scripture Union Book and Resource Centre
87 Georges Street, Dun Laoghaire, Co. Dublin.
Tel: 01 2802300

Siopa Conradh na Gaeilge
6 Sráid Fhearchair, Baile Átha Cliath 2.

Teil: 01 475 7401.
Facs: 01 475 7844.
Ríomhphost: eolas@cnag.ie

Sinn Féin Booksellers
58 Parnell Square, Dublin 1.

Skerries Bookshop
77 Strand Street, Skerries, Co. Dublin.
Tel: 01 8490500

Sub-City Ltd
2 Exchequer Street, Dublin 2.
Tel: 01 6771902

The Rathfarnham Bookshop
Rathfarnham Shopping Centre, Dublin 14.
Tel: 01 4934733

The Rathgar Bookshop
Rathgar road, Dublin 6.
Tel: 01 4928600

The Wise Owl
16 Patrick Street, Dun Laoghaire, Co. Dublin.
Tel: 01 2304675

Third Place Ltd
17 Crow Street, Dublin 2.
Tel: 01 6336964

Usborne Books At Home
5 Cowper Drive, Rathmines, Dublin 6.
Tel: 01 4972787

Veritas Co. Ltd
7-8 Abbey Street Lower, Dublin 1.

Victory Fellowship Book Store
35 Westland Row, Dublin 2.
Tel: 01 6610388

Tuam Bookshop
Vicar Street, Tuam, Co. Galway.
Tel: 093 28907

COUNTY GALWAY

Book Exchange
23 Abbeygate Street, Galway.
Tel: 091 562225

P. Byrne and Son
The Square, Tuam, Co. Galway.
Tel: 093 24159

Charlie Byrnes Bookshop
The Corn Store Middle Street,
Galway.
Tel: 091 561766

Eason and Son Ltd
33 Shop Street, Galway.
Tel: 091 562 284
Fax: 091 561 450
E-mail: galway@easons.com

Joyce Bookstore
52 Dominick Street, Galway, Co.
Galway.
Tel: 091 568227

Laughing Gull Co. Ireland Ltd
Block 3 Ballybrit Bus Pk, Galway, Co.
Galway.
Tel: 091 760800

News 'n' Choose
Main Street, Loughrea, Co. Galway.
Tel: 091 841235

Tara Book Company
Kilcolgan, Co. Galway.
Tel: 091 777070

COUNTY KERRY

The Bookshelf
2 Abbey Court, Tralee, Co. Kerry.
Tel: 066 7125038

An Café Liteartha
An Daingean Chiarraí.
Tel: 066 9152204

The Dingle Bookshop
Green Street, Dingle, Co. Kerry.
Tel: 066 9152433

Dolly McCarthy
22 Main Street, Kenmare, Co. Kerry.
Tel: 064 41009

Eason and Son Ltd
25 The Mall, Tralee, Co. Kerry.
Tel: 066 712 6163
Fax: 066 712 6767
E-mail: tralee@easons.com

Polymaths' Bookstore
Courthouse, Tralee, Co. Kerry.
Tel: 066 7128148

Twinning the Kingdoms Ltd
Tralee Shopping Centre, Tralee,
Tralee, Co. Kerry.
Tel: 085 7163762

COUNTY KILDARE

Barker and Jones
Naas, Co. Kildare.
Tel: 045 856130

Books and Gifts Florists
Church Street, Kilcock, Co. Kildare.
Tel: 01 6287106

Bookstand
Blackhall, Colbinstown, Kildare.
Tel: 045 485451

Browse and Borrow
Liffey Lodge Roseberry Newbridge,
Co. Kildare.
Tel: 045 437067

The Castle Book Shop
Unit 5 Captains hill, Leixlip, Co.
Kildare.
Tel: 01 6243672

Cill Dara Education Supplies
4 Limerick, Newbridge, Co. Kildare.
Tel: 045 434033

Eason and Son Ltd
Whitewater Shopping Centre,
Newbridge, Co. Kildare.
Tel: 045 433347
Fax: 045 433353
E-mail: newbridge@easons.com

Farrell and Nephew
Main Street, Newbridge, Co. Kildare.
Tel: 045 431708

Kilcock Book Shop
The Square, Kilcock, Co. Kildare.
Tel: 01 6287106

The Maynooth Bookshop
68 Main Street, Maynooth, Co.
Kildare.
Tel: 01 6286702

Maynooth University Bookshop
John Hume Building, N.U.I.
Maynooth, Kilcock, Co. Kildare.
Tel: 01 6285629

Village Bookstore
Upper Main Street, Celbridge, Co.
Kildare.
Tel: 087 6102338

COUNTY KILKENNY

Small Stories Bookshop
Main Street, Graiguenamagh, Co.
Kilkenny.
Tel: 059 9725766

COUNTY LAOIS

AllBooks Ltd
Lyster Square, Portlaoise, Laois, Co.
Laois.
Tel: 0502 64300

COUNTY LIMERICK

The Celtic Books Shop
2 Rutland Street, Limerick, Co.
Limerick.
Tel: 061 401155

The Crescent Book Shop
Crescent Shopping Centre,
Dooradoyle, Co. Limerick.
Tel: 061 301389

Dineen's Book Shop
95. Henry Street Limerick.
Tel: 061 413326

Eason and Son Ltd
9 O'Connell Street, Limerick.
Tel: 061 419588
Fax: 061 419932
E-mail: limerick@easons.com

O'Mahony's Booksellers Ltd
120 O'Connell Street, Knocklong,
Co. Limerick.
Tel: 061 418155

COUNTY LOUTH

Ardee Bookshop
Market Street, Ardee, Co. Louth.
Tel: 041 6853665

Carrolls Bookshop
Dundalk, Co. Louth.
Tel: 042 9333719

Eason and Son Ltd
17 West Street, Drogheda, Louth.
Tel: 041 9838654
Fax: 041 9846676
E-mail: drogheda@easons.com

Eason and Son Ltd
Unit 34 The Marshes Shopping
Centre, The Ramparts, Dundalk, Co.
Louth.
Tel: 042 9356527
Fax: 042 9356529
E-mail: dundalk@easons.com

The Wise Owl
Drogheda, Co. Louth.
Tel: 041 984 2847

Usborne Books
Drogheda, Co. Louth.
Tel: 086 823 9486

Waterstones Bookshop
Scotch Hall Shopping Centre, Marsh
Road, Drogheda, Co. Louth.
Tel: 041 983 8527

COUNTY MAYO

Books Etc
Claremorris, Co. Mayo.
Tel: 094 9362730

MJ Joyce and Sons (Foxford) Ltd
Main Street, Foxford, Co. Mayo.
Tel: 094 9256164

McLoughlin Book Shop Ltd
Shop Street, Westport, Co. Mayo.
Tel: 098 27777

COUNTY MEATH

The Bookshop Navan
Trimgate Centre, Navan, Co. Meath.
Tel: 046 9029740

Eason and Son Ltd
Navan Shopping Centre, Navan, Co.
Meath.
Tel: 046 9071696
Fax: 046 9071740
E-mail: navan@easons.com

Wiseowl
Unit 4, Block 4, Ashbourne Business
Park, Ashbourne, Co. Meath.
Tel: 01 8353687

COUNTY MONAGHAN

Readers Paradise
8 Glaslough Street, Monaghan, Co.

Monaghan.
Tel: 047 71432

Stationery Solutions Ltd
77 Main Street, Carrickmacross, Co.
Monaghan.
Tel: 042 9664885

COUNTY OFFALY

The Book Store
O'Connell Street, Birr, Co. Offaly.
Tel: 0509 25926

Midland Books
High Street, Tullamore, Co. Offaly.
Tel: 0506 21797

RM Books
Edenderry, Offaly, Co. Offaly.
Tel: 046 9731282

COUNTY ROSCOMMON

Cormican School Supplies
Abbey Street, Roscommon, Co.
Roscommon.
Tel: 0906 626520

COUNTY SLIGO

Keohanes Bookshop
Castle Street, Sligo.
Tel: 071 9142597

The Book Nest
5, Rockwood Parade, Sligo.
Tel: 071 9146949

COUNTY TIPPERARY

An Stad
21 Main Street, Tipperary, Co.
Tipperary.
Tel: 062 33344

**Book Market New and
Secondhand Books**
Market Place Shopping Centre,
Clonmel, Co. Tipperary.
Tel: 052 29236

Eason and Son Ltd
19/20 Gladstone Street, Clonmel,
Co. Tipperary.
Tel: 052 21 943
Fax: 052 27 832
E-mail: clonmel@easons.com

Mike's Good News
Main Street, Roscrea, Co. Tipperary.
Tel: 0505 21430

Nenagh Bookshop
Friar Street, Nenagh, Co. Tipperary.
Tel: 067 31872

Roscrea Bookshop
Rosemary Square, Roscrea, Co.
Tipperary.
Tel: 0505 22894

Sophie's Bookshop
15 Mitchell Street, Cashel, Co.
Tipperary.
Tel: 052 80752

COUNTY WATERFORD

The Book Centre
John Roberts Square, Waterford, Co.

Waterford.
Tel: 051 873823

Buail Isteach
122 The Quay, Waterford.
Tel: 051 857701

Readers Choice
Lower Main Street, Dungarvan, Co.
Waterford.
Tel: 058 42938

COUNTY WESTMEATH

Byrne's Bookstore and World of Wonder
Lakepoint Retail Park, Mullingar, Co.
Westmeath.
Tel: 044 9331515

Days Bazaar
30-32 Oliver Plunkett Street,,
Mullingar, Co. Westmeath
Tel: 044 48251

Eason and Son Ltd
Unit 23 Athlone Town Centre,
Athlone, Co. Westmeath.
Tel: 090 6484377
Fax: 090 6484378
E- mail: athlonetc@easons.com

Just Books
23 Pearse Street, Mullingar, Co.
Westmeath.
Tel: 044 9332969

Na Linte Bookseller
9 Main Street, Athlone, Co.
Westmeath.
Tel: 0906 494151

Ryan's Bookshop
Mary's Street, Mullingar, Co.
Westmeath.
Tel: 044 42497

Ryans Midland Books
Mary Street, Mullingar, Co.
Westmeath.
Tel: 044 42497

COUNTY WEXFORD

Bargain Books
1 Lowneys Mall Sth Main Street,
Wexford, Co. Wexford.
Tel: 053 44778

The Cenacle Bookshop
25 Henrietta Street, Wexford, Co.
Wexford.
Tel: 053 44365

COUNTY WICKLOW

Books on the Bridge
Main Street, Baltinglass, Co.
Wicklow.
Tel: 086 3366508

The Bookworm
Willowbrook Centre, Kilcoole, Co.
Wicklow.
Tel: 01 2557644

Bride Street Books
Bridge Street, Wicklow Town
Tel: 0404 62240

Dougherty's School Books
Main Street, Bray, Co. Wicklow.
Tel: 01 463 6680

Hilary Hamilton
Bridge Street, Wicklow, Co.
Wicklow.
Tel: 0404 62240

Malone's Bookshop
Main Street, Wicklow, Co. Wicklow.
Tel: 0404 68150 / 086 6048991
Website: www.Schoolbooks4u.ie

MG Gallagher T/A Bookstation
103 Main Street, Bollarney,
Wicklow.
Tel: 01 2761734

Na Cupla Focal
16 Albert Walk, Bray, Co. Wicklow.
Tel: 01 2765120

The Blessington Book Store Ltd
Main Street, Tinahely, Co. Wicklow.
Tel: 045 857730

Town Hall Bookshop
Bray, Co. Wicklow.
Tel: 01 2768574

Village Book Shop
Greystones, Co. Wicklow.
Tel: 01 287 6593

NORTHERN IRELAND

A McAuley
9 Linen Hall Street Ballymoney, Co.
Antrim, BT53 6DP.
Tel: 028 2766 3054

Aras Mhuire
19-25 Shamble Lane Dungannon,
Co. Tyrone, BT70 1BW.
Tel: 028 8772 6852

Ards Evangelical Bookshop
48 Frances Street Newtownards,
Co. Down, BT23 7DN.
Tel: 028 9181 7530
Website: www.ardsbookshop.com

Bargain Books
15 North Street Belfast, Co. Antrim,
BT1 1NA.
Tel: 028 9032 5245

Bargain Books
Connswater Shopping Centre
Bloomfield Avenue Belfast, Co.
Antrim, BT5 5LP.
Tel: 028 9046 1454

Bargain Books
Fair Hill Shopping Centre Fair Hill
Lane Ballymena, Co. Antrim, BT43
6UF.
Tel: 028 2565 8707

Bargain Books
Park Centre Donegall Road Belfast,
Co. Antrim, BT12 6HN.
Tel: 028 9032 1090

Bargain Books
Unit 36/Castle Court Royal Avenue
Belfast, Co. Antrim, BT1 1DD.
Tel: 028 9031 4154

Bargain Books
Unit 42 Abbeycentre, Longwood
Road, Newtownabbey, Co. Antrim,
BT37 9UH.
Tel: 028 9086 1089

Bargain Books
Unit 5/Bloomfield Shopping Centre
South Circular Road Bangor, Co.
Down, BT19 7HB.
Tel: 028 9127 2070

Bargain Books
Unit A4/Bow Street Mall, Bow
Street Lisburn, Co. Antrim, BT28
1AW.
Tel: 028 9267 6018

Bargain Books
Valley Business Centre Church Road
Newtownabbey, Co. Antrim, BT36
7LS.
Tel: 028 9055 1605

BBC Shop
21a Arthur Street Belfast, Co.
Antrim, BT1 4GA.
Tel: 028 9032 5672

Belmont Christian Book Centre
49 Belmont Road Belfast, Co.
Antrim, BT4 2AA.
Tel: 028 9065 3718

Bethel Book Shop
4 Broad Street Magherafelt, Co.
Londonderry, BT45 6EA.
Tel: 028 7963 1446

Bethel Books and Music
15-17 Castlereagh Road Belfast, Co.
Antrim, BT5 5FB.
Tel: 028 9073 1779

Beulah Bookshop
67 Central Promenade Newcastle,
Co. Down, BT33 0HH.
Tel: 028 4372 2629

Bookcity
22 Castle Place Strabane, Co.
Tyrone, BT82 8AW.
Tel: 028 7138 2893

Bookends
Dufferin Court Bangor, Co. Down,
BT20 3BX.
Tel: 028 9147 1919

Bookfinders Belfast
47 University Road Belfast, Co.
Antrim, BT7 1ND.
Tel: 028 9032 8269

Booklore
29 Derrygarve Park Castledawson
Magherafelt, Co. Londonderry, BT45
8EZ Co. Tyrone.
Tel: 028 7946 9389

Bookworm
18-20 Bishop Street Londonderry,
Co. Londonderry, BT48 6PW.
Tel: 028 7128 2727

Bridge Books
3 Bridge Street Dromore, Co. Down,
BT25 1AN.
Tel: 028 9269 9899

The Burning Bush
62 Scotch Street Dungannon, Co.
Tyrone, BT70 1BJ.
Tel: 028 8772 6027

The Carlisle Bookshop
25 High Street Omagh, Co. Tyrone,
BT78 1BA.
Tel: 028 8224 2011

Causeway Books
110 Main Street Bushmills, Co.
Antrim, BT57 8QD.
Tel: 028 2073 2596

Christian Book Centre
18 Rashee Road Ballyclare, Co.

Antrim, BT39 9HJ.
Tel: 028 9335 2170

Covenanter Book Shop
98 Lisburn Road Belfast, Co. Antrim,
BT9 6AG.
Tel: 028 9066 0689

Craodh Rua Books
12 Woodford Gdns Armagh, Co.
Armagh, BT60 2AZ.
Tel: 028 3752 6938

DRC Bookshop
193-195 Donegall Street Belfast, Co.
Antrim, BT1 2FL.
Tel: 028 9023 6249
Website: www.drcbookshop.com

Eason and Son Ltd
14 Tower Centre Wellington Street,
Ballymena, Co. Antrim, BT43 6AH.
Tel: 028 2564 8418

Eason and Son Ltd
Unit 10-12 Fairhill Shopping Centre,
Broughane Street, Ballymena, BT43
6UE.
Tel: 028 2565 8777
E-mail: fairhill@easons.com

Eason and Son Ltd
29-33 Main Street, Bangor, BT20
5AF.
Tel: 028 9147 2042
Fax: 028 9146 9081
E- mail: bangor@easons.com

Eason and Son Ltd
20 Donegall Place, Belfast, BT1 3BA
Tel: 028 9023 5070
Fax: 028 9024 2915
E-mail: donegallplace@easons.com

Eason and Son Ltd
Units 4 and 5 Westwood Shopping
Centre, Kennedy Way, Belfast BT11
9AP.
Tel: 028 9028 2060
E-mail: westwood@easons.com

Eason and Son Ltd
Unit 1 Carryduff Shopping Centre,
Ballynahinch Road, Carryduff, BT8
8RB.
Tel: 028 9081 4568
E-mail: carryduff@easons.com

Eason and Son Ltd
35 Church Street, Coleraine, BT52
1AW
Tel: 028 7034 2497
Fax: 028 7034 2084
E-mail: coleraine@easons.com

Eason and Son Ltd
Unit 28 Rushmere Shopping Centre,
Craigavon, BT64 1AA.
Tel: 028 3834 2031
Fax: 028 3834 1845
E-mail: craigavon@easons.com

Eason and Son Ltd
Units 5 and 6 Market Hill, Market
Street, Downpatrick, BT30 6LP.
Tel: 028 4461 9569
E-mail: downpatrick@easons.com

Eason and Son Ltd
2-3 Buttercrane Shopping Centre
Buttercrane Quay Newry, Co. Down,
BT35 8HJ.
Tel: 028 3026 1037
Fax: 028 3026 1612
E-mail: newry@easons.com

Eason and Son
33-35 Castle Centre Antrim, Co. Antrim, BT41 4DN.
Tel: 028 9442 8975

Eason and Son Ltd
34 Bow Street Lisburn, Co. Antrim, BT28 1BN.
Tel: 028 9267 0561
Fax: 028 9267 4985
E-mail: lisburn@easons.com

Eason and Son Ltd
Units 35-37 Abbeycentre,
Longwood Road, Newtownabbey,
BT37 9UH.
Tel: 028 9036 5647
E-mail: abbeycentre@easons.com

Eason and Son Ltd
Ards Shopping Centre Circular Road
Newtownards, Co. Down, BT23 4EU.
Tel: 028 9181 5366
Fax: 028 9181 7714
E-mail: newtownards@easons.com

Eason and Son Ltd
Foyleside Shopping Centre Orchard
Street Londonderry, Co.
Londonderry, BT48 6XY.
Tel: 028 7137 7133
Fax: 028 7137 7256
E-mail: foyleside@easons.com

Eason and Son Ltd
The Meadows Shopping Centre,
Meadow Lane, Portadown,
Craigavon, Co. Armagh, BT62 3TN.
Tel: 028 3835 1301

Eason and Son Ltd
Unit 16/Castle Court Royal Avenue
Belfast, Co. Antrim,

BT1 1DD.
Tel: 028 9023 5070

Eason and Son Ltd
10 High Street Enniskillen, Co.
Fermanagh, BT74 7EH.
Tel: 028 6632 4341
Fax: 028 6632 4030
E-mail: enniskillen@easons.com

Ebenezer Bible Bookshop
335 Woodstock Road Belfast, Co.
Antrim, BT6 8PT.
Tel: 028 9045 7048

Emerald Isle Books
539 Antrim Road Belfast, Co.
Antrim, BT15 3BU.
Tel: 028 9037 0798

Evangelical Bookshop
15 College Square East Belfast, Co.
Antrim, BT1 6DD.
Tel: 028 9032 0529

The Faith Mission Bookshop
131 Mahon Road Portadown
Craigavon, Co. Armagh, BT62 3SF.
Tel: 028 3833 2806

The Faith Mission Bookshop
17 High Street Lurgan Craigavon,
Co. Armagh, BT66 8AA.
Tel: 028 3832 5304

The Faith Mission Bookshop
20 Oldtown Street Cookstown, Co.
Tyrone, BT80 8EF.
Tel: 028 8676 6569

The Faith Mission Bookshop
20 Thomas Street Portadown
Craigavon, Co. Armagh, BT62 3NP.
Tel: 028 3833 4123

The Faith Mission Bookshop
33 Greencastle Street Kilkeel
Newry, Co. Down, BT34 4BH.
Tel: 028 4176 4934

The Faith Mission Bookshop
36 Market Street Omagh, Co.
Tyrone, BT78 1EH.
Tel: 028 8224 1334

The Faith Mission Bookshop
3b Dobbin Street Armagh, Co.
Armagh, BT61 7QQ.
Tel: 028 3752 7927

The Faith Mission Bookshop
5 Glenavy Gardens, Lisburn, Co.
Antrim, BT28 1PB.
Tel: 028 9266 5888

The Faith Mission Bookshop
57 High Street Ballymena, Co.
Antrim, BT43 6DT.
Tel: 028 2564 9443

The Faith Mission Bookshop
73 High Street Bangor, Co. Down,
BT20 5BD.
Tel: 028 9145 3222

The Faith Mission Bookshop
78 Spencer Road Londonderry, Co.
Londonderry, BT47 6AF.
Tel: 028 7134 5137

The Faith Mission Bookshop
Kings Lane Ballykelly Limavady, Co.
Londonderry, BT49 9JX.
Tel: 028 7776 8871

The Faith Mission Bookshop
43 Bridge Street Banbridge, Co.
Down, BT32 3JL.
Tel: 028 4062 6761

Foyle Bookshop
12 Magazine Street Londonderry,
Co. Londonderry, BT48 6HH.
Tel: 028 7137 2530

Harry Hall
39 Gresham Street Belfast, Co.
Antrim, BT1 1JL.
Tel: 028 9024 1923

Irish Evangelistic Band
8 Dublin Road Enniskillen, Co.
Fermanagh, BT74 6HH.
Tel: 028 6632 2400

J. Gowan
Drumaraw Enniskillen, Co.
Fermanagh, BT74 8AS.
Tel: 028 6634 1239
Website: www.gowanbooks.com

Mizpah Bible and Bookshop
41 Kingsgate Street Coleraine, Co.
Londonderry, BT52 1LD.
Tel: 028 7034 3857

The Music and Book Centre
45 High Street Ballynahinch, Co.
Down, BT24 8AB.
Tel: 028 9756 1679

Northern Ireland Book Service
53 High Street Ballymena, Co.
Antrim, BT43 6DT.
Tel: 028 2564 5010

Oasis Bookshop
59 Main Street Lisnaskea Enniskillen,
Co. Fermanagh, BT92 0JD.
Tel: 028 6772 2677

The Old Book Shop
3 Bridge Street Lisburn, Co. Antrim,

BT28 1XZ.
Tel: 028 9266 8450

The Readers Room
21 Cennick Road Gracehill
Ballymena, Co. Antrim, BT42 2NH.
Tel: 028 2564 1187
Website:
www.thereadersroom.co.uk

Shipquay Books
10 Shipquay Street Derry, Co.
Londonderry, BT48 6DN.
Tel: 028 7137 1747

Smyth and Ryan
Church Lodge Centre Moneyrea
Newtownards, Co. Down, BT23 6EX.
Tel: 028 9044 8333

**Usborne Books at Home and
School**
10 Greenfield Drive, Annalong, Co.
Down.
Tel: 028 4376 7215

War on Want
13 Campsie Road Omagh, Co.
Tyrone, BT79 0AE.
Tel: 028 8225 9986

Waterstone's Booksellers
Cromore Road Coleraine, Co.
Londonderry, BT52 1SA.
Tel: 028 7034 3942

World of Books
Railway Street Newcastle, Co.
Down, BT33 0AL.
Tel: 028 4372 3060

World of Learning
6 Corcreechy Road Newry, Co.

Down, BT34 1LP.
Tel: 028 3025 2856
Website:
www.worldoflearning.uk.com

BOOK DISTRIBUTORS

Argosy
Unit 12 North Park, North Road,
Finglas, Dublin 11.
Tel: 01 8239500
Fax: 01 8239599
Email : info@argosybooks.ie
Website: www.argosybooks.ie

CMD Booksource
55a Spruce Avenue, Stillorgan
Industrial Park, Blackrock, Co.
Dublin
Tel: 01 2942560
Fax: 01 2942564

Eason and Son Ltd
Wholesale Book Division, Dublin
Airport Logistics Park, St Margaret's
Road, Co. Dublin.
Tel: 01 8448888
Fax: 01 8448018

Gill & Macmillan Ltd
10 Hume Avenue, Park West, Dublin
12.
Tel: 01 5009506
Fax: 01 5009597
Website: www.gillmacmillan.ie

K. Libraries

COUNTY CARLOW

Carlow Central Library
Tullow Street, Carlow, Co. Carlow
Tel: 059 9170094
Fax: 059 9740548
E-mail: library@carlowcoco.ie
Website: www.countycarlow.ie

Muinebheag Library
Main Street, Bagenalstown, Co.
Carlow
Tel: 059 972 2208
Website: www.countycarlow.ie

COUNTY CAVAN

**Cavan County Library
Headquarters**
Farnham Centre, Farnham Street,
Cavan
Tel: 049 4378505
Fax: 049 4326987
E-mail: library@cavancoco.ie
Website: www.cavancoco.ie

Arva Public Library
Market House, Arvagh, Co. Cavan
Tel: 049 4335905

Bailieborough Library
Market House, Bailieborough, Co.
Cavan
Tel: 042 9665779
E-mail:
bailieboroughlibrary@cavancoco.ie
Website: www.bailieborough.com

Ballinagh Library
Community Centre, Ballinagh, Co.

Cavan
Tel: 049 436 7041

Ballyconnell Library
Church Street, Ballyconnell, Co.
Cavan
Tel: 049 9526844

Ballyjamesduff Library
Health Centre, Ballyjamesduff, Co.
Cavan
Tel: 049 8545184

Belturbet Public Library
Town Hall, Belturbet, Co. Cavan
Tel: 049 9522683

Cootehill Library
Bridge Street, Cootehill, Co. Cavan
Tel: 049 5559873
E-mail:
cootehilllibrary@cavancoco.ie

Johnston Central Library
Farnham Centre, Farnham Street,
Cavan
Tel: 049 4378500
Fax: 049 4326987
E-mail: library@cavancoco.ie

Killeshandra Library
Community Centre, Railway Road,
Killeshandra, Co. Cavan
Tel: 049 31799

Kilnaleck Library
Community Centre, Kilnaleck, Co.
Cavan
Tel: 049 31799

Kingscourt Library
St Mary's Hall, Kingscourt, Co.
Cavan
Tel: 049 31799

Virginia Library
Health Centre, Bailieborough Road,
Virginia, Co. Cavan
Tel: 049 8548456

COUNTY CLARE

Clare County Library
Headquarters
Mill Road, Ennis, Co. Clare
County Librarian: Helen Walsh
Tel: 065 6821616 / 6846350.
Fax: 065 6842462
E-mail: mailbox@clarelibrary.ie
Website: www.clarelibrary.ie

Corofin Public Library
Corofin, Co. Clare
Tel: 065 6837219
Website: www.clarelibrary.ie

Cranny Virtual Public Library
Cranny Rural Renewal Centre,
Cranny, Co. Clare.
Tel: (065) 6832070

De Valera Public Library
Harmony Row, Ennis, Co. Clare
Tel: 065 6846353
Fax: 065 6842462
Website: www.clarelibrary.ie

Ennistymon Public Library
The Square, Ennistymon, Co. Clare
Tel: 065 7071245
Website: www.clarelibrary.ie

Kildysart Public Library
St John Bosco's Community College,
Kildysart, Co. Clare.
Tel: 065 6832113
Website: www.clarelibrary.ie

Kilfinaghty Public Library
Kilfinaghty, Church Street,
Sixmilebridge, Co. Clare
Tel: 061 369678
Fax: 061 369678
Website: www.clarelibrary.ie

Killaloe Public Library
The Lock House, Killaloe, Co. Clare
Tel: 061 376062
Fax: 061 376062
Website: www.clarelibrary.ie

Kilmihil Public Library
St Michael's Community Centre,
Church Street, Kilmihil, Co. Clare.
Tel: 065 9050528
Website: www.clarelibrary.ie

Kilrush Library
O Gorman Street, Kilrush, Co. Clare
Tel: 065 9051504
Website: www.clarelibrary.ie

Lisdoonvarna Public Library
Kincora Road, Lisdoonvarna, Co.
Clare
Tel: 065 7074029
Website: www.clarelibrary.ie

Hillery Public Library (Miltown Malbay)
Ballard Road, Miltown Malbay, Co.
Clare
Tel: 065 7084822
Website: www.clarelibrary.ie

Newmarket-on-Fergus Public Library

Kilnasoolagh Park, Newmarket-on-Fergus, Co. Clare
Tel: 061 368411
Website: www.clarelibrary.ie

Scariff Public Library

Mountshannon Road, Scariff, Co. Clare
Tel: 061 922893
Website: www.clarelibrary.ie

Sean Lemass Public Library (Shannon)

Town Centre, Shannon, Co. Clare
Tel: 061 364 266
Website: www.clarelibrary.ie

Sweeney Memorial Public Library (Kilkee)

O'Connell Street, Kilkee, Co. Clare
Tel: 065 9056034
Website: www.clarelibrary.ie

Tulla Public Library

The Market House, Tulla, Co. Clare
Tel: 065 6835919
Website: www.clarelibrary.ie

CORK CITY

Central Library

Central Library, 57-61 Grand Parade, Cork
City Librarian: Liam Ronayne
Tel: 021 4924900
Fax: 021 4275684
E-mail: libraries@corkcity.ie
Website: www.corkcitylibraries.ie

Bishopstown Library

Wilton, Cork
Executive Librarian: David G. O'Brien
Tel: 021 4924959 (Desk Phone Exec Librarian 086 8597712)
Fax: 021 4345428
E-mail: david_obrien@corkcity.ie / bishopstown_library@corkcity.ie
Website: www.corkcitylibraries.ie/bishopstown/

Douglas Library

Douglas Village Shopping Centre, Douglas, Cork
Acting Executive Librarian: Deirbhile Dennehy
Tel: 021 4924931/32
Fax: 021 4366524
E-mail: douglas_library@corkcity.ie
Website: www.corkcitylibrary.ie

Hollyhill Library

Foyle Avenue, Knocknaheeny, Cork
Tel: 021 4924928
Fax: 021 4393032
E-mail: hollyhill_library@corkcity.ie
Website: www.corkcitylibraries.ie/hollyhill/

Frank O'Connor Library, Mayfield

Old Youghal Road, Mayfield, Cork
Tel: 4924935
E-mail: mayfield_library@corkcity.ie
Website: www.corkcitylibraries.ie/mayfield/

St Mary's Road Library

St Mary's Road, Cork
Executive Librarian: Eibhlín Cassidy
Tel: 021 4924933 (Adults), 021

4924937 (Children and Teens)
Fax: 021 427 5684
E-mail: stmarys_library@corkcity.ie
(for Adults) or
stmaryskids_library@corkcity.ie
(for Children and Teens)
Website:
www.corkcitylibraries.ie/stmarysr
oad/

Tory Top Library

Ballyphehane, Cork
Executive Librarian: Mary Corcoran
Tel: 021 4924934 / 4924946
Fax: 021 4966029
E-mail: torytop_library@corkcity.ie
Website:
www.corkcitylibraries.ie/torytop/

Mobile Library

c/o Frank O'Connor Library, Old
Youghal Road, Mayfield, Cork
Executive Librarian: Mary
FitzGerald
Tel: 021 4924935
E-mail:
mayfield_library@corkcity.ie
Website:
www.corkcitylibraries.ie/mobilelib
rary/

COUNTY CORK

Cork County Library
Headquarters

Carrigrohane Road, Cork.
Tel: 021 4546499
Fax: 021 4343254
E-mail:
corkcountylibrary@corkcoco.ie
(Lending),
reference.library@corkcoco.ie

(Reference)
Website: www.corkcoco.ie

Ballincollig Public Library

The Village Shopping Centre,
Ballincollig, Co. Cork.
Tel: 021 4873024
E-mail:
ballincollig.library@corkcoco.ie
Website: www.corkcoco.ie

Leabharlann Bhaile Bhuirne
(Ballyvourney)

Baile Mic Ire, Co. Chorcaí
Teil: 026 45767
Ríomhphost:
leabharlannbhailebhuirne@corkcoc
o.ie
Website: www.corkcoco.ie

Bantry Library

Bridge Street, Bantry, Co. Cork.
Tel: 027 50460
Fax: 021 51389
E-mail: bantrylibrary@corkcoco.ie
Website: www.corkcoco.ie

Bandon Library

Shopping Centre, South Main Street,
Bandon.
Tel: 023 8844830
E-mail: bandonlibrary@corkcoco.ie
Website: www.corkcoco.ie

Blarney Library

The Square, Blarney, Co. Cork
Tel: 021 4382115
E-mail:
blarneylibrary@hotmail.com
Website: www.corkcoco.ie

Carrigaline Public Library

Main Street, Carrigaline, Co. Cork

Tel: 021 4371888
E-mail:
carrigalinelibrary@corkcoco.ie
Website: www.corkcoco.ie

Castletownbere Library
Bank Place, Castletownbere, Co.
Cork
Tel: 027 70233
E-mail:
castletownberelibrary@eircom.net
Website: www.corkcoco.ie

Charleville Branch Library
Main Street, Charleville, Co. Cork
Tel: 063 89769
E-mail:
charlevillelibrary@eircom.net
Website: www.corkcoco.ie

Clonakilty Library
Kent Street, Clonakilty, Co. Cork
Tel: 023 88 34275
E-mail:
clonakiltylibrary@corkcoco.ie
Website: www.corkcoco.ie

Cobh Public Library
Arch Building, Casement Square,
Cobh, Co. Cork
E-mail: cobh.library@corkcoco.ie
Tel: 021 4811130
Website: www.corkcoco.ie

Dunmanway Library
The Square, Dunmanway, Co. Cork
Tel: 023 8855411
E-mail:
dunmanway.library@corkcoco.ie
Website: www.corkcoco.ie

Fermoy Public Library
Connolly Street, Fermoy, Co. Cork

Tel: 025 31318
E-mail: fermoylibrary@eircom.net
Website: www.corkcoco.ie

Glanmire Library
Hazelwood Shopping Centre,
Glanmire, Co. Cork
Tel: 021 4821627
E-Mail:
glanmirelibrary@eircom.net
Website: www.corkcoco.ie

Kanturk Library
Methodist Hall, Kanturk, Co. Cork
Tel: 029 51384
E-mail:
kanturk.library@corkcoco.ie
Website: www.corkcoco.ie

Kinsale Library
Market Quay, Kinsale, Co. Cork
Tel: 021 4774266
E-mail: kinsalelibrary@eircom.net
Website: www.corkcoco.ie

Macroom Branch Library
Briery Gap Cultural Centre, Main
Street, Macroom, Co. Cork
Tel: 026 42483
E-mail:
macroomlibrary@corkcoco.ie
Website: www.corkcoco.ie

Mallow Public Library
Thomas Davis Street, Mallow, Co.
Cork.
Tel: 022 21821
E-mail: mallow.library@corkcoco.ie
Website: www.corkcoco.ie

Midleton Library
Main Street, Midleton, Co. Cork
Tel: 021 4613929

E-mail:
midletonlibrary@corkcoco.ie
Website: www.corkcoco.ie

Millstreet Library
Carnegie Hall, County Council
Offices, Millstreet, Co. Cork.
Tel: 029 21920
E-mail:
millstreetlibrary@corkcoco.ie
Website: www.corkcoco.ie

Mitchelstown Library
County Council Offices, Georges
Street, Mitchelstown, Co. Cork.
Tel: 025 41939
E-mail:
mitchelstown.library@corkcoco.ie
Website: www.corkcoco.ie

Newmarket Library
Scarteen Street, Newmarket, Co.
Cork
Tel: 029 61090
E-mail:
newmarketlibrary@eircom.net
Website: www.corkcoco.ie

**An Leabharlann Oileán Chléire
(Cape Clear)**
An Sciobairín, Co. Chorcaí.
Tel: 021 546 499
E-mail: cleirelibrary@corkcoco.ie
Website: www.corkcoco.ie

Passage West Library
Main Street, Passage West, Co. Cork
Tel: 021 4863727
E-mail:
passagewestlibrary@eircom.net
Website: www.corkcoco.ie

Schull Public Library
Main Street, Schull, Co. Cork
Tel: 028 28290
E-mail: schull.library@corkcoco.ie
Website: www.corkcoco.ie

Sherkin Library Library
Adjacent to the Church, Sherkin
Island, Co. Cork.
Tel: 028 20009
E-mail: sherkinlibrary@eircom.net
Website: www.corkcoco.ie

Skibbereen Public Library
North Street, Skibbereen, Co. Cork
Tel: 028 22400
E-mail:
skibbereenlibrary@corkcoco.ie
Website: www.corkcoco.ie

Youghal Public Library
River Gate Mall, North Main Street,
Youghal, Co. Cork
Tel: 024 93459
E-mail:
youghal.library@corkcoco.ie
Website: www.corkcoco.ie

COUNTY DONEGAL

Donegal County Library
County Library Administrative
Centre, Rosemount, Letterkenny,
Co. Donegal
Librarian: Eileen Burgess
Tel: 074 9121968 (2 Lines)
Fax: 074 9121740
E-mail: library@donegalcoco.ie /
email: eburgess@donegalcoco.ie
Web: www.donegalcoco.ie

Central Library
Oliver Plunkett Road, Letterkenny,
Co. Donegal
Tel: 074 9124950
Fax: 074 9124950
E-mail: dglcolib@iol.ie
Website: www.donegalcoco.ie

Ballybofey Library
Butt Hall, Ballybofey, Co. Donegal
Tel: 074 9131822
Website: www.donegalcoco.ie

Ballyshannon Library
Ballyshannon Town Council,
Abbeyview, Ballyshannon, Co.
Donegal
Tel: 071 9252044
Fax: 071 985 8271
Website: www.donegalcoco.ie

Buncrana Community Library
St Orans Road, Buncrana, Co.
Donegal
Tel: 074 936 1941
Fax: 074 936 1980
E-mail:
bunclibrary@donegalcoco.ie
Website: www.donegalcoco.ie

Bundoran Library
UDC Offices, Main Street, Bundoran,
Co. Donegal
Tel: 071 984 1146
Website: www.donegalcoco.ie

Carndonagh Library
Carndonagh, Co. Donegal
Tel: 074 9373701
Website: www.donegalcoco.ie

Clonmany Library
Parochial Hall, Clonmany, Co.

Donegal
Tel: 074 912 1968
Website: www.donegalcoco.ie

Donegal Town Library
Tel: 074 9735380
Website: www.donegalcoco.ie

Leabharlann Phobail na Rosann
Dungloe, Co. Donegal
Tel: 074 952 2500
Fax: 074 952 2124
E-mail: lpnarosann@hotmail.com
Website: www.donegalcoco.ie

Glenties Library
Courthouse, Glenties, Co. Donegal
Tel: 074 915 1165
Website: www.donegalcoco.ie

Leabharlann Gaoth Dobhair
Sean tSeipeal, Gweedore, Co.
Donegal
Tel: 074 9560862
Website: www.donegalcoco.ie

Killybegs Library
Bruach Na Mara, Killybegs, Co.
Donegal
Tel: 074 9732860
Website: www.donegalcoco.ie

Lifford Community Library
Courthouse, Lifford, Co. Donegal
Tel: 074 9172726
Website: www.donegalcoco.ie

Milford Library
Millford, Co. Donegal
Tel: 074 9153927
Website: www.donegalcoco.ie

Moville Library
Moville, Co. Donegal
Tel: 074 9385110
Website: www.donegalcoco.ie

Ramelton Community Library
Old Meetinghouse, Rathmelton, Co. Donegal
Tel: 074 9151414
Website: www.donegalcoco.ie

Raphoe Library
The Diamond, Raphoe, Co. Donegal
Tel: 074 9144115
Website: www.donegalcoco.ie

DUBLIN CITY COUNCIL

Dublin City Library and Archive
138 - 144 Pearse Street, Dublin 2.
Tel: 01 6744999
Fax: 01 6744879
E-mail:
dublinpubliclibraries@dublincity.ie
/ dublinstudies@dublincity.ie /
cityarchives@dublincity.ie
Website:
www.dublincitypubliclibraries.ie

Ballyfermot Library
Ballyfermot Road, Ballyfermot,
Dublin 10
Tel: 01 6269324 / 6269325
Fax: 01 623 0706
E-mail:
ballyfermotlibrary@dublincity.ie
Website:
www.dublincitypubliclibraries.ie

Ballymun Library
Main Street, Ballymun, Dublin 11
Tel: 01 8421890

Fax: 01 842 1762
E-mail:
ballymunlibrary@dublincity.ie
Website:
www.dublincitypubliclibraries.ie

Business Information Centre
Central Library, Ilac Centre, Henry
Street, Dublin 1
Tel: 01 8733996 / 8734333
E-mail:
businesslibrary@dublincity.ie
Website:
www.dublincitypubliclibraries.ie

Cabra Library
Navan Road, Dublin 7
Tel: 01 8691414
E-mail: cabralibrary@dublincity.ie
Website:
www.dublincitypubliclibraries.ie

Central Library
ILAC Centre, Henry Street, Dublin 1
Tel: 01 8734333
Fax: 01 8721451
E-mail: centrallibrary@dublincity.ie
Website:
www.dublincitypubliclibraries.ie

Charleville Mall Library
North Strand, Dublin 1
Tel: 01 8749619
E-mail:
charlevillemalllibrary@dublincity.ie
Website:
www.dublincitypubliclibraries.ie

Children's and Schools' Library Service
18 Lower Kevin Street, Dublin 8
Tel: 01 475 8791
Fax: 01 478 5698

E-mail:
childrens.library@dublincity.ie
Website:
www.dublincitypubliclibraries.ie

Coolock Library
Barryscourt Road, Coolock, Dublin 17
Tel: 01 8477781
Fax: 01 8674304
E-mail:
coolocklibrary@dublincity.ie
Website:
www.dublincitypubliclibraries.ie

Dolphins Barn Library
Parnell Road, Dolphins Barn, Dublin 12
Tel: 01 454 0681
E-mail:
dolphinsbarnlibrary@dublincity.ie
Website:
www.dublincitypubliclibraries.ie

Dublin City Public Libraries and Archive
138-144 Pearse Street, Dublin 2
Tel: 01 674 4800
Fax: 01 677 5954
E-mail: cityarchives@dublincity.ie /
dublinstudies@dublincity.ie
Website:
www.dublincitypubliclibraries.ie

Donaghmede Library
Donaghmede Shopping Centre,
Grange Road, Dublin 13
Tel: 01 848 2833
E-mail:
donaghmedelibrary@dublincity.ie
Website:
www.dublincitypubliclibraries.ie

Drumcondra Library
Milmount Avenue, Drumcondra,
Dublin 9
Librarian: Emma Kelly
Tel: 01 8377206
E-mail:
drumcondralibrary@dublincity.ie
Website:
www.dublincitypubliclibraries.ie

Finglas Library
Main Shopping Centre, Jamestown
Road, Finglas, Dublin 11
Tel: 01 8344906
Fax: 01 8642085
E-mail: finglaslibrary@dublincity.ie
Website:
www.dublincitypubliclibraries.ie

Inchicore Library
34 Emmet Road, Inchicore, Dublin 8
Tel: 01 4533793
E-mail:
inchicorelibrary@dublincity.ie
Website:
www.dublincitypubliclibraries.ie

Kevin Street Library
18 Lower Kevin Street, Dublin 8
Tel: 01 4753794
E-mail:
kevinstreetlibrary@dublincity.ie
Website:
www.dublincitypubliclibraries.ie

Marino Public Library
14 - 20 Marino Mart, Fairview,
Dublin 3
Tel: 01 8336297
E-mail: marinolibrary@dublincity.ie
Website:
www.dublincitypubliclibraries.ie

Mobile Libraries Headquarters
Bibliographic Centre, Navan Road,
Dublin 7
Tel: 01 8691415
E-mail:
mobilelibraries@dublincity.ie
Website:
www.dublincitypubliclibraries.ie

Pearse Street Library
138 - 144 Pearse Street, Dublin 2
Tel: 01 6744888
E-mail:
pearsestreetlibrary@dublincity.ie
Website:
www.dublincitypubliclibraries.ie

Pembroke Library
Angelsea Road, Ballsbridge, Dublin
4
Tel: 01 6689575
E-mail:
pembrokelibrary@dublincity.ie
Website:
www.dublincitypubliclibraries.ie

Phibsboro Library
Blacquiere Bridge, Off North
Circular Road, Phibsboro, Dublin 7
Librarian: Maria Sheahan
Tel: 01 8304341
E-mail:
phibsborolibrary@dublincity.ie
Website:
www.dublincitypubliclibraries.ie

Raheny Library
Howth Road, Raheny, Dublin 5
Tel: 01 8315521
E-mail: rahenylibrary@dublincity.ie
Website:
www.dublincitypubliclibraries.ie

Rathmines Library
157 Lower Rathmines Road, Dublin
6
Tel: 01 4973539
E-mail:
rathmineslibrary@dublincity.ie
Website:
dublincitypubliclibraries.ie

Ringsend Library
Fitzwilliam Street, Dublin 4
Tel: 01 668 0063
E-mail:
ringsendlibrary@dublincity.ie
Website:
www.dublincitypubliclibraries.ie

Terenure Library
Templeogue Road, Terenure, Dublin 6
Tel: 01 4907035
E-mail:
terenurelibrary@dublincity.ie
Website:
www.dublincitypubliclibraries.ie

Walkinstown Library
Percy French Road, Walkinstown,
Dublin 12
Tel: 01 4558159
Fax: 01 4558159
E-mail:
walkinstownlibrary@dublincity.ie
Website:
www.dublincitypubliclibraries.ie

DUBLIN - FINGAL COUNTY COUNCIL

Balbriggan Library
George's Square, Balbriggan, Co.
Dublin
Senior Librarian: Assumpta Hickey

Tel: 01 8704409
Fax: 01 8411128
E-mail:
balbrigganlibrary@fingalcoco.ie
Website: www.fingalcoco.ie/library

Baldoyle Library
Strand Road, Baldoyle, Fingal,
Dublin 13
Tel: 01 8906793
E-mail:
baldoylelibrary@fingalcoco.ie
Website: www.fingalcoco.ie/library

Blanchardstown Library
Civic Centre, Blanchardstown
Centre, Dublin 15
Tel: 01 8905560/8905563
Fax: 01 8905574
E-mail: blanchlib@fingalcoco.ie
Website:
www.fingalcoco.ie/Library/Library
Services/BlanchardstownLibrary/

Fingal Mobile Libraries Services
34 Coolmine, Industrial Estate,
Coolmine, Dublin 15
Tel: 01 822 1564
Fax: 01 822 1568
Website:
www.fingalcoco.ie/LivingInFingal/
Libraries/

Fingal Housebound Library Service
Unit 34, Coolmine Industrial Estate,
Coolmine, Dublin 15
Librarian: Lynda Beasley or Marian
Caulfield

Garristown Library
Main Street, Garristown, Fingal, Co.
Dublin

Tel: 01 8355020
Fax: 01 8355554
E-mail:
garristownlibrary@fingalcoco.ie
Website: www.fingalcoco.ie/library

Howth Library
Main Street, Howth, Co. Dublin
Tel: 01 8322130
Fax: 01 8322277
E-mail: howthlibrary@fingalcoco.ie
Website: www.fingalcoco.ie
Website: www.fingalcoco.ie/library

Malahide Library
P.O. Box 11336, Main Street,
Malahide, Fingal, Co. Dublin
Tel: 01 8704430 / 4431
Fax: 01 8283526
E-mail:
malahidelibrary@fingalcoco.ie
Website: www.fingalcoco.ie/library

Skerries Library
Strand Street, Skerries, Co. Dublin
Tel: 01 8491900
Fax: 01 8495142
E-mail:
skerrieslibrary@fingalcoco.ie
Website: www.fingalcoco.ie/library

Swords Library
Rathbeale Road, Rathbeale, Swords,
Co. Dublin
Tel: 01 8404179
Fax: 01 8404417
E-mail:
swordslibrary@fingalcoco.ie
Website: www.fingalcoco.ie/library

SOUTH COUNTY DUBLIN

South Dublin Libraries' Headquarters

Unit 1, Square Industrial Complex,
Tallaght, Dublin 24
Librarian: Georgina Byrne
Tel: 01 4597834
Fax: 01 4597872
E-mail: libraries@sdublincoco.ie
Website:
www.southdublinlibraries.ie

Ballyroan Library

Orchardstown Avenue,
Rathfarnham, Dublin 16
Senior Librarian: Ann Dunne
Tel: 01 4941900
Fax: 01 4947083
E-mail: ballyroan@sdublincoco.ie
Website:
www.southdublinlibraries.ie

Castletymon Library

Castletymon Shopping Centre, Tymon
Road North, Tallaght, Dublin 24
Senior Librarian: Helen Brennan
Tel: 01 4524888
Fax: 01 4597873
E-mail:
castletymon@sdublincoco.ie
Website:
www.southdublinlibraries.ie

Clondalkin Library

Monastery Road, Clondalkin, Dublin 22
Acting Senior Librarian: Catherine
Gallagher
Tel: 01 4593315
Fax: 01 4595509
E-mail: clondalkin@sdublincoco.ie
Website:
www.southdublinlibraries.ie

Lucan Library

Superquinn Shopping Centre,
Newcastle Road, Lucan, Co. Dublin
Senior Librarian: Henry Morrin
Tel: 01 6216422
Fax: 01 6216433
E-mail: lucan@sdublincoco.ie
Website:
www.southdublinlibraries.ie

Tallaght Library

Library Square, Tallaght, Dublin 24
Senior Executive Librarian: Una
Phelan
Tel: 01 4620073
Fax: 01 4149207
E-mail: talib@sdublincoco.ie
Website:
www.southdublinlibraries.ie

The John Jennings Library,

Stewarts Hospital, Palmerstown,
Dublin 20
Senior Librarian: Siobhan McCrystal
Tel: 01 6264444 (extn. 1129)
Fax: 01 6261707
E-mail:
library@stewartshospital.com
Website:
www.stewartshospital.com

Whitechurch Library

Taylor's Lane, Rathfarnham, Dublin 16
Librarian: Breda Bollard
Tel: 01 4930199
E-mail:
whitechurch@sdublincoco.ie
Website:
www.southdublinlibraries.ie

Mobile Libraries

South Dublin County Libraries, Unit
1 The Square Industrial Complex,

Tallaght, Dublin 24
Senior Librarian: Bernie
Meenaghan
Tel: 01 4597834
E-mail: mobiles@sdublincoco.ie
Website:
www.southdublinlibraries.ie

DÚN LAOGHAIRE-RATHDOWN

Dún Laoghaire-Rathdown County Library Headquarters
2 Harbour Square, Dun Laoghaire, Co. Dublin
Librarian: Laura Higgins, Clerical Officer
Tel: 01 2781788 Ext: 3700
Fax: 01 2781792
E-mail: lhiggins@dlrcoco.ie
Website: www.dlrcoco.ie/library

Blackrock Library
Valentine House, Temple Road, Blackrock, Co. Dublin
Librarian: Jonathan Duggan
Tel: 01 2888117
Fax: 01 2780075
E-mail: blackrocklib@dlrcoco.ie
Website: www.dlrcoco.ie/library

Cabinteely Library
Old Bray Road, Cabinteely, Dublin 18
Librarian: Patricia Byrne
Tel: 01 2855363
Fax: 01 2353000
E-mail: cabinteelylib@dlrcoco.ie
Website: www.dlrcoco.ie/library

Dalkey Library
Castle Street, Dalkey, Co. Dublin
Librarian: Fiona Doherty
Tel: 01 2855317 / 2855277

Fax: 01 2855789
E-mail: dalkeylib@dlrcoco.ie
Website: www.dlrcoco.ie/library

Deansgrange Library
Clonkeen Drive, Deansgrange, Dublin 18
Librarian: Mary McCaughan
Tel: 01 2850860
Fax: 01 2898359
E-mail: deansgrangelib@dlrcoco.ie
Website: www.dlrcoco.ie/library

Dún Laoghaire Library
Lower Georges Street, Dún Laoghaire, Co. Dublin
Librarian: Detta O'Connor
Tel: 01 2801147
Fax: 01 2846141
E-mail: dunlaoghairelib@dlrcoco.ie
Website: www.dlrcoco.ie/library

Dundrum Library
Upper Churchtown Road, Dundrum, Dublin 14
Librarian: Lisa Murphy
Tel: 01 2985000
Fax: 01 2963216
E-mail: dundrumlib@dlrcoco.ie
Website: www.dlrcoco.ie/library

Sallynoggin Library
Senior College, Sallynoggin, Co. Dublin
Librarian: Yvonne Quigley
Tel: 01 2850127
Fax: 01 2850127
E-mail: sallynogginlib@dlrcoco.ie
Website: www.dlrcoco.ie/library

Shankill Library
Library Road, Shankill, Co. Dublin
Librarian: Mary Reynolds

Tel: 01 2823081
Fax: 01 2824555
E-mail: shankilllib@dlrcoco.ie
Website: www.dlrcoco.ie/library

Stillorgan Library
St Laurence's Park, Stillorgan, Co. Dublin
Librarian: Anne Millane
Tel: 01 2889655
Fax: 01 2781794
E-mail: stillorganlib@dlrcoco.ie
Website: www.dlrcoco.ie/ibraries

GALWAY - CITY

Galway City Library
Hynes Building, St Augustine Street, Galway
Tel: 091 561666
Fax: 091 566852
E-mail: info@galwaylibrary.ie
Website: www.galwaylibrary.ie

Ballybane Library
Ballybane, Co. Galway
Tel: 091 380590
E-mail: ballybane@galwaylibrary.ie
Website: www.galwaylibrary.ie

Oranmore Library
Main Street, Oranmore, Co. Galway
Librarian: John Lawlor
Tel: 091 792117
E-mail: oranmore@galwaylibrary.ie
Website: www.galwaylibrary.ie

Westside Library
Seamus Quirke Road, Galway
Tel: 091 520616
Fax: 091 565039
E-mail: westside@galwaylibrary.ie
Website: www.galwaylibrary.ie

COUNTY GALWAY

Athenry Library
Main Street, Athenry, Co. Galway
Tel: 091 845592
E-mail: athenry@galwaylibrary.ie
Website: www.galwaylibrary.ie

Ballinasloe Library
Fairgreen, Ballinasloe, Co. Galway
Librarian: Mrs. Mary Dillon
Tel: 090 9643464
E-mail: ballinasloe@galwaylibrary.ie
Website: www.galwaylibrary.ie

Ballygar Branch Library
Ballygar, Co. Galway
Librarian: Mrs. M. O'Malley
Tel: 090 6624919
E-mail: ballygar@galwaylibrary.ie
Website: www.galwaylibrary.ie

Carraroe Library
An Scailp Chultúrtha, An Cheathrú Rua, Co. na Gaillimhe
Librarian: Bernie Kelly
Tel: 091 595733
E-mail: anceathrurua@galwaylibrary.ie
Website: www.galwaylibrary.ie

Clifden Library
Market Street, Clifden, Co. Galway
Librarian: Paul Keogh
Tel: 095 21092
E-mail: clifden@galwaylibrary.ie
Website: www.galwaylibrary.ie

Dunmore Library
Main Street, Dunmore, Co. Galway
Librarian: Linda Morris
Tel: 093 38923

E-mail: dunmore@galwaylibrary.ie
Website: www.galwaylibrary.ie

Eyrecourt Library
Main Street, Eyrecourt, Co. Galway
Librarian: Laura Flynn
Tel: 090 9675056
E-mail: eyrecourt@galwaylibrary.ie
Website: www.galwaylibrary.ie

Glenamaddy Library
Glennamaddy, Co. Galway
Librarian: Mary Donelan
Tel: 094 9659734
E-mail:
glenamaddy@galwaylibrary.ie
Website: www.galwaylibrary.ie

Gort Branch Library
Old Church of Ireland, Queen Street,
Gort, Co. Galway
Tel: 091 631224
E-mail: gort@galwaylibrary.ie
Website: www.galwaylibrary.ie

Headford Library
Library, Headford, Co. Galway
Librarian: Edel Talbot
Tel: 093 36406
E-mail: headford@galwaylibrary.ie
Website: www.galwaylibrary.ie

Inishbofin Library
Inishbofin, Co. Galway
Librarian: Paul Kehoe
Tel: 095 45861
Website: www.galwaylibrary.ie

Inis Meáin
Inis Meain Library, Inis Meáin, Co.
Galway
Librarian: Máirín Uí Chonghaile
Tel: 099 73136

E-mail: inismeain@galwaylibrary.ie
Website: www.galwaylibrary.ie

Inis Oirr Library
Inis Oirr, Co. Galway
Librarian: Áine Ní Coistealbha
Tel: 099 75154
E-mail: inisoirr@galwaylibrary.ie
Website: www.galwaylibrary.ie

Kilimor Library
Main Street, Killimor, Co. Galway
Librarian: Marie Mullins
Tel: 090 9676062
E-mail: killimor@galwaylibrary.ie
Website: www.galwaylibrary.ie

Kilronan Library
Kilronan, Inis Mór, Co. Galway
Librarian: Mairín Ní Fhlaithearta
Tel: 099 20937
E-mail: inismor@galwaylibrary.ie
Website: www.galwaylibrary.ie

Leenane Library
Leenane, Co. Galway
Librarian: Catherine O'Neill
Tel: 095 42920
E-mail: leenane @galwaylibrary.ie
Website: www.galwaylibrary.ie

Letterfrack Library
Letterfrack Furniture College,
Letterfrack Co. Galway
Librarian: Sigi Gilger
Tel: 095 41660
E-mail:
letterfracklibrary@eircom.net
Website: www.galwaylibrary.ie

Loughrea Branch Library
Church Street, Loughrea, Co. Galway
Librarian: Ms. Ann Callanan

Tel: 091 847220
E-mail: loughrea@galwaylibrary.ie
Website: www.galwaylibrary.ie

Moylough Library
Main Street, Moylough, Co. Galway
Librarian: Patricia Conneely
Tel: 090 9679072
E-mail: moylough@galwaylibrary.ie
Website: www.galwaylibrary.ie

Oughterard Library
Main Street, Oughterard, Co. Galway
Librarian: Ruth Meally
Tel: 091 557002
E-mail:
oughterard@galwaylibrary.ie
Website: www.galwaylibrary.ie

Portumna Library
Main Street, Portumna, Co. Galway
Librarian: Teresa Tierney
Tel: 090 9741261
E-mail: portumna@galwaylibrary.ie
Website: www.galwaylibrary.ie

Roundstone Library
Seaview, Roundstone, Co. Galway
Librarian: Caroline Sweeney
Tel: 095 35518
E-mail:
roundstonelibrary@eircom.net
Website: www.galwaylibrary.ie

Spiddal Library
Main Street, Spiddal, Co. Galway
Librarian: Máire Breathnach
Tel: 091 504028
E-mail: anspideil@galwaylibrary.ie
Website: www.galwaylibrary.ie

Tiernea Library
Tiernea, Lettermore, Co. Galway

Librarian: Margaret Vaughan
Tel: 091 551610
E-mail: tiernealibrary@eircom.net
Website: www.galwaylibrary.ie

Tuam Library
Main Street, Tuam, Co. Galway
Librarian: Emer Donoghue
Tel: 093 24287
E-mail: tuam@galwaylibrary.ie
Website: www.galwaylibrary.ie

Woodford Library
Main Street, Woodford, Co. Galway
Tel: 090 9749200
E-mail: woodford@galwaylibrary.ie
Website: www.galwaylibrary.ie

COUNTY KERRY

**Kerry County Library
Headquarters**
Moyderwell, Tralee, Co. Kerry
County Librarian: Tommy O'Connor
Tel: 066 7121200
Fax: 066 7129202
E-mail: info@kerrylibrary.ie
Website: www.kerrylibrary.ie

Ballybunion Library
Sandhill Road, Ballybunion, Co.
Kerry
Librarian: Dolores McKenna
Tel: 068 27615
E-Mail:
ballybunion@kerrylibrary.ie
Website: www.kerrylibrary.ie

Caherciveen Library
Caherciveen, Co. Kerry
Librarians: Noreen O'Sullivan and
Hazel Joy

Tel: 066 9472287
E-mail: cahirciveen@kerrylibrary.ie
Website: www.kerrylibrary.ie

Castleisland Library
Area Services Centre, Station Road,
Castleisland, Co. Kerry
Librarians: Eamon Browne, Lucy
Kerins, Eileen Murphy
Tel: 066 7163403
E-mail: castleisland@kerrylibrary.ie
Website: www.kerrylibrary.ie

Dingle Library - Leabharlann an Daingin
Sráid an Dóirín, An Daingean, Co.
Chiarraí
Librarians: Bernard MacBrádaigh,
Niamh Doyle, Kathleen Carroll
Tel: 066 9151499
E-mail: dingle@kerrylibrary.ie
Website: www.kerrylibrary.ie

Kenmare Library
Shelbourne Street, Kenmare, Co.
Kerry
Librarians: Carmel Moriarty and
Mary O'Grady
Tel: 064 6641416
E-mail: kenmare@kerrylibrary.ie
Website: www.kerrylibrary.ie

Killarney Library
Rock Road, Killarney, Co. Kerry
Librarian: Mary Murray
Tel: 064 6632655
Fax: 064 6632967
E-mail: killarney@kerrylibrary.ie
Website: www.kerrycountylibrary.ie

Killorglin Library
Library Place, Killorglin, Co. Kerry
Librarians: Eibhlín Hayes, Margaret

Riordan
Tel: 066 9761272
E-mail: killorglin@kerrylibrary.ie
Website: www.kerrycountylibrary.ie

Listowel Library
Civic Centre, Listowel, Co. Kerry
Librarians: Martina Daly, Patti-Ann
O'Leary, Laureen Moriarty, Mary B.
Quirke
Tel: 068 23044
E-mail: listowel@kerrylibrary.ie
Website: www.kerrycountylibrary.ie

Tralee Library
Moyderwell, Tralee, Co. Kerry
Librarian: Ann Ferguson
Tel: 066 7121200
Fax: 066 7129202
E-Mail: tralee@kerrylibrary.ie
Website: www.kerrycountylibrary.ie

COUNTY KILDARE

Kildare County Library Headquarters
Riverbank Newbridge Co. Kildare.
Tel: 045 431109
Fax: 045 432490
E-mail: colibrary@kildarecoco.ie
Website: www.kildare.ie/library

Athy Library
Emily Square, Athy, Co. Kildare
Tel: 059 8631144
E-mail: athylib@kildarecoco.ie
Website: www.kildare.ie/library

Ballitore Public Library and Museum
Mary Leadbetter House, Ballitore,
Co. Kildare

Tel: 059 8623344
E-mail: ballitorelib@kildarecoco.ie
Website: www.kildare.ie/library

Castledermot Public Library
Main Street, Castledermot, Co.
Kildare
Tel: 059 9144483
E-mail:
castledermotlib@kildarecoco.ie
Website: www.kildare.ie/library

Celbrige Community Library
St Patrick's Park, Celbridge, Co.
Kildare
Tel: 01 6272207
E-mail: Celbridgelib@kildarecoco.ie
Website: www.kildare.ie/library

Clane Public Library
The Woods, Clane, Co. Kildare
Tel: 045 892716
E-mail: Clanelib@kildarecoco.ie
Website: www.kildare.ie/library

Clocha Rince Library
Clocha Rince, Co. Kildare
Tel: 046 9553428
E-mail:
clocharincelib@kildarecoco.ie
Website: www.kildare.ie/library

Kilcock Branch Library
New Lane, Main Street, Kilcock, Co.
Kildare
Tel: 01 6284403
E-mail: Kilcocklib@kildarecoco.ie
Website: www.kildare.ie/library

Kilcullen Community Library
New Abbey Road, Kilcullen, Co.
Kildare
Tel: 045 482193

E-mail: Kilcullenlib@kildarecoco.ie
Website: www.kildare.ie/library

Kildare Library
Kildare Business Park, Melitta Road,
Kildare, Co. Kildare
Tel: 045 520235
E-mail: Kildarelib@kildarecoco.ie
Website: www.kildare.ie/library

Leixlip Public Library
Captain's Hill, Leixlip, Co. Kildare
Tel: 01 6060050
Fax: 01 6245970
E-mail: Leixliplib@kildarecoco.ie
Website: www.kildare.ie/library

Maynooth Community Library
Main Street, Maynooth, Co. Kildare
Tel: 01 6285530
E-mail:
Maynoothlib@kildarecoco.ie
Website: www.kildare.ie/library

Monasterevin Public Library
Watermill Place, Monasterevin, Co.
Kildare
Tel: 045 529239
E-mail:
Monasterevinlib@kildarecoco.ie
Website: www.kildare.ie/library

Coill Dubh Public Library
Naas, Co. Kildare
Tel: 045 431 486
E-mail: coilldubhlib@eircom.net
Website: www.kildare.ie/library

Naas Community Library
Harbour View, Naas, Co. Kildare
Tel: 045 879111
Fax: 045 881766
E-mail: Naaslib@kildarecoco.ie
Website: www.kildare.ie/library

Newbridge Public Library

Athgarvan Road, Newbridge, Co. Kildare
Tel: 045 436453
E-mail:
Newbridgelib@kildarecoco.ie
Website: www.kildare.ie/library

Rathangan Public Library

Canal Court, Rathangan, Co. Kildare
Tel: 045 528078
E-mail:
rathanganlib@kildarecoco.ie
Website: www.kildare.ie/library

Mobile Library Service Point

Library Headquarters, Riverbank
Arts Centre, Main Street,
Newbridge, Co. Kildare
Tel: 045 448304 / 087 2399215
Website: www.kildare.ie/library

COUNTY KILKENNY

Kilkenny Library Headquarters and Local Studies Department

John's Green House, John's Green
Kilkenny
Tel: 056 7794160
E-mail:info@kilkennylibrary.ie
Website:
www.kilkennylibrary.kilkenny.ie

Callan Library

Clonmel Road, Callan, Co. Kilkenny
Tel: 056 7794183
E-mail: callan@kilkennylibrary.ie
Website:
www.kilkennylibrary.kilkenny.ie

Castlecomer Library

Kilkenny Street, Castlecomer, Co.
Kilkenny
Tel: 056 4440651
E-mail:
castlecomer@kilkennylibrary.ie
Website:
www.kilkennylibrary.kilkenny.ie

Graiguenamanagh Library

Convent Road, Graiguenamanagh,
Co. Kilkenny
Tel: 056 7794178
E-mail:
graiguenamanagh@kilkennylibrary.ie
Website:
www.kilkennylibrary.kilkenny.ie

Kilkenny City Library

John's Quay, Kilkenny
Tel: 056 7794174
E-mail:
citylibrary@kilkennylibrary.ie
Website:
www.kilkennylibrary.kilkenny.ie

Loughboy Branch

Loughboy Shopping Centre,
Waterford Road, Kilkenny
Tel: 056 7794176
E-mail:
loughboy@kilkennylibrary.ie
Website:
www.kilkennylibrary.kilkenny.ie

Thomastown Library

Marshes Street, Thomastown, Co.
Kilkenny
Tel: 056 7724911
E-mail:
thomastown@kilkennylibrary.ie
Website:
www.kilkennylibrary.kilkenny.ie

Urlingford Library
The Courthouse, Urlingford, Co.
Kilkenny
Tel: 056 7794182
E-mail:
urlingford@kilkennylibrary.ie
Website:
www.kilkennylibrary.kilkenny.ie

COUNTY LAOIS

Laois County Library
Headquarters
Aras an Chontae, James Fintan Lalor
Avenue, Portlaoise, Co. Laois.
Tel: 057 8674315
Fax: 057 8674381
E-mail: library@laoiscoco.ie
Website: www.laois.ie/library

Abbeyleix Public Library
Abbeyleix, Co. Laois
Assistant Librarian: Laura Brett
Tel: 057 873 0020
Website: www.laois.ie/library

Ballylinan Library
Librarian: Niamh Boyce
Tel: 059 8625007
Website: www.laois.ie/library

Borris in Ossory Library
Librarian: Pauline Gardner
Tel: 057 8674315
Website: www.laois.ie/library

Clonaslee Library
Librarian: Maureen Cusack
Tel: 057 8648437
Website: www.laois.ie/library

Durrow Library
Librarian: Catherine Hutchinson
Tel: 057 8736090
Website: www.laois.ie/library

Mountmellick Library
Irishtown, Mountmellick, Co. Laois
Librarian: Fiona Lynch
Tel: 057 8624733
Website: www.laois.ie/library

Mountrath Public Library
Mountrath, Co. Laois
Assistant Librarian: Breda Connell
Tel: 057 8756378
Website: www.laois.ie/library

Portlaoise Library
Executive Librarian: Jacqueline
McIntyre
Tel: 057 8622333
Website: www.laois.ie/library

Portarlington Library
Portarlington, Co. Laois
Librarian: Patricia Norton
Tel: 057 8643751
Website: www.laois.ie/library

Rathdowney Library
Rathdowney, Co. Laois
Librarian: Catherine Fitzpatrick
Tel: 0505 46852
Website: www.laois.ie/library

Stradbally Public Library
Stradbally, Co. Laois
County Librarian: Gerry Maher
Tel: 057 8674313
Website: www.laois.ie/library

Timahoe Library
Branch Librarian: Mairin Scully

Tel: 057 8627231
Website: www.laois.ie/library

COUNTY LEITRIM

Leitrim County Library Headquarters
Main Street, Ballinamore, Co. Leitrim
Librarian: Gabrielle Flynn
Tel: 071 9645582
Fax: 071 964 4425
E-mail: leitrimlibrary@leitrimcoco.ie
Website: www.leitrimcoco.ie

Ballinamore Library
Main Street, Ballinamore, Co. Leitrim
Librarians: Hilda King, Mary Bohan, Veronica Mc Keon
Tel: 071 9645566
E-mail: ballinamorelibrary@leitrimcoco.ie
Website: www.leitrimcoco.ie

Carrick-on-Shannon Library
Park Lane House, Carrick-on-Shannon, Co. Leitrim
Librarians: Mary Gannon & Anna McKiernan
Tel: 071 9620789
E-mail: carrickonshannonlibrary@leitrimcoco.ie
Website: www.leitrimcoco.ie

Carrigallen Library
Librarian: Helen Corcoran
Tel: 049 4339188
E-mail: carrigallenlibrary@leitrimcoco.ie
Website: www.leitrimcoco.ie

Dromahaire Library
Dromahaire, Co. Leitrim
Librarian : Breda Sweeney
Tel: 071 9164364
E-mail: dromahairlibrary@leitrimcoco.ie
Website: www.leitrimcoco.ie

Drumshanbo Branch Library
Main Street, Drumshanbo, Co. Leitrim
Librarian : Marian Mulvey
Tel: 071 9641258
E-mail: drumshanbolibrary@leitrimcoco.ie
Website: www.leitrimcoco.ie

Kiltyclogher Branch Library
Kiltyclogher, Co. Leitrim
Librarian: Orla Parkinson
Tel: 071 9854891
E-mail: kiltyclogherlibrary@leitrimcoco.ie
Website: www.leitrimcoco.ie

Kinlough Library
Bundoran Road, Kinlough, Co. Leitrim
Librarian: Mary McGowan
Tel: 071 9842554
E-mail: kinloughlibrary@leitrimcoco.ie
Website: www.leitrimcoco.ie

Manorhamilton Branch Library
Library Corner, Manorhamilton, Co. Leitrim
Librarian: Caroline Farrell, Teresa Kelly, Martina Feeney
Tel: 071 9856180
E-mail: manorhamiltonlibrary@leitrimcoco.ie
Website: www.leitrimcoco.ie

Mohill Library

Castle Street, Mohill, Co. Leitrim
Librarian: Evelyn Kelly
Tel: 071 9631360
E-mail:
mohilllibrary@leitrimcoco.ie
Website: www.leitrimcoco.ie

LIMERICK - CITY

Limerick City Library

The Granary, Michael Street,
Limerick City
Tel: 061 407510
Fax: 061 411506
E-mail: citylib@limerickcorp.ie
Website:
www.limerickcity.ie/Library

Roxboro Branch Library

Roxboro Shopping Centre, Roxboro,
Limerick City
Librarian: Fiona Ismail
Tel: 061 417906
E-mail: fismail@limerickcity.ie
Website:
www.limerickcity.ie/Library

Watch House Cross Commuity Library

Watch House Cross, Limerick City
Librarian: Patricia Cusack
Tel: 061 457726
E-mail: pcusack@limerickcity.ie
Website:
www.limerickcity.ie/Library

COUNTY LIMERICK

Limerick County Library Headquarters

Lissanalta House, Dooradoyle Road,
Limerick
Tel: 061 496526
Fax: 061 583135
E-mail: libinfo@limerickcoco.ie
Website: www.lcc.ie/library

Abbeyfeale Library

Bridge Street, Abbeyfeale, Co.
Limerick
Senior Library Assistant: Mike
Sweeney
Tel: 068 32488
E-mail:
abbeyfealelibrary@eircom.net
Website: www.lcc.ie/Library

Adare Library

Main Street, Adare, Co. Limerick
Executive Librarian: Margaret
O'Reilly
Tel: 061 396822
E-mail: adarelibrary@excite.com
Website: www.lcc.ie/Library

Askeaton Library

Librarian: Maria Sheehan
Tel: 061 392256
Website: www.lcc.ie/Library

Athea Library

Librarian: Noreen Tierney
Tel: 068 52810
Website: www.lcc.ie/Library

Ballingarry Library

Librarian: Eileen O'Connor
Tel: 069 68059
Website: www.lcc.ie/Library

Broadford Library
Librarian: Mary O'Gorman
Tel: 063 84274
Website: www.lcc.ie/Library

Ballylanders Library
Ballylanders
Co. Limerick
Tel: 063 91300
Website: www.lcc.ie/Library

Caherconlish Library
Caherconlish, Co. Limerick
Librarian: Mary Bogue
Tel: 061 352314
Website: www.lcc.ie/Library

Caherdavin Library
Community Centre, Whitethorn
Drive, Caherdavin, Co. Limerick
Tel: 061 325 496
Website: www.lcc.ie/Library

Cappamore Library
Cappamore, Co. Limerick
Librarian: Justine O'Malley
Tel: 061 381586
Website: www.lcc.ie/Library

Dooradoyle Library
The Cresent Shopping Centre,
Dooradoyle, Limerick
Librarian: Noreen O'Neill
Tel: 061 496860
Fax: 061 301144
Website: www.lcc.ie/Library

Drumcollogher Library
Dromcollogher, Co. Limerick
Librarian: Mary O'Gorman
Tel: 063 83011
E-mail: dromcolib@eircom.net
Website: www.lcc.ie/Library

Feenagh Library
Librarian: Mary Cronin
Tel: 063 85298
Website: www.lcc.ie/Library

Foynes Library
Foynes, Co. Limerick
Librarian: Catherine Griffin
Tel: 069 65365
E-mail: foyneslib@eircom.net
Website: www.lcc.ie/Library

Galbally Library
Galbally, Co. Limerick
Librarian: Mary Daly
Tel: 062 37100
Website: www.lcc.ie/Library

Glin Library
Librarian: Peg Prendiville
Tel: 068 26910
Website: www.lcc.ie/Library

Hospital Library
Librarian: Mary Bogue
Tel: 061 383060
Website: www.lcc.ie/Library

Kilfinane Library
Main Street, Kilfinnane, Co.
Limerick
Librarian: Mary Daly
Tel: 063 91002
Website: www.lcc.ie/Library

Kilmallock Library
Kilmallock, Co. Limerick
Tel: 063 20306
Fax: 063 31120
E-mail:
kilmallocklib@limerickcoco.ie
Website: www.lcc.ie/Library

Newcastle West Library

Gortboy, Newcastle West, Co. Limerick
Executive Librarian: Aileen Dillane
Tel: 069 62273
Fax: 069 61859
E-mail: newcastlewest@excite.com
Website: www.lcc.ie/Library

Pallaskenry Library

Pallaskenry, Limerick City
Librarian: Emer Bowen
Tel: 061 220974
Website: www.lcc.ie/Library

Rathkeale Library

Carnegie Library Building, New Line, Rathkeale, Co. Limerick
Librarian: Joan O'Toole
Tel: 069 64505
Website: www.lcc.ie/Library

Shanagolden Library

Assistant Librarian: Sarah Prendeville
Tel: 069 60818
Website: www.lcc.ie/Library

COUNTY LONGFORD

Longford Library Headquarters

Town Centre, Longford
County Librarian: Mary Reynolds
Tel: 043 3341124
E-mail: library@longfordcoco.ie
Website: www.longfordlibrary.ie

Ballymahon Library

Ballymahon, Co. Longford
Tel: 090 643 2546
E-mail: mahonlib@eircom.net
Website: www.longfordlibrary.ie

Drumlish Library

Mary Street, Drumlish, Co. Longford
Librarian: Isabella Mallon
Tel: 043 3324760
E-mail: drumlishlibrary@longfordcoco.ie
Website: www.longfordlibrary.ie

Edgeworthstown Library

Pound Street, Edgeworthstown, Co. Longford
Librarian: Sheila Walsh
Tel: 043 6671927
E-mail: Edgeworthstownlibrary@longfordcoco.ie
Website: www.longfordlibrary.ie

Granard Library

Market House, Granard, Co. Longford
Librarian: Rosemary Gaynor
Tel: 043 6686164
E-mail: Granardlibrary@longfordcoco.ie
Website: www.longfordlibrary.ie

Lanesboro Library

Main Street, Lanesborough, Co. Longford
Contact: Stella O'Sullivan
Tel: 043 3321291
E-mail: lanesborolibrary@longfordcoco.ie
Website: www.longfordlibrary.ie

Longford Library

Town Centre, Longford
Librarian: Willie O'Dowd
Tel. 043 3340727
E-mail: longfordbranchlibrary@longfordcoco.ie
Website: www.longfordlibrary.ie

COUNTY LOUTH

Louth County Library Headquarters
Roden Place, Dundalk, Co. Louth
County Librarian: Bernadette Fennell
Tel: 042 9353190
Fax: 042 9337635
E-mail:
bernadette.fennell@louthcoco.ie /
peter.murphy@louthcoco.ie
Website:
www.louthcoco.ie/Services/Library

Ardee Library
Market Square, Ardee, Co. Louth
Tel: 041 6856080
Website:
www.louthcoco.ie/Services/Library

Carlingford Library
Newry Street, Carlingford, Co. Louth
Tel: 042 9383020
Website:
www.louthcoco.ie/Services/Library

Drogheda Library
Stockwell Street, Drogheda, Co. Louth
Tel: 041 9836649
Fax: 041 9836649
Website:
www.louthcoco.ie/Services/Library

Dunleer Library
Station House, Dunleer, Co. Louth
Tel: 041 6861270
Website:
www.louthcoco.ie/Services/Library

Dundalk Library
Roden Place, Dundalk, Co. Louth
Tel: 042 9353190
Fax: 042 9337635
E-mail:
referencelibrary@louthcoco.ie
Website:
www.louthcoco.ie/Services/Library

COUNTY MAYO

Mayo County Library Headquarters
John Moore Road, Castlebar Co. Mayo
Librarian: Austin Vaughan
Tel: 094 9047921
Fax: 094 9026491
E-mail: avaughan@mayococo.ie
Website: www.mayolibrary.ie

Achill Library
The Library, Achill Sound, Co. Mayo
Librarian: Pauline Briody
Tel: 098 20910
E-mail: pbriody@mayococo.ie
Website: www.mayolibrary.ie

Ballina Library
Pearse Street, Ballina, Co. Mayo
Librarian: Barbara Varley
Tel: 096 70833
Fax: 096 22180
E-mail: bvarley@mayococo.ie
Website: www.mayolibrary.ie

Ballinrobe Library
Main Street, Ballinrobe, Co. Mayo
Librarian: Mary Farragher
Tel: 094 9541896
E-mail: mfarragher@mayococo.ie
Website: www.mayolibrary.ie

Ballyhaunis Public Library
Clare Street, Ballyhaunis, Co. Mayo
Librarian: Eleanor Freyne
Tel: 094 9630161
E-mail: efreyne@mayococo.ie
Website: www.mayolibrary.ie

Belmullet Library
Civic Centre, Belmullet, Co. Mayo
Librarian: Brid Lavelle
Tel: 097 82555
E-mail: blavelle@mayococo.ie
Website: www.mayolibrary.ie

Castlebar Library
John Moore Road, Castlebar, Co. Mayo
Librarian: Paula Leavy McCarthy
Tel: 094 9047925 / 9047936
Fax: 094 9024774
E-mail: plmccart@mayococo.ie
Website: www.mayolibrary.ie

Charlestown Library
Charlestown Library, Charlestown, Co. Mayo
Librarian: Noreen Gannon
Tel: 094 9255934
E-mail: ngannon@mayococo.ie
Website: www.mayolibrary.ie

Clare Island Library
The Library, Clare Island, Co. Mayo
Librarian: Catharina Jager
Tel: 098 29838
E-mail: cliara@anu.ie
Website: www.mayolibrary.ie

Claremorris Library
Dalton Street, Claremorris, Co. Mayo
Tel: 094 9371666
E-mail: claremorrislib@mayococo.ie
Website: www.mayolibrary.ie

Crossmolina Library
Ballina Street, Crossmolina, Co. Mayo
Librarian: Maureen Gallagher
Tel: 096 31939
E-mail: mgallagh@mayococo.ie
Website: www.mayolibrary.ie

Foxford Library
Main Street, Foxford, Co. Mayo
Librarian: Kathie Joyce
Tel: 094 9256040
E-mail: kjoyce@mayococo.ie
Website: www.mayolibrary.ie

Kilkelly Library
Kilkelly, Co. Mayo,
Librarian: Dolores Power
Tel: 094 9367758
E-mail: dpower@mayococo.ie
Website: www.mayolibrary.ie

Kiltimagh Library
Aidan Street, Kiltimagh, Co. Mayo
Librarian: Bridie Wimsey
Tel: 094 9381786
E-mail: bwimsey@mayococo.ie
Website: www.mayolibrary.ie

Louisburg Library
Main Street, Louisburg, Co. Mayo
Librarian: Mary Keane
Tel: 098 66658
E-mail: mkeane@mayococo.ie
Website: www.mayolibrary.ie

Swinford Public Library
Bridge Street, Swinford, Co. Mayo
Librarian: Ann O'Brien
Tel: 094 9252065

E-mail: aobrien@mayococo.ie
Website: www.mayolibrary.ie

Westport Library
The Crescent, Westport, Co. Mayo
Librarian: Marguerite Foy
Tel: 098 25747
Fax: 098 25747
E-mail: westportlib@mayococo.ie
Website: www.mayolibrary.ie

COUNTY MEATH

Meath County Library
Railway Street, Navan, Co. Meath
Librarian: Ciaran Mangan
Tel: 046 9021134
Fax: 046 9021463
E-mail: cmangan@meathcoco.ie
Website: www.meath.ie/library

Ashbourne Library
1-2 Killegland Square Upper,
Killegland Street, Ashbourne, Co.
Meath
Tel: 01 8358185
E-mail:
ashbournelib@meathcoco.ie
Website: www.meath.ie/library

Athboy Library
Main Street, Athboy, Co. Meath
Tel: 046 9432539
E-mail: athboylib@meathcoco.ie
Website: www.meath.ie/library

Duleek Library
Main Street, Duleek, Co. Meath
Tel: 041 9880709
E-mail: duleeklib@meathcoco.ie
Website: www.meath.ie/library

Dunboyne Library
Castle View, Dunboyne, Co. Meath
Tel: 01 8251248
E-mail: dunboynelib@meathcoco.ie
Website: www.meath.ie/library

Dunshauglin Library
Main Street, Dunshaughlin, Co.
Meath
Tel: 01 8250504
E-mail: dunshlib@meathcoco.ie
Website: www.meath.ie/library

Kells Library
Maudlin Street, Kells, Co. Meath
Tel: 046 9241592
E-mail: kellslib@meathcoco.ie
Website: www.meath.ie/library

Navan Library
Railway Street, Navan, Co. Meath
Tel: 046 9021134
E-mail: navanlib@meathcoco.ie
Website: www.meath.ie/library

Nobber Library
Main Street, Nobber, Co. Meath
Tel: 046 9052732
E-mail:
nobberlibrary@meathcoco.ie
Website: www.meath.ie/library

Oldcastle Library
Millbrook Road, Oldcastle, Co.
Meath
Tel: 049 8542084
E-mail: oldcastlelib@meathcoco.ie
Website: www.meath.ie/library

Leabharlann Rathcairn
Seoladh: Ráth Cairn, Baile Átha Buí,
Co. na Mí
Teil 046-9430929

Ríomhphoist:
rathcairnlib@meathcoco.ie
Suíomh Gréasáin:
www.meath.ie/library

Slane Library
Castle Hill, Slane, Co. Meath
Tel: 041 9824955
E-mail: slanelib@meathcoco.ie
Website: www.meath.ie/library

Trim Library
High Street, Trim, Co. Meath
Tel: 046 9436014
E-mail: trimlib@meathcoco.ie
Website: www.meath.ie/library

COUNTY MONAGHAN

Monaghan County Library Headquarters
98th Avenue, Clones, Co. Monaghan
Tel: 047 51143
Fax: 047 51863
E-mail: moncolib@eircom.net
Website: www.monaghan.ie

Ballybay Library
Main Street, Ballybay, Co. Monaghan
Tel: 042 9741256
E-mail:
ballybaylibrary@monaghancoco.ie
Website: www.monaghan.ie

Carrickmacross Library
Market Square, Carrickmacross, Co. Monaghan
Tel: 042 9661148
E-mail:
carrickmacrosslibrary@monaghanc
oco.ie
Website: www.monaghan.ie

Castleblayney Library
Iontas Arts Resource Centre,
Conabury, Castleblaney, Co. Monaghan
Tel: 042 9740281
E-mail:
castleblayneylibrary@monaghanco
co.ie
Website: www.monaghan.ie

Clones Library
98 Avenue, Clones, Co. Monaghan
E-mail:
cloneslibrary@monaghancoco.ie
Website: www.monaghan.ie

Monaghan Library
North Road, Monaghan
Tel: 047 81830
Fax: 047 38688
E-mail:
monaghanlibrary@monaghancoco.ie
Website: www.monaghan.ie

Mobile Library
Library Headquarters, 98 Avenue,
Clones, Monaghan
Contact: Niall Greenan
Tel: Mondays at 047 74700.
Tuesday to Friday on 087 1385798
Website: www.monaghan.ie

COUNTY OFFALY

Offaly County Library Headquarters

O'Connor Square, Tullamore, Co. Offaly
County Librarian: Mary Stuart
Tel: 057 9346833 / 087 6887996
Fax: 057 935 2769
E-mail: mstuart@offalycoco.ie
Website: www.offalycoco.ie

Banagher Library

Moore's Corner, Banagher, Co. Offaly
Tel: 057 9151471
E-mail:
banagherlibrary@offalycoco.ie
Website: www.offalycoco.ie

Birr Library

Wilmer Road, Birr, Co. Offaly
Tel: 057 9124950
E-mail: birrlibrary@offalycoco.ie
Website:
www.offalycountylibrary.ie

Clara Library

Clara, Co. Offaly
Tel: 057 9331389
E-mail: claralibrary@offalycoco.ie
Website:
www.offalycountylibrary.ie

Daingean Library

Main Street, Daingean, Co. Offaly
Tel: 057 9353005
E-mail:
daingeanlibrary@offalycoco.ie
Website: www.offalycoco.ie

Edenderry Library

JKL Street, Edenderry, Co. Offaly
Tel: 046 9731028
E-mail:
edenderrylibrary@offalycoco.ie
Website: www.offalycoco.ie

Ferbane Library

Gallen, Ferbane, Co. Offaly
Tel: 090 6454259
E-mail:
ferbanelibrary@offalycoco.ie
Website: www.offalycoco.ie

Kilcormac Library

Main Street, Kilcormac, Co. Offaly
Tel: 057 9135086
E-mail:
kilcormaclibrary@offalycoco.ie
Website: www.offaly.ie

Tullamore Library

O'Connor Square, Tullamore, Co. Offaly.
Tel: 057 93 46832
E-mail:
tullamorelibrary@offalycoco.ie
Website:
www.offalycountylibrary.ie

Shinrone Library

Brosna Road, Shinrone, Co. Offaly
Tel: 0505 47045
E-mail:
shinronelibrary@offalycoco.ie
Website: www.offaly.ie

COUNTY ROSCOMMON

Roscommon County Library

Abbey Street, Roscommon
Librarian: Richard Farrell
Tel: 090 6637277
Fax: 090 6637101
E-mail: roslib@roscommoncoco.ie

Website:
www.roscommoncoco.ie/services/
library

Ballaghdereen Library
Main Street, Ballaghaderreen, Co.
Roscommon
Senior Library Assistant: Deirdre
Creighton
Tel: 094 9877044
E-mail:
ballaghaderreenlibrary@roscommo
ncoco.ie
Website:
www.roscommoncoco.ie/services/
library

Ballyforan Library
Courthouse, Ballyforan, Co.
Roscommon
Tel: 090 662 6100
Website:
www.roscommoncoco.ie/services/
library

Boyle Library
King House, Boyle. Co. Roscommon
Senior Library Assistant: Patricia
O'Flaherty
Tel: 071 9662800
E-mail:
boylelibrary@roscommoncoco.ie
Website:
www.roscommoncoco.ie/services/
library

Castlerea Library
Main Street, Castlerea, Co.
Roscommon
Librarian: Maura Carroll
Tel: 094 9620745
E-mail:
castlerealibrary@roscommoncoco.ie

Website:
www.roscommoncoco.ie/services/
library

Elphin Library
Main Street, Elphin, Co. Roscommon
Tel: 071 9635775
E-mail: ebllib@eircom.net
Website:
www.roscommoncoco.ie/services/
library

Roscommon Branch Library
Abbey Street, Roscommon
Senior Library Assistant: Caitlin
Browne
Website:
www.roscommoncoco.ie/services/
library

Strokestown Library
Bawn Street, Strokestown, Co.
Roscommon
Tel: 071 9634027
E-mail:
strokestownlibrary@roscommonco
co.ie
Website:
www.roscommoncoco.ie/services/
library

**Roscommon Mobile Library
Service**
Contact: Meliosa Moran, Senior
Library Assistant
Tel: 090 6637279 / 087 9943508
Website:
www.roscommoncoco.ie/services/
library

COUNTY SLIGO

Sligo Library Headquarters
Stephen Street, Sligo
County Librarian: Donal Tinney,
Tel: 071 9111850
Fax: 071 914 6798
E-mail: sligolib@sligococo.ie
Website: www.sligolibrary.ie

Ballymote Library
The Courthouse, Ballymote, Co.
Sligo
Librarian: Louise McGrath
Tel: 071 9111663
E-mail:
ballymotebranchlibrary@sligococo.ie
Website: www.sligolibrary.ie

Enniscrone Library
Pier Road, Enniscrone, Co. Sligo
Librarians: Dympna Egan, Ann
Melia
Tel: 071 9111653
E-mail:
enniscronebranchlibrary@sligococ
o.ie
Website: www.sligolibrary.ie

**Local Studies and Reference
Library**
Westward Town Centre, Bridge
Street, Sligo
Tel: 071 9111858
Fax: 071 9146798
E-mail: sligolib@sligococo.ie
Website: www.sligolibrary.ie

Sligo Central Library,
Stephen Street, Sligo
Executive Librarian: Caroline
Morgan,
Tel: 071 9111675

E-mail:
sligocentrallibrary@sligococo.ie
Website: www.sligolibrary.ie

Tubbercurry Library
Teach Laighne, Humbert Street,
Tubbercurry, Co. Sligo
Senior Library Assistant: Grainne
Mahon
Tel: 071 9111705
E-mail: tubberlibrary@sligococo.ie
Website: www.sligolibrary.ie

COUNTY TIPPERARY

**Tipperary Libraries
Headquarters**
Castle Avenue, Thurles Co.
Tipperary
County Librarian: Martin Maher
Tel: 0504 21555
Fax: 0504 23442
E-mail: info@tipperarylibraries.ie
Website: www.tipperarylibraries.ie

Borrisokane Library
Main Street, Borrisokane, Co.
Tipperary
Librarian: Noirín Duggan
Tel: 067 27199
Website: www.tipperarylibraries.ie

Cahir Library
The Square, Cahir, Co. Tipperary
Librarian: Ann Tuohy
Tel: 052 7442075
Website: www.tipperarylibraries.ie

Carrick-on-Suir Library
Fair Green, Carrick-on-Suir, Co.
Tipperary
Senior Library Assistant: Orla

O'Connor
Tel: 051 640591
Fax: 051 640591
Website: www.tipperarylibraries.ie

Cashel Library
Friar Street, Cashel, Co. Tipperary
Tel: 062 63825
Fax: 062 63948
E-mail:
cashel@tipperarylibraries.ie
Website: www.tipperarylibraries.ie

Clonmel Library
Emmet Street, Clonmel, Co.
Tipperary
Executive Librarian: Marie Boland
Tel: 052 6124545
Fax: 052 6127336
E-mail:
clonmel@tipperarylibraries.ie
Website: www.tipperarylibraries.ie

Cloughjordan Library
Main Street, Cloughjordan, Co.
Tipperary
Librarian: Marie Brady
Tel: 0505 42425
Website: www.tipperarylibraries.ie

Fethard Library
Main Street, Fethard, Co. Tipperary
Tel: 052 31728
Website: www.tipperarylibraries.ie

Killenaule Library
Slieveardagh Centre, River Street,
Killenaule, Co. Tipperary
Librarian: Maura Barrett
Tel: 052 9157906
Website: www.tipperarylibraries.ie

Nenagh Library
O'Rahilly Street, Nenagh, Co.
Tipperary
Executive Librarian: Breffni
Hannon
Tel: 067 34404
Fax: 067 34405
E-mail:
nenagh@tipperarylibraries.ie
Website: www.tipperarylibraries.ie

Templemore Library
Old Mill Court, Templemore, Co.
Tipperary
Librarians: Anne Loughnane,
Margaret Looby.
Tel: 0504 32555 / 32556
Fax: 0504 32545
E-mail:
templemore@tipperarylibraries.ie
Website: www.tipperarylibraries.ie

Thurles Library
The Source, Cathedral Street,
Thurles, Co. Tipperary
Executive Librarian: Ann Marie
Brophy
Tel: 0504 29720
Fax: 0504 21344
E-mail:
thurles@tipperarylibraries.ie
Website: www.tipperarylibraries.ie

Tipperary Town Library
Davis Street, Tipperary Town
Librarians: Gerardine Hughes,
Nollaig Butler
Tel: 062 51761
Fax: 062 51761
E-mail:
tipperary@tipperarylibraries.ie
Website: www.tipperarylibraries.ie

Roscrea Library
Birr Road, Roscrea, Co. Tipperary
Tel: 0505 22032
Website: www.tipperarylibraries.ie

Tipperary Studies,
The Source, Cathedral Street,
Thurles, Co. Tipperary
Senior Library Assistant: John
O'Gorman,
Tel: 0504 29278
Fax: 0504 21344
E-mail:
studies@tipperarylibraries.ie
Website: www.tipperarylibraries.ie

WATERFORD - CITY

Waterford City Council Library Service
Waterford City Council Depot,
Northern Extension Industrial
Estate, Old Kilmeaden Road,
Waterford City
City Librarian: Jane Cantwell
Tel: 051 849839
Fax: 051 850031
E-mail: library@waterfordcity.ie
Website:
www.waterfordcity.ie/library

Waterford City Central Library
Lady Lane, Waterford City
Librarian: Sinead O'Higgins
Tel: 051 849975
E-mail: sohiggins@waterfordcity.ie
Website:
www.waterfordcity.ie/library

Ardkeen Library
1st Floor, Ardkeen Shopping Centre,
Dunmore Road, Waterford

Librarian: Sinead Cummins
Tel: 051 849844
E-mail: scummins@waterfordcity.ie
Website:
www.waterfordcity.ie/library

Brown's Road Library
Paddy Brown's Road, Waterford
Librarian: Sinead Cummins
Tel: 051 - 849845
E-mail: scummins@waterfordcity.ie
Website:
www.waterfordcity.ie/library

COUNTY WATERFORD

Waterford County Library Headquarters
Ballyanchor Road, Lismore, Co.
Waterford.
County Librarian: Donald Brady
Tel: 058 21370
E-mail: libraryhq@waterfordcoco.ie
Website:
www.waterfordcountylibrary.ie

Cappoquin Library
Cappoquin, Co. Waterford
Librarian: Mary Tobin
Tel: 058 52263
E-mail:
cappoquinlibrary@waterfordcoco.ie
Website:
www.waterfordcountylibrary.ie

Dungarvan Central Library
Davitt's Quay, Dungarvan, Co.
Waterford
Executive Librarian: Ger Croughan
Tel: 058 41231
E-mail:
dungarvanlibrary@waterfordcoco.ie
Website: www.waterfordcoco.ie

Dunmore East Branch Library
Fisherman's Hall, Dunmore East,
Co. Waterford
Librarian: Claire O Mulláin
E-mail:
dunmorelibrary@waterfordcoco.ie
Website:
www.waterfordcountylibrary.ie

Kilmacthomas Library
Kilmacthomas, Co. Waterford
Librarian: Laura Kirwan
Tel: 051-294270
E-mail:
kilmacthomaslibrary@waterfordco
co.ie
Website:
www.waterfordcountylibrary.ie

Lisduggan Library
Paddy Brown's Road, Lisduggan, Co.
Waterford
Tel: 051 860 845
Website:
www.waterfordcountylibrary.ie

Lismore Library
West Street, Lismore, Co. Waterford
Executive Librarian: Eddie Byrne
Tel: 058 21377
E-mail:
lismorelibrary@waterfordcoco.ie
Website:
www.waterfordcountylibrary.ie

Portlaw Public Library
Brown Street, Portlaw, Co.
Waterford
Tel: 051 381479
E-mail:
portlawlibrary@waterfordcoco.ie
Website:
www.waterfordcountylibrary.ie

Tallow Library
Tallow, Co. Waterford
Librarian: Sheila Curtin
Tel: 058-56347
E-mail:
tallowlibrary@waterfordcoco.ie
Website:
www.waterfordcountylibrary.ie

Tramore Library
Market Street, Tramore, Co.
Waterford
Executive Librarian (Acting): Tracy
McEneaney
Tel: 051 381479
E-mail:
tramorelibrary@waterfordcoco.ie
Website:
www.waterfordcountylibrary.ie

COUNTY WESTMEATH

**Westmeath County Library
Headquarters**
Dublin Road, Mullingar, Co.
Westmeath
Tel: 044 9332162
E-mail: library@westmeathcoco.ie
Website:
www.westmeathcoco.ie/en/service
sa-z/library

Athlone Library
Aidan Heavey Public Library,
Athlone Civic Centre, Athlone, Co.
Westmeath
Senior Executive Librarian: Gearoid
O'Brien
Tel: 090 644 2157/8/9
E-mail: athlib@westmeathcoco.ie
Website:
www.westmeathcoco.ie/en/service
sa-z/library

Ballynacarrigy Library
2 Kilmurray's Corner,
Ballynacarrigy, Co. Westmeath
Librarian: Cecilia Connolly
Tel: 044 9373882
E-mail: bnclib@westmeathcoco.ie
Website:
www.westmeathcoco.ie/en/service
sa-z/library

Castlepollard Library
Civic Offices, Mullingar Road,
Castlepollard, Co. Westmeath
Tel: 044 9332199
E-mail: cpdlib@westmeathcoco.ie
Website:
www.westmeathcoco.ie/en/service
sa-z/library

Kilbeggan Library
The Square, Kilbeggan, Co.
Westmeath
Senior Library Assistant: Margaret
Crentsil
Tel: 057 9333148
E-mail: Killib@westmeathcoco.ie
Website:
www.westmeathcoco.ie/en/service
sa-z/library

Killucan Library
Rathwire Hall, Killucan, Co.
Westmeath
Librarian: Cecilia Connolly
Tel: 057 9374260
E-mail: klnlib@westmeathcoco.ie
Website:
www.westmeathcoco.ie/en/service
sa-z/library

Moate Library
Main Street, Moate, Co. Westmeath
Librarian: Lorna Farrell
Tel: 090 6481888
Fax: 090 6481888
E-mail:
moatelib@westmeathcoco.ie
Website:
www.westmeathcoco.ie/en/service
sa-z/library

Mullingar Library
County Buildings, Mount Street,
Mullingar, Co. Westmeath
Executive Librarian: Cailin
Gallagher
Tel: 044 9332161
E-mail: mgarlib@westmeathcoco.ie
Website:
www.westmeathcoco.ie/en/service
sa-z/library

COUNTY WEXFORD

Wexford County Library Headquarters
Library Management Services, 6A
Ardcavan Business Park, Ardcavan,
Wexford.
County Librarian: Fionnuala
Hanrahan
Tel: 053 9124922/9124928
Fax: 053 9121097
E-mail: libraryhq@wexfordcoco.ie
Website: www.wexford.ie/Library

Bunclody Library
Millwood, Carrigduff, Bunclody, Co.
Wexford
Executive Librarian: Patricia
Keenan
Tel: 053 9375466
E-mail:
bunclodylib@wexfordcoco.ie
Website: www.wexford.ie/Library

Enniscorthy Public Library

Lymington Road, Enniscorthy, Co. Wexford
Executive Librarian: Jarlath Glynn
Tel: 053 9236055
Fax: 053 9236164
E-mail: enniscorthylib@wexfordcoco.ie
Website: www.wexford.ie/Library

Gorey Library

Market house, Main Street, Gorey, Co. Wexford
Tel: 053 9421481
E-mail: goreylib@wexfordcoco.ie
Website: www.wexford.ie/Library

New Ross Library

Barrack Lane, New Ross, Co. Wexford
Executive Librarian: Sinead O'Gorman
Tel: 051 421877
E-mail: newrosslib@wexfordcoco.ie
Website: www.wexford.ie/Library

Wexford Town Library

McCauley's Car Park, Off Redmond Square, Wexford
Executive Librarian: Hazel Percival
Tel: 053 9121637
E-mail: wexfordlib@wexfordcoco.ie
Website: www.wexford.ie/Library

COUNTY WICKLOW

Wicklow County Library

Boghall Road, Bray, Co. Wicklow
Librarian: Brendan Martin
Tel: 01 2866566
Fax: 01 2865811
E-mail: library@wicklowcoco.ie
Website: www.wicklow.ie

Arklow Library

St Mary's Road, Arklow, Co. Wicklow
Librarian: Ann Murduff
Tel: 0402 39977
E-mail: AMurdiff@wicklowcoco.ie

Aughrim Public Library

Rathdrum Road, Aughrim, Co. Wicklow
Librarian: Mary Carty
Tel: 0402 36036
E-mail: MCarty@wicklowcoco.ie
Website: www.wicklow.ie

Avoca Library

IT Centre, Main Street, Avoca, Co. Wicklow
Librarian: Helen Maher
Tel: 0402 35022
Website: www.wicklow.ie

Ballywaltrim Library

Boghall Road, Bray, Co. Wicklow
Librarian: Ciara Brennan
Tel: 01 2723205
Fax: 01 2866581
E-mail: CBRennan@wicklowcoco.ie
Website: www.wicklow.ie

Baltinglass Library

Weaver Square, Baltinglass, Co. Wicklow
Librarian: Catherine Walshe
Tel: 059 6482300
E-mail: CWalshe@wicklowcoco.ie
Website: www.wicklow.ie

Blessington Library

New Town Centre, Blessington, Co. Wicklow
Librarian: Gillian Misstear
Tel: 045 891740

E-mail: GMisstear@wicklowcoco.ie
Website: www.wicklow.ie

Bray Public Library
Eglinton Road, Bray, Co. Wicklow
Librarian: Fiona Scannell
Tel: 01 2862600
E-mail: FScannell@wicklowcoco.ie
Website: www.wicklow.ie

Carnew Library
Main street, Carnew, Co. Wicklow
Librarian: Lena Elliot
Tel: 053 9426088
E-mail: LElliot@wicklowcoco.ie
Website: www.wicklow.ie

Dunlavin Library
Market House, Dunlavin, Co.
Wicklow
Librarian: Maura Greene
Tel: 045 401100
E-mail: MGreene@wicklowcoco.ie
Website: www.wicklow.ie

Enniskerry Library
Dublin Road, Enniskerry, Co.
Wicklow
Librarian: Peggy Byrne
Tel: 01 2864339
E-mail: PegByrne@wicklowcoco.ie
Website: www.wicklow.ie

Greystones Public Library
Mill Road, Greystones, Co. Wicklow
Librarian: Mary Murphy
Tel: 01 2873548
E-mail: Greylib@wicklowcoco.ie
Website: www.wicklow.ie

Local History Collection
(Located in Ballywaltrim Library)
For Enquiries or appointments

address correspondence to:
Ciara Brennan, Wicklow County
Library Headquarters, Boghall
Road, Bray, Co. Wicklow,
Tel: 01 2866566
E-mail: cbrennan@wicklowcoco.ie
Website: www.wicklow.ie

Rathdrum Library
Gilbert's Road, Rathdrum, Co.
Wicklow
Librarian: Margaret Byrne
Tel: 0404 43232
E-mail: MgtByrne@wicklowcoco.ie
Website: www.wicklow.ie

Tinahely Branch Library
Market House, Tinahely, Co.
Wicklow
Librarian: Miriam Barton
Tel: 0402 38080
E-mail: MBarton@wicklowcoco.ie
Website: www.wicklow.ie

Wicklow Library
Market Square, Wicklow
Librarian: Emer O'Grady
Tel: 0404 67025
E-mail: EOGrady@wicklowcoco.ie
Website: www.wicklow.ie

Wicklow Family History Centre
Wicklow's Historic Gaol, Killmantin
Hill, Wicklow Town
Tel: 0404 20126
Fax: 0404 61612
E-mail: wfh@eircom.net
Website:
www.wicklow.ie/FamilyHistoryCen
tre/

Mobile Library
Contact the library at:

library@wicklowcoco.ie
Website: www.wicklow.ie

NORTHERN IRELAND

Libraries NI - Headquarters
Office Suite 1, First Floor, Lisburn
Square House, 8 Haslem's Lane,
Lisburn, BT28 1TW
Chief Executive: Irene Knox
Tel: 028 9260 6750
Fax: 028 9267 9106
E-mail:
enquiries@librariesni.org.uk
Website: www.ni-libraries.net

Andersonstown Library
Slievegallion Drive, Belfast, Co.
Antrim, BT11 8JP
Librarian: Tinya Parkes
Tel: 028 9050 9200
Fax: 028 9050 9200
E-mail:
andersonstown.library@librariesni.
org.uk
Website: www.ni-libraries.net

Antrim Library
10 Railway Street, Antrim, Co.
Antrim, BT41 4AE
Librarian: Gerdette Doyle
Tel: 028 9446 1942
Fax: 028 9446 7931
E-mail:
antrim.library@librariesni.org.uk
Website: www.ni-libraries.net

Ardoyne Library
446 - 450 Crumlin Road, Belfast, Co.
Antrim, BT14 7GH
Librarian: Trevor Gordon
Tel: 028 9050 9202

Fax: 028 9050 9202
E-mail:
ardoyne.library@librariesni.org.uk
Website: www.ni-libraries.net

Armagh Library
2 Market Street, Armagh, Co.
Armagh, BT61 7BU
Librarian: Helen Grimes
Tel: 028 3752 4072
E-mail:
armaghlibrary@librariesni.org.uk
Website: www.ni-libraries.net

Ballycastle Library
5 Leyland Road, Ballycastle, Co.
Antrim, BT54 6DT
Librarian: Maura O'Loan
Tel: 028 2076 2566
E-mail: ballycastle.librariesni.org.uk
Website: www.ni-libraries.net

Ballyclare Library
Market House, School Street,
Ballyclare, Co. Antrim, BT39 9BE
Librarian: Josephine Patten
Tel: 028 9335 2269
Fax: 028 9335 2269
E-mail:
ballyclare.library@librariesni.org.uk
Website: www.ni-libraries.net

Ballyhackamore Library
1-3 Eastleigh Drive, Belfast, Co.
Down, BT4 3DX
Librarian: Maureen King
Tel: 028 9050 9204
E-mail:
ballyhackamore.library@librariesni
.org.uk

Ballymacarrett Library
19-35 Templemore Avenue, Belfast,

Co. Down, BT5 4FP
Librarian: Carol James
Tel: 028 9050 9207
E-mail:
ballymacarrett.library@librariesni.
org.uk
Website: www.ni-libraries.net

Ballymena Library
5 Pat's Brae, Ballymena, Co. Antrim,
BT43 5AX
Librarian: Maria Higgins
Tel: 028 2563 3950
Fax: 028 2563 3953
E-mail:
ballymena.library@librariesni.org.uk
Website: www.ni-libraries.net

Ballymoney Library
Rodden Foot, Queen Street,
Ballymoney, Co. Antrim, BT53 6JB
Librarian: Leah Tweed
Tel: 028 2766 3589
Fax: 028 2766 3589
E-mail:
ballymoney.library@librariesni.org.
uk
Website: www.ni-libraries.net

Ballynahinch Library
Main Street, Ballynahinch, Co.
Down, BT24 8DN
Tel: 028 9756 4282
Fax: 028 9756 4282
E-mail:
ballynahinchlibrary@librariesni.org
.uk
Website: www.ni-libraries.net

Banbridge Library
23 Scarva Road, Banbridge, Co.
Down, BT32 3AD
Librarian: Evelyn Hanna

Tel: 028 4062 3973
E-mail:
banbridgelibrary@librariesni.org.uk
Website: www.ni-libraries.net

Bangor Carnegie Library
Hamilton Road, Bangor, Co. Down,
BT20 4LH
Librarian: Diane McCready/Pamela
Macrory
Tel: 028 91270591
E-mail:
bangorcarnegie.library@librariesni.
org.uk
Website: www.ni-libraries.net

Belfast Central Library
Royal Avenue, Belfast, Co. Antrim,
BT1 1EA
Tel: 028 9050 9150
Fax: 028 9033 2819
E-mail: infobelb@librariesni.org.uk
Website: www.ni-libraries.net

Belfast Ulster and Irish Studies
Belfast Central Library, Royal
Avenue, Belfast, Co. Antrim
BT1 1 EA
Tel: 028 9050 9199
Fax: 028 9033 2819
E-mail: buis.belb@librariesni.org.uk
Website: www.ni-libraries.net

Belvoir Park Library
Drumart Square, Belfast, Co. Down,
BT8 7EY
Tel: 028 9064 4331
Fax: 028 9064 4331
E-mail:
belvoirpark.library@librariesni.org.
uk
Website: www.ni-libraries.net

Bessbrook Library
22 Church Road, Bessbrook, Co.
Armagh, BT35 7AQ
Librarian: Ann Morgan
Tel: 028 3083 0424
E-mail:
bessbrooklibrary@librariesni.org.uk
Website: www.ni-libraries.net

Braniel Library
Glen Road, Belfast, Co. Down, BT5
7JH
Tel: 028 9079 7420
Fax: 028 9079 7420
E-mail:
braniellibrary@librariesni.org.uk
Website: www.ni-libraries.net

Broughshane Library
Main Street, Broughshane, Co.
Antrim, BT42 4JW
Librarian: Beth Clyde
Tel: 028 2586 1613
Fax: 028 2586 1613
E-mail:
broughshane.library@librariesni.or
g.uk
Website: www.ni-libraries.net

Brownlow Library
2 Brownlow Road, Craigavon, Co.
Armagh, BT65 5DP
Librarian: Lynda Stewart
Tel: 028 3834 1946
E-mail:
brownlowlibrary@librariesni.org.uk
Website: www.ni-libraries.net

**Cardinal Tomás Ó Fiaich Library
and Archive**
15 Moy Road, Armagh, Co. Armagh,
BT61 7LY
Tel: 028 3752 2981

Fax: 028 3751 1944
Web: www.ofiaich.ie
E-mail: eolas@ofiaich.ie
Website: www.ni-libraries.net

Carnlough Library
Town Hall, Carnlough, Co. Antrim,
BT44 0EU
Librarian: Sandra Hook
Tel: 028 2888 5552
Fax: 028 2888 5552
E-mail:
carnlough.library@librariesni.org.uk
Website: www.ni-libraries.net

Carrickfergus Library
2 Joymount Court, Carrickfergus,
Co. Antrim, BT38 7DQ
Librarian: Dawn Young
Tel: 028 9336 2261
Fax: 028 9336 0589
E-mail:
carrickfergus.library@librariesni.or
g.uk
Website: www.ni-libraries.net

Carryduff Library
Church Road, Carryduff, Co. Down,
BT8 8DT
Tel: 028 9081 3568
Fax: 028 9081 3568
E-mail:
carrydufflibrary@librariesni.org.uk
Website: www.ni-libraries.net

Castlederg Library
1A Hospital Road, Castlederg, Co.
Tyrone, BT81 7BU
Tel: 028 8167 1419
Fax: 028 8167 9048
E-mail:
castlederglibrary@librariesni.org.uk
Website: www.ni-libraries.net

Castlewellan Library
3 Upper Square, Castlewellan, Co.
Down, BT31 9DA
Librarian: Ann Crilly
Tel: 028 4377 8433
Fax: 028 4377 8433
E-mail:
castlewellanlibrary@librariesni.org.uk
Website: www.ni-libraries.net

Centre for Migration Studies at
Ulster American Folk Park
1A Hospital Road, Castlederg, Co.
Tyrone, BT81 7BU
Tel: 028 8167 1419
Fax: 028 8167 9048
E-mail:
castlederglibrary@librariesni.org.uk
Website: www.ni-libraries.net

Chichester Library
Salisbury Avenue, Belfast, Co.
Antrim, BT15 5EB
Librarian: Julie Todd
Tel: 028 9050 9210
E-mail:
chichester.library@librariesni.org.uk
Website: www.ni-libraries.net

Cloughfern Library
2A Kings Crescent, Newtownabbey,
Co. Antrim, BT37 0DH
Librarian: Maureen Weir
Tel: 028 9085 4789
Fax: 028 9085 4789
E-mail:
cloughfern.library@librariesni.org.
uk
Website: www.ni-libraries.net

Coleraine Library
Queen Street, Coleraine, Co.
Londonderry, BT52 1BE

Librarian: Bernadette Kennedy
Tel: 028 7034 2561
Fax: 028 7034 2561
E-mail:
coleraine.library@librariesni.org.uk
Website: www.ni-libraries.net

Coalisland Library
2-4 Lineside, The Cornmill,
Coalisland, Co. Tyrone, BT71 4LT
Librarian: Mary Quinn
Tel: 028 8774 0569
E-mail:
coalislandlibrary@librariesni.org.uk
Website: www.ni-libraries.net

Colin Glen Library
Unit 17 Dairy Farm Centre,
Stewartstown Road, Dunmurry, Co.
Antrim, BT17 0AW
Tel: 028 9043 1266
Fax: 028 9043 1266
E-mail:
colin.glen@librariesni.org.uk
Website: www.ni-libraries.net

Comber Library
Newtownards Road, Comber, Co.
Down, BT23 5AU
Tel: 028 9187 2610
Fax: 028 9187 1759
E-mail:
comberlibrary@librariesni.org.uk
Website: www.ni-libraries.net

Cookstown Library
13 Burn Road, Cookstown, Co.
Tyrone, BT80 8DJ
Librarian: Bernie McCann
Tel: 028 8676 3702
E-mail:
cookstownlibrary@librariesni.org.uk
Website: www.ni-libraries.net

Cregagh Library
409-413 Cregagh Road, Belfast, Co.
Down, BT6 0LF
Tel: 028 9040 1365
Fax: 028 9079 8911
E-mail:
cregaghlibrary@librariesni.org.uk
Website: www.ni-libraries.net

Creggan Library
59 Central Drive, Derry, Co.
Londonderry, BT48 9QH
Tel: 028 7126 6168
Fax: 028 7130 8939
E-mail:
creggan.library@librariesni.org.uk
Website: www.ni-libraries.net

Crossmaglen Library
44 The Square, Crossmaglen, Co.
Armagh, BT35 9AA
Librarian: Susan Cumiskey
Tel: 028 30861951
E-mail:
crossmaglenlibrary@librariesni.org.uk
Website: www.ni-libraries.net

Crumlin Library
Orchard Road, Crumlin, Co. Antrim,
BT29 4SD
Librarian: Claire Keag
Tel: 028 9442 3066
Fax: 028 9442 3066
E-mail:
crumlin.library@librariesni.org.uk
Website: www.ni-libraries.net

Cushendall Library
Mill Street, Cushendall, Co. Antrim,
BT44 0RR
Librarian: Anne Blaney
Tel: 028 2177 1297
Fax: 028 2177 1297

E-mail:
cushendall.library@librariesni.org.
uk
Website: www.ni-libraries.net

Derry Central Library
35 Foyle Street, Derry, Co.
Londonderry, BT48 6AL
Tel: 028 7127 2300
Fax: 028 7126 9084
E-mail:
derrycentrallibrary@librariesni.org
.uk
Website: www.ni-libraries.net

Donaghadee Library
5 Killaughey Road, Donaghadee, Co.
Down, BT21 0BL
Tel: 028 9188 2507
Fax: 028 9188 2507
E-mail:
donaghadeelibrary@librariesni.org.
uk
Website: www.ni-libraries.net

Downpatrick Library
Market Street, Downpatrick, Co.
Down, BT30 6LZ
Tel: 028 4461 2895
Fax: 028 4461 1444
E-mail:
downpatricklibrary@librariesni.org
.uk
Website: www.ni-libraries.net

Draperstown Library
High Street, Draperstown, Co.
Londonderry, BT45 7AD
Librarian: Elizabeth Sewell
Tel: 028 7962 8249
E-mail:
draperstown.library@librariesni.or
g.uk
Website: www.ni-libraries.net

Dromore Library
38 Market Square, Town Hall,
Dromore, Co. Down, BT25 1AW
Tel: 028 9269 2280
E-mail:
dromorelibrary@librariesni.org.uk
Website: www.ni-libraries.net

Dundonald Library
16 Church Road, Dundonald,
Belfast, Co. Down, BT16 2LN
Tel: 028 9048 3994
E-mail:
dundonaldlibrary@librariesni.org.uk
Website: www.ni-libraries.net

Dungannon Library
36 Market Street, Dungannon, Co.
Tyrone, BT70 1JD
Librarian: Monica Montgomery
Tel: 028 8772 2952
E-mail:
dungannonlibrary@librariesni.org.
uk
Website: www.ni-libraries.net

Dungiven Library
74 Main Street, Dungiven, Co.
Londonderry, BT47 4LD
Tel: 028 7774 1475
Fax: 028 7774 1475
E-mail:
dungivenlibrary@librariesni.org.uk
Website: www.ni-libraries.net

Dunmurry Library
Upper Dunmurry Lane, Dunmurry,
Belfast, Co. Antrim, BT17 0AA
Tel: 028 9062 3007
Fax: 028 9062 3007
E-mail:
dunmurrylibrary@librariesni.org.uk
Website: www.ni-libraries.net

Enniskillen Library
Halls Lane, Enniskillen, Co.
Fermanagh, BT74 7DR
Tel: 028 6632 2886
Fax: 028 6632 4685
E-mail:
enniskillenlibrary@librariesni.org.uk
Website: www.ni-libraries.net

Falls Road Library
49 Falls Road, Belfast, Co. Antrim,
BT12 4PD
Librarian: Anne Maxwell
Tel: 028 9050 9212
E-mail:
fallsroad.library@librariesni.org.uk
Website: www.ni-libraries.net

Finaghy Library
38B Finaghy Road South, Belfast,
Co. Antrim, BT10 0DR
Librarian: Margaret Mulholland,
Barbara McCabe
Tel: 028 9050 9214
E-mail:
finaghyroad.library@librariesni.org.
uk
Website: www.ni-libraries.net

Fintona Library
112-114 Main Street, Fintona, Co.
Tyrone, BT78 2AE
Tel: 028 8284 1774
Fax: 028 8284 1774
E-mail:
fintonalibrary@librariesni.org.uk
Website: www.ni-libraries.net

Fivemiletown Library
67 Main Street, Fivemiletown, Co.
Tyrone, BT75 0PG
Tel: 028 8952 1409
E-mail:

fivemiletownlibrary@librariesni.org.uk
Website: www.ni-libraries.net

Garvagh Library
Bridge Street, Garvagh, Co.
Londonderry, BT51 5AF
Librarian: Eugenie Murphy
Tel: 028 2955 8500
E-mail:
garvagh.library@librariesni.org.uk
Website: www.ni-libraries.net

Gilford Library
43 Main Street, Gilford, Co. Down,
BT63 6HY
Tel: 028 3883 1770
E-mail:
gilfordlibrary@librariesni.org.uk
Website: www.ni-libraries.net

Gilnahirk Library
Gilnahirk Rise, Belfast, Co. Down,
BT5 7DT
Tel: 028 9079 6573
Fax: 028 9079 6573
E-mail:
gilnahirklibrary@librariesni.org.uk
Website: www.ni-libraries.net

Glengormley Library
40 Carnmoney Road,
Newtownabbey, Co. Antrim, BT36
6HP
Librarian: Rosemary Hope
Tel: 028 9083 3797
Fax: 028 9083 3797
E-mail:
glengormley.library@librariesni.org.uk
Website: www.ni-libraries.net

Greenisland Library
17 Glassillan Grove, Greenisland,
Co. Antrim, BT38 8PE
Librarian: Angela Campbell
Tel: 028 9086 5419
E-mail:
greenisland.library@librariesni.org.uk
Website: www.ni-libraries.net

Greystone Library
Greystone Road, Antrim, Co.
Antrim, BT41 1JW
Librarian: Vivien Carlisle
Tel: 028 9446 3891
Fax: 028 9446 3891
E-mail:
greystone.library@librariesni.org.uk
Website: www.ni-libraries.net

Grove Library
Grove Wellbeing Centre, 120 York
Road, Belfast, Co. Antrim, BT15 3HF
Librarian: Diane Lee
Tel: 028 9050 9244
E-mail:
grove.library@librariesni.org.uk
Website: www.ni-libraries.net

Holywood Arches Library
Holywood Arches Library, 4 - 12
Holywood Road, Belfast, Co. Antrim,
BT4 1NT
Librarian: Janet Watt
Tel: 028 9050 9216
E-mail:
holywoodarches.library@librariesni.org.uk
Website: www.ni-libraries.net

Holywood Library
Sullivan Building, 86-88 High
Street, Holywood, Co. Down, BT18

9AE
Tel: 028 9042 4232
Fax: 028 9042 4194
E-mail:
holywoodlibrary@librariesni.org.uk
Website: www.ni-libraries.net

Irish and Local Studies Library, Armagh

39c Abbey Street, Armagh, Co.
Armagh, BT61 7EB
Tel: 028 3752 7851
Website: www.ni-libraries.net

Irvinestown Library

Main Street, Irvinestown, Co.
Fermanagh, BT94 1GT
Tel: 028 6862 1383
Fax: 028 6862 1383
E-mail:
irvinestownlibrary@librariesni.org.
uk
Website: www.ni-libraries.net

Keady Library

3 Bridge Street, Keady, Co. Armagh,
BT60 3SY
Librarian: Bernie Vallely
Tel: 028 3753 1365
E-mail:
keadylibrary@librariesni.org.uk
Website: www.ni-libraries.net

Kells and Connor Library

5 Main Street, Kells, Co. Antrim,
BT42 3JH
Librarian: Frances Reid
Tel: 028 2589 0019
E-mail:
kellsandconnor.library@librariesni.
org.uk
Website: www.ni-libraries.net

Kilkeel Library

49 Greencastle Street, Kilkeel, Co.
Down, BT34 4BH
Tel: 028 4176 2278
E-mail:
kilkeellibrary@librariesni.org.uk
Website: www.ni-libraries.net

Killyleagh Library

High Street, Killyleagh, Co. Down,
BT30 9QF
Tel: 028 4482 8407
Fax: 028 4482 8407
E-mail:
killyleaghlibrary@librariesni.org.uk
Website: www.ni-libraries.net

Kilrea Library

Town Hall, 27 The Diamond, Kilrea,
Co. Londonderry, BT51 5QN
Librarian: Anne Wilson
Tel: 028 2954 0630
Fax: 028 2954 0630
E-mail:
kilrea.library@librariesni.org.uk
Website: www.ni-libraries.net

Larne Library

36 Pound Street, Larne, Co. Antrim,
BT40 1SQ
Tel: 028 2827 7047
Fax: 028 2827 7047
E-mail:
larne.library@librariesni.org.uk
Website: www.ni-libraries.net

Ligoniel Library

53-55 Ligoniel Road, Belfast, Co.
Antrim, BT14 8BW
Librarian: Gary Ferris
Tel: 028 9050 9221
E-mail:
ligoniel.library@librariesni.org.uk
Website: www.ni-libraries.net

Limavady Library
5 Connell Street, Limavady, Co.
Londonderry, BT49 0EA
Tel: 028 7776 2540
Fax: 028 7772 2006
E-mail:
limavadylibrary@librariesni.org.uk
Website: www.ni-libraries.net

Lisburn City Library
23 Linenhall Street, Lisburn, Co.
Antrim, BT28 1FJ
Tel: 028 9263 3350
E-mail:
lisburncity.library@librariesni.org.
uk
Website: www.ni-libraries.net

Lisburn Road Library
440 Lisburn Road, Belfast, Co.
Antrim, BT9 6GR
Librarian: Maura Barron
Tel: 028 9050 9223
E-mail:
lisburnroad.library@librariesni.org.
uk
Website: www.ni-libraries.net

Lisnaskea Library
Drumhaw, Lisnaskea, Co.
Fermanagh, BT92 0GT
Tel: 028 6772 1222
Fax: 028 6772 1222
E-mail:
lisnaskealibrary@librariesni.org.uk
Website: www.ni-libraries.net

Area Local Studies Collection - Ballymena
Ballymena Central Library, 5 Pat's
Brae, Ballymena, Co. Antrim, BT43
5AX
Development Officer: Michael Lynn

Tel: 028 2563 3964/2563 3960
Fax: 028 2563 2038
E-mail:
localstudies.neelb@librariesni.org.uk
Website: www.ni-libraries.net

Local Studies - Ballynahinch
Library Headquarters, Windmill
Hill, Ballynahinch, Co. Down, BT24
8DH
Tel: 028 9756 6400
Fax: 028 9756 5072
E-mail:
seelb.localstudies@librariesni.org.uk
Website: www.ni-libraries.net

Lurgan Library
1 Carnegie Street, Lurgan, Co.
Armagh, BT66 6AS
Tel: 028 3832 3912
E-mail:
lurganlibrary@librariesni.org.uk
Website: www.ni-libraries.net

Maghera Library
1 Church Street, Maghera, Co.
Londonderry, BT46 5EA
Librarian: Carol O'Doherty
Tel: 028 7964 2578
Fax: 028 7964 2578
E-mail:
maghera.library@librariesni.org.uk
Website: www.ni-libraries.net

Magherafelt Library
The Bridewell, 6 Church Street,
Magherafelt, Co. Londonderry, BT45
6AN
Librarian: Mildred Jones
Tel: 028 7963 2278
Fax: 028 7963 2278
E-mail:
magherafelt.library@librariesni.org.uk
Website: www.ni-libraries.net

Moira Library
Backwood Road, Moira, Co. Down,
BT67 0LJ
Tel: 028 9261 9330
Fax: 028 9261 9330
E-mail:
moiralibrary@librariesni.org.uk
Website: www.ni-libraries.net

Moneymore Library
8 Main Street, Moneymore, Co.
Londonderry, BT45 7PD
Tel: 028 8674 8380
E-mail:
moneymorelibrary@librariesni.org.
uk
Website: www.ni-libraries.net

Moy Library
1 The Square, Moy, Co. Tyrone,
BT71 7SG
Tel: 028 8778 4661
E-mail:
moylibrary@librariesni.org.uk
Website: www.ni-libraries.net

Newcastle Library
141-143 Main Street, Newcastle, Co.
Down, BT33 0AE
Tel: 028 4372 2710
Fax: 028 4372 6518
E-mail:
newcastlelibrary@librariesni.org.uk
Website: www.ni-libraries.net

Newry City Library
79 Hill Street, Newry, Co. Down,
BT34 1DG
Tel: 028 3026 4683
Fax: 028 3025 1739
E-mail:
newrylibrary@librariesni.org.uk
Website: www.ni-libraries.net

Newtownards Library
Queens Hall, Regent Street,
Newtownards, Co. Down, BT23 4AB
Tel: 028 9181 4732
Fax: 028 9181 0265
E-mail:
newtownardslibrary@librariesni.or
g.uk
Website: www.ni-libraries.net

Newtownbreda Library
Saintfield Road, Belfast, Co. Down,
BT8 7HL
Tel: 028 9070 1620
Fax: 028 9070 1780
E-mail:
newtownbredalibrary@librariesni.
org.uk
Website: www.ni-libraries.net

Newtownstewart Library
2 Main Street, Newtownstewart, Co.
Tyrone, BT78 9AA
Librarian: Kieran McGuigan
Tel: 028 8166 2060
Fax: 028 8166 2060
E-mail:
newtownstewart.library@libraries
ni.org.uk
Website: www.ni-libraries.net

Oldpark Road Library
46 Oldpark Road, Belfast, Co.
Antrim, BT14 6FR
Librarian: Mark Knowles
Tel: 028 9050 9226
E-mail:
oldparkroad.library@librariesni.or
g.uk
Website: www.ni-libraries.net

Ormeau Road Library
247 Ormeau Road, Belfast, Co.

Antrim, BT7 3GG
Librarian: Karen Woods
Tel: 028 9050 9228
E-mail:
ormeauroad.library@librariesni.org.uk
Website: www.ni-libraries.net

Omagh Library
1 Spillars Place, Irishtown Road,
Omagh, Co. Tyrone, BT78 1HL
Tel: 028 8224 4821
Fax: 028 8224 6772
E-mail:
omaghlibrary@librariesni.org.uk
Website: www.ni-libraries.net

Portadown Library
24-26 Church Street, Portadown,
Co. Armagh, BT63 3LQ
Tel: 028 3833 6122
Fax: 028 3833 2499
E-mail:
portadownlibrary@librariesni.org.uk
Website: www.ni-libraries.net

Portaferry Library
47 High Street, Portaferry, Co.
Down, BT22 1QU
Tel: 028 4272 8194
Fax: 028 4272 8194
E-mail:
portaferrylibrary@librariesni.org.uk
Website: www.ni-libraries.net

Portglenone Library
19 Townhill Road, Portglenone, Co.
Antrim, BT44 8AD
Librarian: Deirdre Carty
Tel: 028 2582 2228
E-mail:
portglenone.library@librariesni.org
.uk
Website: www.ni-libraries.net

Portrush Library
12 Causeway Street, Portrush, Co.
Antrim, BT56 8AB
Librarian: Elizabeth Cameron
Tel: 028 7082 3752
Fax: 028 7082 3752
E-mail:
portrush.library@librariesni.org.uk
Website: www.ni-libraries.net

Portstewart Library
Town Hall, The Crescent,
Portstewart, Co. Londonderry,
BT55 7AB
Librarian: Doreen Moreland
Tel: 028 7083 2712
Fax: 028 7083 2712
E-mail:
portstewart.library@librariesni.org.uk
Website: www.ni-libraries.net

Randalstown Library
34 New Street, Randalstown, Co.
Antrim, BT41 3AF
Librarian: Freda Watson
Tel: 028 9447 2725
Fax: 028 9447 2725
E-mail:
randalstown.library@librariesni.or
g.uk
Website: www.ni-libraries.net

Rathcoole Library
2 Rosslea Way, Newtownabbey, Co.
Antrim, BT37 9BJ
Librarian: Amanda Wardle
Tel: 028 9085 1157
Fax: 028 9085 1157
E-mail:
rathcoole.library@librariesni.org.uk
Website: www.ni-libraries.net

Rathfriland Library
12 John Street, Rathfriland, Co.
Armagh, BT34 5QH
Tel: 028 4063 0661
E-mail:
rathfrillandlibrary@librariesni.org.uk
Website: www.ni-libraries.net

Richhill Library
1 Maynooth Road, Richhill, Co.
Armagh, BT61 9PE
Tel: 028 3887 0639
E-mail:
richilllibrary@librariesni.org.uk
Website: www.ni-libraries.net

Saintfield Library
Ballynahinch Road, Saintfield, Co.
Down, BT24 7AD
Tel: 028 9751 0550
Fax: 028 9751 0550
E-mail:
saintfieldlibrary@librariesni.org.uk
Website: www.ni-libraries.net

Sandy Row Library
127 Sandy Row, Belfast, Co. Antrim,
BT12 5ET
Tel: 028 9050 9230
E-mail:
sandyrow.library@librariesni.org.uk
Website: www.ni-libraries.net

Shankill Road Library
298-300 Shankill Road, Belfast, Co.
Antrim, BT13 2BN
Librarian: Mark Knowles
Tel: 028 9050 9232
E-mail:
shankillroad.library@librariesni.or
g.uk
Website: www.ni-libraries.net

Shantallow Library
92 Racecourse Road, Shantallow,
Derry, Co. Londonderry, BT48 8DA
Tel: 028 7135 4185
Fax: 028 7135 4122
E-mail:
shantallowlibrary@librariesni.org.uk
Website: www.ni-libraries.net

Strathfoyle Library
22 Temple Road, Strathfoyle, Derry,
Co. Londonderry, BT47 6TJ
Tel: 028 7186 0385
Fax: 028 7186 0385
E-mail:
strathfoylelibrary@librariesni.org.uk
Website: www.ni-libraries.net

Strabane Library
1 Railway Street, Strabane, Co.
Tyrone, BT82 8EF
Tel: 028 7188 3686
Fax: 028 7138 2745
E-mail:
strabanelibrary@librariesni.org.uk
Website: www.ni-libraries.net

Suffolk Library
Stewartstown Road, Belfast, Co.
Antrim, BT11 9JP
Librarian: Mary Grieve
Tel: 028 9050 9234
Fax:
E-mail:
suffolkroad.library@librariesni.org.
uk
Website: www.ni-libraries.net

Tandragee Library
84 Market Street, Tandragee, Co.
Armagh, BT62 2BW
Tel: 028 3884 0694
E-mail:

tandrageelibrary@librariesni.org.uk
Website: www.ni-libraries.net

Tullycarnet Library
Kinross Avenue, Kings Road,
Belfast, Co. Down, BT5 7GF
Tel: 028 9048 5079
Fax: 028 9048 2342
E-mail:
tullycarnet.library@librariesni.org.
uk
Website: www.ni-libraries.net

Warrenpoint Library
61 Summerhill, Warrenpoint, Co.
Down, BT34 3JB
Tel: 028 4175 3375
E-mail:
warrenpointlibrary@librariesni.org.uk
Website: www.ni-libraries.net

Waterside Library
The Workhouse, 23 Glendermott
Road, Derry, Co. Londonderry,
BT47 6BG
Tel: 028 7134 2963
Fax: 028 7131 8283
E-mail:
watersidelibrary@librariesni.org.uk
Website: www.ni-libraries.net

Whitehead Library
17B Edward Road, Whitehead, Co.
Antrim, BT38 9QB
Librarian: Hazel Black
Tel: 028 9335 3249
Fax: 028 9335 3249
E-mail:
whitehead.library@librariesni.org.uk
Website: www.ni-libraries.net

Whiterock Library
Whiterock Road, Belfast, Co.

Antrim, BT12 7FW
Tel: 028 9050 9236
E-mail:
whiterock.library@librariesni.org.uk
Website: www.ni-libraries.net

Whitewell Library
Ballygolan Primary School, Belfast,
Co. Antrim, BT36 7HB
Librarian: Diane Lee
Tel: 028 9050 9242
E-mail:
whitewell.library@librariesni.org.uk
Website: www.ni-libraries.net

Woodstock Library
358 Woodstock Road, Belfast, Co.
Down, BT6 9DQ
Librarian: Anita Mulholland
Tel: 028 9050 9239
E-mail:
woodstock.library@librariesni.org.uk
Website: www.ni-libraries.net

L. Literary Festivals and Events

Aspects Irish Literature Festival
Co. Down. Contact: Gail Prentice, Arts Officer/Festival Director Town Hall,
The Castle, Bangor Co. Down BT20 4BT. Tel: 028 9127 8032 / 9127 1200
(Box Office).

Athlone Literary Festival
E-mail: literaryathlone@gmail.com.
Website: www.athlone.ie/literaryfestival.
Date: Late September

Ballymena Arts Festival
The Braid, Ballymena Town Hall, Museums and Arts Centre, 1-29 Bridge
Street, Ballymena Co. Antrim BT43 5EJ. Tel: 028 2565 7161. E-mail:
rosalind.lowry@ballymena.gov.uk. Contact: Rosalind Lowry, Festival
Director.

Cork Spring Literary Festival
The Munster Literature Centre, Frank O'Connor House, 84 Douglas Street,
Cork. Website: www.munsterlit.ie Tel: 021 4312955. E-mail
info@munsterlit.ie.
Date: 17th-20th February.

Cuisle - Limerick International Poetry Festival
Arts Office Limerick City Council, City Hall Merchants Quay, Limerick.
Telephone: 061 40 7421. Fax: 061 41 5266. E-mail: artsoff@limerickcity.ie
or sdeegan@limerickcity.ie.
Date: Mid October.

Cúirt International Festival of Literature, Galway
Contact: Maura Kennedy, Programme Director. Galway Arts Centre, 47
Dominick Street, Galway. Tel: 091 565886. E-mail:
info@galwayartscentre.ie. Website: www.galwayfestivals.com.
Date: Late Spring

Sean Dunne Writers' Festival, Waterford
Telephone 051 849856/7. E-mail: seandunne@waterfordcity.ie. Website:
www.seandunne.ie.
Date: Late March

Dromnineer Literary Festival
Website: www.dromineerliteraryfestival.ie. Contacts:

Chairman - Pat Kelly. E-mail: pat.kelly6@gmail.com. Tel: 087 6908099.
Secretary - Deborah Powell. E-mail: deborahpowell01@hotmail.com. Tel:
087 2315851
PRO: Eleanor Hooker. E-mail: emhooker@eircom.net. Tel: 087 7535207.
Presents readings (poetry and prose), workshops, poetry and prose
competitions (Prizes worth €2000). Target audience is lovers of writing in
all genres. Location: Beautiful village on eastern shore of Lough Derg,
North Tipperary, Ireland. Weather permitting, at least one event is held
afloat on the lake. See website for full details on travel directions to
Dromineer, local accomodation, eating/drinking venues, etc.
Date: 1 - 3 October 2010

Dublin Writers' Festival
Contact: Dublin City Council, Arts Office, The Lab, Foley Street, Dublin 1.
Tel: 01 2227847. E-mail: info@dublinwritersfestival.com. Website:
www.dublinwritersfestival.com.
Date: Mid June.

Dun Laoghaire-Rathdown Poetry Now Festival
Contact: Arts Office, Dún Laoghaire-Rathdown County Council, Marine
Road, Dún Laoghaire, Co. Dublin. Tel: 01 2719531. E-mail: arts@dlrcoco.ie.
Website: www.poetrynow.ie. Venue: The Pavilion Theatre, Dún Laoghaire.
Date: March.

Ennis Book Club Festival
Contact: Frances O'Gorman, Clare Library Headquarters, Mill Road, Ennis,
Co. Clare. Tel: 087 2262259. E-mail: info@ennisbookclubfestival.com

Egdeworth Literary Festival
Website: www.edgeworthliteraryfestival.com. Usually held in the Spring.

The Flatlake Literary Festival, Monaghan
E-mail: flatlakeinfo@eircom.net. Website: www.theflatlakefestival.com.
Date: Mid August

Franco-Irish Literary Festival
Alliance Française, The French Institute, 1 Kildare Street, Dublin 2. Tel. (01)
638 14 41. E-mail: cweld@alliance-francaise.ie. Website:
www.francoirishliteraryfestival.com. Irish and European writers. Held in
Chester Beatty Museum and Dublin Castle's Coach House in early summer.

The Forge at Gort, Co. Galway
E-mail: sylfredcar@iolfree.ie. Website: www.twwc.ie.
Date: Late March

The Glór Sessions
Music and Poetry. The International Bar, 23 Wicklow Street, Dublin 2.
Contact: Stephen James Smith, organiser, poet and MC of The Glór. 56
Dunmore Lawns, Kingswood Heights, Tallaght, Dublin 24. Tel: 01 6779250.
TheGlorSessions@gmail.com. Website: www.stephenjamessmith.com/Glor.
The Glór Sessions is Dublin's only weekly poetry night. It has hosted many
musicians and poets from all around Ireland and the world. It was featured
in The Irish Times' Cultural Review 2009 and on RTÉ Radio One's Arts
Show Arena. Open Mic.

IMRAM
Literay festival held in spring in Derry in conjunction with Bláthana
Festival.

Immrama Lismore Festival of Travel Writing
Waterford. Website: www.lismoreimmrama.com.
Date: Mid June

Listowel Writers Week
24 The Square, Listowel, Co. Kerry. Tel: 068 21074. Website:
www.writersweek.ie. E-mail: info@writersweek.ie.
Date: Late May

The Frank O'Connor International Short Story Festival
The Munster Literature Centre, Frank O'Connor House, 84 Douglas Street,
Cork. Tel: 021 4312955. E-mail info@munsterlit.ie. Website:
www.munsterlit.ie.
Date: Mid September

Oireachtas na Gaeilge
6 Sráid Fhearchair, Baile Átha Cliath 2. Teil: 01 475 3857. Facs: 01 475
8767. Ríomhphost: eolas@antoireachtas.ie. Suíomh Gréasáin:
www.antoireachtas.ie. Eagraíonn Oireachtas na Gaeilge raon leathan
imeachtaí i rith na bliana chun na healaíona dúchasacha, trí mheán na
Gaeilge, a cheiliúradh. Tugtar aire do gach aon ealaín thraidisiúnta -
amhránaíocht, ceol, rince, scéalaíocht, lúibíní, agallaimh beirte agus
drámaíocht - ag na féilte, Oireachtas na Cásca agus Oireachtas na Samhna.
Déanann Comórtais Liteartha an Oireachtais cúram don litríocht
chomhaimseartha - seo sraith comórtas a eagraítear gach bliain do
scríbhneoirí óga agus do scríbneoirí fásta. Tugann Gradaim Chumarsáide
an Oireachtais aitheantas do dhaoine atá ag saothrú sna meáin Ghaeilge a
bhaineann ardchaighdeán amach i réimsí éagsúla oibre.

Siar Scéal Festival

Roscommon. E-mail: siarsceal@live.ie. Website: siarsceal.com.
Date: Early April.

Ranelagh Arts Festival

Tel: 085 7437212. E-mail: info@ranelagharts.org. Website:
www.ranelagharts.org.

Strokestown Poetry Festival

E-mail: patcompton@live.ie. Website: www.strokestownpoetry.org.
Date: Early May

Jonathan Swift Festival

Trim, Co. Meath. Contacts: Barbara Nestor or Shane Dempsey. Tel: 087
9268066. E-mail: info@trimswiftfestival.com. Website:
www.trimswiftfestival.com
Date: 1st to 4th July, 2010

Ulster Bank Belfast Festival at Queen's University Belfast

Contact: Graeme Farrow Director. Culture and Arts Unit, Queen's
University, 8 Fitzwilliam Street, Belfast BT9 6AW. E-mail:
festival.operations@qub.ac.uk.
Date: October.

West Cork Literary Festival

E-mail: sarawcm@eircom.net. Website: www.westcorkliteraryfestival.ie.
Date: Early July

M. Literary Competitions

PRIZES AND AWARDS

Arts Council/ An Chomhairle Ealaíon
70 Merrion Square, Dublin 2. Tel: 01 618 0296. E-mail: artistsservices@artscouncil.ie. Website: www.artscouncil.ie. Publishes Supports for Artists, a guide to Arts Council bursaries and awards.

Bryan MacMahon Short Story Award
24 The Square, Listowel, Co. Kerry. Tel: 068 21074. E-mail: info@writersweek.ie. Website: www.writersweek.ie.

Cork City-Frank O'Connor Short Story Award
The Munster Literature Centre, Frank O'Connor House, 84 Douglas Street, Cork. Tel: 021 4312955. E-mail info@munsterlit.ie. Website: www.munsterlit.ie

The CBI Bisto Book of the Year Awards
Children's Books Ireland, 17 North Great Georges Street, Dublin 1. Tel: 01 8727475. E-mail: info@childrensbooksireland.ie. Website: www.childrensbooksireland.ie. Annual awards to authors and illustrators resident in Ireland.

The Glen Dimplex New Writers Awards
Run in conjunction with the Irish Writers' Centre.

Fish Publishing
Durrus, Bantry, Co. Cork. E-mail: info@fishpublishing.com. Website: www.fishpublishing.com. Fish runs three international competitions annually: The Fish Short Story Prize, The Fish One-Page Prize, and the Fish Poetry Prize. The winners of each competition are published in the annual Fish Anthology. Well known writers judge the competitions to ensure independence. There are large cash prizes. Entry is mostly online but also by post. The Fish Prize was set up in 1994 to encourage and publish new and exciting literary talent. Hon Patrons Roddy Doyle, Colum McCann, Dermot Healy.

International IMPAC Dublin Literary Award
Dublin City Library and Archive 138-144 Pearse Street Dublin 2. Tel: 01 6744802. Website: www.impacdublinaward.ie. E-mail: literaryaward@dublincity.ie.

The Irish Book Awards
Website: www.irishbookawards.ie. The awards will move from their traditional spring date to November in 2010. Categories include:
- Hughes & Hughes Irish Novel of the Year
- The Argosy Irish Non-Fiction Book of the Year
- The Dublin Airport Authority Irish Children's Book of the Year - Junior
- The Dublin Airport Authority Irish Children's Book of the Year - Senior
- International Education Services Ltd Best Irish Newcomer of the Year
- The Best Irish-Published Book of the Year
- The Energise Sport Irish Sports Book of the Year
- The Tubridy Show Listeners' Choice Book of the Year
- The Easons Irish Popular Fiction Book of the Year
- Ireland AM Crime Fiction Award
- Lifetime Achievement in Literary Ireland Award

Irish PEN Award
Website: www.irishpen.com/award.htm

Irish Times Poetry Now Award
See Dun Laoghaire Rathdown International Poetry Festival.

Kerry Group Irish Fiction Award
24 The Square, Listowel, Co. Kerry. Tel: 068 21074. E-mail: info@writersweek.ie. Website: www.writersweek.ie.

The Rooney Prize for Irish Literature
Strathin, Templecarrig, Delgany, Co. Wicklow. Tel: 01 287 4769. E-mail: rooneyprize@ireland.com. Contact: J.A. Sherwin.

RTÉ PJ O'Connor Radio Drama Award
RTÉ Radio Drama, Dublin 4. Tel: 01 2083111. E-mail: radiodrama@rte.ie. Website: www.rte.ie/radio1/drama. Annual competition for 30 minute plays, open to writers living in Ireland.

RTÉ Radio 1 Francis MacManus Short Story Competition
RTÉ Radio 1, RTÉ Radio Centre, Features and Drama Dept, Dublin 4. Tel: 01 2083111. E-mail: radiodrama@rte.ie. Website: www.rte.ie/radio1/francismcmanus. Annual short-story competition open to writers born or living in Ireland.

The Sean O'Faolain Short Story Competition
The Munster Literature Centre, Frank O'Connor House, 84 Douglas Street, Cork. Tel: 021 4312955. E-mail info@munsterlit.ie. Website: www.munsterlit.ie

Writers' Week Poetry Competition
24 The Square, Listowel, Co. Kerry. Tel: 068 21074. E-mail: info@writersweek.ie. Website: www.writersweek.ie.

N. Literary and Publishing Blogs

The Irish Blog Directory includes listings for more than 200 blogs under the 'Literature' category alone. On closer inspection however, not all the blogs listed were active when we clicked on the links. The directory itself looks like it could use some updating. Nevertheless, it is quite a useful resource for anyone who wants to take up blogging. Make it your first port of call to register your blog for free. The Irish Blog Directory can be found at www.irishblogdirectory.com.

We have included here, just a few blogs that might whet the appetite of anyone with an interest in literary and publishing themes; or blogging as an art in itself.

Ask About Writing
The resource site for writers of all abilities. Useful source for news and general information.
www.askaboutwriting.net

The Author's Friend News Blog
News Blog of The Author's Friend. For anyone with an interest in writing and publishing, whether professionally or as a hobby. Promotes Assisted Publishing and new Irish writing produced in this way. Contributions are also invited from writers groups, community organisations, libraries, schools, colleges, local history societies, etc., who want to publicise their activities.
www.theauthorsfriend.blogspot.com

Beaut.ie
Ireland's premier online resource for women who are into cosmetics and makeup, and who enjoy a bit of banter in a welcoming, supportive environment, making the site a buzzy, fun place to be.
www.beaut.ie

Brightspark Consulting
Whether you are starting out new to the web, or you already have a website and are looking for better results, we can provide sound strategic advice on how to succeed online.
www.brightspark-consulting.com/blog

Catherine Caffeinated
A blog by an an "occasionally delusional twenty-something from Cork,

Ireland. She's trying to get somebody - ANYBODY! Anybody? - to publish her first novel."
www.catherineryanhoward.com

Damien Mulley
Damien Mulley owns Cork based Mulley Communications and teaches organisations and enterprises how to communicate amongst themselves and with the greater world. He is also the organiser of the Irish Blog Awards and Irish Web Awards, wrote a technology column for the Sunday Tribune from Jan 07 to Jan 08 and is the former chairman of broadband lobby group IrelandOffline.
www.mulley.net

Daily Lit
Allows you to read books, in serialisation form by email or RSS.
www.dailylit.com

David Maybury
David Maybury is a writer and person who lives in Dublin. This is his blog about about writing, children's books and other bits. Mostly it is about writing and children's books.
www.davidmaybury.ie

Emerging Writer
The struggles of an emerging writer to get published. What exactly is it that I'm emerging from? Some kind of primeval literary goo?
www.emergingwriter.blogspot.com

Eoin Purcell's Blog
It is a blog for my thoughts on publishing, books, the future of books and publishing, with a little history, the web, politics and whatever else takes my fancy.
www.eoinpurcellsblog.com

Galway Public Libraries Blog
Keep up to date with what's happening at the library. A weblog of library news, book chat, events, websites and more!
www.galwaylibrary.blogspot.com

The Irish Economy
Provides commentary and information about the Irish economy.
www.irisheconomy.ie

Irish Publishing News
News and Features about Irish Publishing. Aims to have the most up to date news about the issues, authors and companies that affect publishing in Ireland.
www.irishpublishingnews.com

Irish Writers Online
A no-frills, basic bio-bibliographical database of over 570 Irish writers, and related resources. It is now accessed by students, academics, media and lovers of Irish Literature from more than 100 countries.
www.irishwriters-online.com

The Job Seekers Union
A social network for job seekers and the unemployed. Set up in 2009 in response to massive job losses and spiralling levels of unemployment. The Job Seekers Union manage a couple of blogs which allow members to share information, advice, ideas, find work or promote business ventures.
www.thejobseekersunion.com

Michael Farry
Literary blog from a retired teacher and ICT Advisor who has written history and now mostly writes poetry. A native of Co. Sligo now living in Meath. A member of Boyne Writers, Trim, Co. Meath and editor of their magazine *Boyne Berries*.
www.michaelfarry.blogspot.com

Overheard in Dublin
An interesting take on life in the capital. Amusing quotes and anecdotes.
www.overheardindublin.com

POD, Self Publishing and Independent Publishing
Contact: Mick Rooney, Researcher and Publishing Consultant. Tel: 086 6028453. E-mail: mickrooney777@gmail.com. Online news, features and reviews of publishing services for independent and self-publishing authors. Consultancy services also available.
www.mickrooney.blogspot.com

Scribd
Document sharing website. Describes itself as the largest social publishing and reading site in the world. Allows you to upload and share any file - such as PDF, Word and PowerPoint - into a web document and immediately connect with passionate readers and information-seekers
www.scribd.com

Stony River
A place for stories small and tall, and some very stupid things
www.stonyriver.ie

Tipperary Libraries News
Brings you all the very latest information regarding events, clubs and news
from all the Libraries in the county.
www.tipperarylibrarynews.ie

Tor.com
Science Fiction, Fantasy, The Universe and related subjects.
www.tor.com

Twenty Major
I come from Dublin, Ireland. This is my blog. I am a kind, considerate,
gentle person who always sees the good in the world ...
www.twentymajor.net

wait til i tell ye
a Northern Irish literary journal (of sorts)
Interests: Books Culture Films Poetry Reading Theatre Writing
www.itellye.blogspot.com

The Word Cloud
A social networking site run by writers, for writers.
www.thewordcloud.org

Words and Comments
An occasional journal of thoughts and opinions on matters of interest and
concern. News commentary and current affairs blog for anyone with an
opinion; and who is not afraid to share it.
www.wordsandcomments.com

Write and Review
Is writing your passion? Do you love to comment on other aspiring writers
work as well as getting reviews on your own work at the same time? If
you're looking for constructive criticism, some inspiration or would just
like to chat to people that share the same interest as you Write and Review
is the place for you!
www.shaz532.webs.com

Writing4all.ie
Spade Enterprise Centre, North King Street, Smithfield, Dublin 7. Contact:

John Kenny, Managing Director. Tel: 01 6174863. Fax: 01 6771558. E-mail: john@writing4all.ie. Website: www.writing4all.ie. Members can post their work (fiction, non-fiction, poetry) to our website for feedback from other members.

Writing and Publishing
A free information site packed with helpful hints and advice for everyone interested in writing and getting published.
www.WritingandPublishing.info

Appendix
Directory Submission Form

If you would like to include your organisation in future editions of *The Irish Writers, Authors and Poets Handbook*; or if you would like to amend an existing listing; please fill in the form below and return it to:

The Editors, *Lámhleabhar do Scríbhneoirí, d'Údar agus d'Fhilí Gaelacha*, TAF Publishing, c/o 52 Cardiffsbridge Avenue, Finglas, Dublin 11, Éire-Ireland

You can also fill it in online at:
www.tafpublishing.com/titles/irish-writers-handbook/directory-listings

GENERAL INFO

Business Name:

Other Business Names, Publisher Imprints, etc:

Business

Main Business Contact:

Contact Telephone Number:

Fax

E-mail

Website:

Additional Information:
Other factual information that you would like to appear in the listings

MAIN BUSINESS ACTIVITY: *Please choose one only*

○ Publisher - Books
○ Publisher - Magazines
○ Literary Agent
○ Literary Magazine/Journal
○ Other Specialist Publication
○ Daily Newspaper
○ Sunday Newspaper
○ Local Newspaper
○ Literary or Publishing Blog
○ Book Shop
○ Book Distributor
○ Library
○ Book Club
○ Writers Group
○ Creative Writing Course
○ Literary Festival/Competition/Event
○ Scholarship/Bursary/Grant
○ Editorial Services Provider
○ Printer/Printing Services
○ Other: *please specify* ....

PUBLISHERS AND LITERARY AGENTS

Please complete this section if you are a publishers or literary agents. The purpose is to help authors and writers identify publishers they might wish to approach with their manuscripts, proposals, etc.

Do you accept unsolicited manuscripts?
○ Yes
○ No

Contact details and procedure for submitting a manuscript:
Type of manuscripts you accept, don't accept, format for submissions, etc

Genre Fiction: *Tick all that apply*

- ❑ Crime
- ❑ Thriller
- ❑ Science Fiction
- ❑ Fantasy
- ❑ Horror
- ❑ Humour
- ❑ Children
- ❑ Young Adult
- ❑ Satire
- ❑ Chick Lit
- ❑ Lads' Lit
- ❑ Historical
- ❑ Romantic
- ❑ Erotic
- ❑ Other: *please specify* ....

Genre - Non Fiction: *Tick all that apply*

- ❑ Crime
- ❑ Politics/Current Affairs
- ❑ History
- ❑ Biography/Autobiography
- ❑ Business and Finance
- ❑ Humour
- ❑ Satire
- ❑ Lifestyles
- ❑ Fashion
- ❑ Cookery
- ❑ Sport
- ❑ Nature
- ❑ Religious/Spiritual
- ❑ Self-Help
- ❑ Education
- ❑ Gardening
- ❑ DIY
- ❑ Technical
- ❑ Computers
- ❑ Photography
- ❑ Other: *please specify* ....

OTHER BUSINESS ACTIVITIES
If you have more than one type of business activity please use this section to tell us about it. You may be eligible for more than one listing

Other Business Activities: *Tick all that apply*

❑ Publisher - Books
❑ Publisher - Magazines
❑ Literary Agent
❑ Literary Magazine/Journal
❑ Other Specialist Publication
❑ Daily Newspaper
❑ Sunday Newspaper
❑ Local Newspaper
❑ Literary or Publishing Blog
❑ Book Shop
❑ Book Distributor
❑ Library
❑ Book Club
❑ Writers Group
❑ Creative Writing Course
❑ Literary Festival/Competition/Event
❑ Scholarship/Bursary/Grant
❑ Editorial Services Provider
❑ Printer/Printing Services
❑ Other: *please specify* ....

....

Details about your 'Other Business Activities':
Information that will help to ensure that our listings are accurate and complete